PUBLIC OPINION AND EUROPEAN INTEGRATION

For Gillian

Public Opinion and European Integration

ROBERT J. *ames* SHEPHERD

SAXON HOUSE | LEXINGTON BOOKS

Published by

SAXON HOUSE, D. C. Heath Ltd.
Westmead, Farnborough, Hants., England.

Jointly with

LEXINGTON BOOKS, D. C. Heath & Co.
Lexington, Mass. U.S.A.

ISBN 0 347 01053 9
Library of Congress Catalog Card Number 74-34529

Printed in Great Britain
by Unwin Brothers Limited
The Gresham Press, Old Woking, Surrey
A member of the Staples Printing Group

Contents

List of tables

List of figures

Preface

The purpose of this book is to facilitate a fuller understanding of the nature of public opinion toward European integration. This demands an effort to accomplish two objectives, which T.B. Bottomore believes to be the twin elements in the scientific intention of sociology. These two objectives, or elements, are: '(i) exact description, by the analysis of the properties and relations of social phenomena, and (ii) explanation by the formulation of general statements.'[1] It is worth emphasising that it is in the achievement of the second objective that social scientists encounter greatest difficulty, 'because of the complexity or interrelatedness of social happenings and because of human creativity'.[2] Despite these major limitations, reasonable predictions can sometimes be made even when a full explanation of the phenomena has not been accomplished.

To present a study on public opinion towards European integration at a time when the public debate over the future of the Community has grown ever more intense and urgent throughout the Nine, presents the author, fairly and squarely, with the question of his own opinions. But the problem of bias is universal to the social scientist. Indeed, the unusual immediacy of the European debate has been beneficial for me — each day, I have been made aware of my own deeply-held beliefs.

I do support moves toward further European integration — in the jargon of the debate in Britain, I am a 'pro-Marketeer'. In the preface of *Diplomacy and Persuasion: How Britain joined the Common Market,* Uwe Kitzinger informs the reader of his active commitment to the Marketeers' cause. He states, 'I can only warn the reader of my open bias. As one of my informants put it: "On this issue, silence would have been the only neutrality".'[3]

Today, few social scientists share Durkheim's recommendation that 'social facts' ought to be treated *comme des choses.* Instead, the assessment of value-freedom in social science given by Max Weber is more widely accepted although this too now has its critics. The Weberian view holds that freedom from value-judgments is an ideal which the social scientist must try to achieve. Salvador Giner argues that 'Complete value-freedom may be unattainable, but a serious level of scientific objectivity results from a sustained effort towards it.'[4] But secondly, since the social scientist is bound to possess some ultimate assumptions or commitments, these values must influence at the very least his selection of 'problems' or 'issues' for study.

As man contemplates the world, he also evaluates it. Thus, the evaluative element may limit the degree of objectivity attainable, but to follow the phenomenological critique is to shun the view that knowledge of society has increased through the studies of social scientists deeply committed to various causes. If the aim of social scientific research is the description of the nature of certain social phenomena, with the ability to make limited predictions, and even to attempt to explain social phenomena, then the methods of research must obey the rules of logical consistency and scientific enquiry.

The plan of the present study is as follows. In Chapter One, I review the definitions of public opinion and discuss the role of public opinion polls in social scientific research. I also discuss the three main dimensions in the analysis of public opinion — psychological, sociological and historical. In Chapter Two there is a brief survey of the historical dimension of this particular study. Chapter Three is concerned with an analysis of the role of public opinion in European integration — I present a full discussion on the significance attached to public opinion by the various theorists of international integration. In conclusion, I list six propositions which form the basis for the detailed review of public opinion which follows. Chapters Four to Nine comprise a discussion on the theoretical sources of the six main propositions and an examination of the evidence from the polls, along with the conclusions which we are able to reach. Chapter Ten presents the general conclusions which can be drawn from the examination of the polls, and, finally, there is a discussion in which I sketch some plausible scenarios for the development of European integration.

For their assistance in the preparation of this book I should like to thank Brigitte Bonnet, Rick Cox, Kate Gibbons, Muriel Lloyd, Tessa Osborne, Jim Sumerfield and Vera Williams. In particular, I am indebted to Roger Osborne and to my colleagues at Cambridge Tutors, while I must thank my students, past and present, for their constant encouragement. The task of collecting a vast amount of opinion poll data was greatly facilitated by the courteous and efficient help rendered by Lolli du Vivier and Valerie Williams of the European Communities' Office, London, Jacques-René Rabier of the European Commission, Brussels and also Bob Wybrow and Leslie Austen of Gallup Social Surveys Ltd., London. The advice and criticism offered to me by Michael Hodges, Richard Mayne, Richard Bone and John Pinder was of immense value. However, the responsibility for the work remains, of course, entirely mine.

Notes

1   T.B. Bottomore, *Sociology: a Guide to Problems and Literature,* 2nd edition, Geo. Allen and Unwin, 1971, p.63.
2   Ibid.
3   Uwe Kitzinger, *Diplomacy and Persuasion: How Britain joined the Common Market,* Thames and Hudson, 1973, p.13.
4   Salvador Giner, *Sociology,* Martin Robertson, 1972, p.19.

1 Introduction: Public Opinion, the Polls and European Integration

There is a certain paradox in much of the discussion on European integration. Apologists of integration frequently claim that the creation of a European Community has strengthened the foundations of liberal-democracy and has removed the fierce national rivalries that divided Western Europe. Yet the fact remains that, although integration is often seen as the bulwark of liberal-democracy, integration has been almost totally a creature of the 'elite'. Monnet, Schuman, de Gasperi and Adenauer were the leading members of this elite, who created the European Community with no direct consultation of the people, while the experiment of integration came nearest to collapse as a result of de Gaulle's intransigence.

As living standards soared and liberal-democracies could prosper in peace, the question of European integration failed to become a controversial political issue amongst the publics of the 'Common Market'. If integration was seen to be desirable, for whatever reasons, its elitist origins seemed unimportant. But all this changed with the enlargement of the Community. In 1972, when the people were allowed a say, they showed in Norway that they could check the apparent inevitability of integration. The Danes wavered before assenting to the Treaty of Rome, while the British remained decidedly cool, limited in the expression of their views to opinion polls as a result of their government's evocation of the Burkean view of the constitution.

The significance of the Norwegian vote was that it constituted the first major rebuff for the European Community at the hands of an electorate. Analysing the significance of the British and Danish publics' attitudes toward integration, Johann Galtung has argued that,

> The situation is different from that in the six current member states, where the integration has never been made a political issue at the mass level: it is something made by and for the elite. This may now change: there may be a growing awareness among people in the Six

that the European Community is something else, something more than just a natural and inevitable attempt at harmonization and integration.[1]

Bearing in mind Galtung's view, it must be stressed that a crucial feature of the member-states of the European Community is that they are liberal-democracies. Indeed, it is essential for the method of making decisions within the Community that its member-states should be liberal-democracies. This is because the Community method consists of a most complex procedure of lobbying, negotiating and bargaining, which involves not only the national governmental elites, but also the various non-governmental elites — businessmen, farmers and trade unionists participate in Community institutions, and not only politicians and civil servants. In this way, there is the possibility that, as a result of the common heterogeneity of the member-states, alliances will be struck up across national boundaries by those with a common interest and it will not be too easy for respective member-states to adopt nationalistic postures on every issue. Therefore, in the present framework of the Community, it is impossible to conceive of a non-democratic state attaining full membership.

It is because the European Community necessarily comprises liberal-democracies that the rebuff by the Norwegians and the reluctant entry of the British and the Danes is especially important. Galtung's view that the role of the public may well come to be a consideration of vital importance throughout the Community is strengthened still further by the emergence of 'political sovereignty' as an issue in the future development of integration. Enshrined in the preamble to the Treaty of Rome is the statement that the aim of the European Community is 'ever closer union'. This refers to the eventual political unification of the Community — economic integration is acknowledged to be a stepping-stone to a more fully united political community.

Clearly, the Treaty of Rome envisages that, at some specific point in the future, sovereignty will pass from the member-states to the Community. However, given that the member-states are liberal-democracies, it is impossible to foresee the transfer of sovereignty from Bonn, Paris, London or Rome to Brussels, without the approval of the various publics. In Britain in particular, the debate over sovereignty tends to focus on the niceties of legal-constitutional practice, but the real issue at stake throughout the Nine, at some point in the future, would be the political acceptability of an 'ever closer union'.[2] To attempt to create this union without public approval would be to invite secession, as Andrew Shonfield

2

has argued so lucidly, and this could in itself deal a death-blow to the proposed union.[3]

It would be remarkably naïve to assume that the question of political sovereignty will become an issue of public concern only on the eve of the final step toward some full political union of the Community. The enlargement of the Six sparked off the debate on sovereignty in the applicant-states, and there seems every reason to agree with Galtung and to foresee 'a growing awareness among the people in the Six' of the wider implications of integration.[4] It is feasible that the economic crises of 1974 may prove to be the spark as far as the publics in the member-states are concerned.

What is public opinion?

There is no adequate, single definition of public opinion. In the words of V.O. Key, 'To speak with precision of public opinion is a task not unlike coming to grips with the Holy Ghost.'[5] Nonetheless, many people have tried to come to grips with public opinion and a critical discussion of the varied definitions of the concept will help us to clarify the meaning of public opinion which we shall employ in this study.

'Opinion' itself is a word which has generated much discussion among psychologists and social scientists. Hodder-Williams provides us with a useful initial definition when he states that opinion is 'an expression, either actual or potential, on a topic admitting of controversy'.[6] We shall return to a fuller discussion of the nature of opinion and the meanings of 'attitude' and 'personality' later in this chapter.

To define opinion is one thing, but to introduce the notion of 'public opinion' is a very different matter and presents a range of fresh complications. For those Victorians writing before the extension of the franchise, public opinion meant the views of a small, informed elite.[7] Depending on the issue involved, this elite might include Members of Parliament, civil servants, the professions, landowners, industrialists and so on. Because of the very nature of the political system, there was little recognition of a mass public opinion – the majority of the population were limited to demonstrations or petitions, organised by the pressure groups of the time.

In a sense the Victorian definition of public opinion persists, reflecting the indirect form of democracy, which exists in modern liberal-democratic political systems of the type comprising the member-states of the European Community. Formal participation by the people in government is limited to the election of representatives and, in some countries, to infrequent referenda. Direct democracy of the type advocated by Rousseau is impracticable in the twentieth century because of the sheer size of our political systems (in terms of population), the multiplicity of decisions to be made and the specialist knowledge now demanded of all modern governments. In fact, on different issues there are, so to speak, different publics – normally 'the public' means only a segment of the electorate. To quote Ian Gilmour, 'The public, in the sense of the people with a capital P, as Joe Chamberlain called it, is not often involved'.[8] Thus, together with the views of the governmental elite, it is the public in the sense of the motoring public, the farming interest or the trade union movement, whose particular opinion holds sway on specific issues.

In a different context, 'public opinion' assumes a much wider meaning than that given above. Even in political systems which have inherited more from the utilitarian writers than from Rousseau, some concept of a single, 'public interest' is still incorporated in much of the political debate. When public opinion is conceived in terms of an identifiable 'public interest', an element of Rousseau's General Will enters the discussion. For instance, according to A.L. Lowell, for public opinion to be said to exist 'a majority is not enough, and unanimity is not required, but the opinion must be such that while the minority may not share it, they feel bound, by conviction, not by fear, to accept it'.[9] The implication of Lowell's definition is that certain opinions are held by the public in common, and, '. . . therefore public opinion becomes some kind of General Will'.[10] The difference between this sense of public opinion and the meaning given to public opinion by the Victorians is reflective of the different political philosophies of Rousseau and Bentham respectively.[11]

Like Rousseau, Bentham did conceive of a single public interest, but for Bentham this 'public interest consists in securing to each group in society the maximum of what it desires consistent with all other groups securing the maximum of what each one of them desires also'.[12] As Finer points out, the Benthamite doctrine is very much that practised by ministers and civil servants, 'when they finally have to decide after consulting all interested parties'.[13]

At the crux of Rousseau's conception of the public interest is his distinction between, on the one hand, the sum of sectional interests and, on the other hand, the General Will. Finer summarises this distinction by stating that,

> Where every person or interest said, 'what is *my* interest', the result
> was the mere 'will of all', the aggregate of selfish desires. The general

will – which in this context is the same as 'the public interest' – could only be reached when each man (or interest) asked himself: 'What is for the *public* advantage?' and voted accordingly. [14]

Society's interest is thus seen to be different from those of its constituent parts, and it is this societal or public interest which is 'the most potent check on the otherwise unmoderated claims of the various lobbies', because most people, in Finer's experience, hold Rousseau's belief in a public interest 'with rare passion'. [15]

Every individual has his own vision of this public interest, stemming from the common, shared assumptions of the time. Thus, public opinion in the sense of the 'public interest' is referring to the current moral and intellectual assumptions and to the wider social and cultural attitudes within which the assumptions exist. Examples of these 'standards' existing as public opinion would be the widespread acceptance of pacificism in Britain in the 1930s, and (to date) the immorality of unemployment since 1945. Only massive social forces can undermine standards, which define the terms within which the 'public interest' is couched by politicians and lobby-spokesmen alike.

However, the above definitions of public opinion are not suitable as a definition of the public opinion which is measured by the opinion polls. Of course, the pollsters do conduct research on the opinions of particular publics, for instance the views of the motoring public on speed limits, and opinion polls can also give some clues to the 'standards' of a nation. But the meaning of public opinion to the pollsters was stated by Henry Durant, when he wrote, 'Public opinion can be considered to mean what the pollsters say it means . . . a conventional yardstick which imparts to one person an opinion more or less equal in weight to the opinion of other individual persons.'[16] Thus, the public is seen to be co-extensive with the electorate and, to quote Hodder-Williams,

> . . . this public does not necessarily have one opinion as though some form of General Will existed, but a number of opinions, one of which may or may not be held by a majority; finally, these opinions are made public to interviewers on request and are not volunteered. [17]

As far as the pollsters are concerned, public opinion can be said to consist of whatever views a community makes public. In contrast with private opinions, the assumption is that public opinion is an overt 'response or judgement', and not necessarily a candid reflection of a man's private opinion. A weakness of opinion polls is that they cannot measure accurately, whether by different relative weightings or any other method, the fundamental difference between expressions of opinion that are made on a man's own initiative and those opinions elicited only after questioning by interviewers.

Yet the polls do now constitute a channel of communication where previously the mass were very limited in their ability to communicate their views. General elections, by-elections and referenda were the only channels open to the mass who did not otherwise participate in the political system. In liberal-democracies, only small minorities actually belong to political parties, and research has shown that even in the USA, a supposedly pluralistic state, only 40 per cent of the electorate belonged to voluntary associations. [18] Schattschneider commented,

> The business and upper class bias of the pressure system shows up everywhere ... large areas of the population appear to be wholly outside the system of private organisation. ... The flaw in the pluralist heaven is that the heavenly chorus sings with a strong upper class accent. [19]

Interpreting the implications of a particular election result, of course, is quite another matter, despite the increased interest in electoral research since 1945. In Britain, the nature of the electoral system and the lack of referenda has made it impossible to deduce the state of public opinion on a particular issue from voting figures, but even in Western Europe, where referenda are sometimes held and where the electoral systems allow more scope for the expression of interests, the inference of public opinion from voting returns remains an extremely difficult task.

According to Teer and Spence, it is in recent years that, 'The opinion poll has emerged as a means of communicating the unformulated opinion of a mass electorate so that the opinions of special publics can be set in a wider context.'[20] Central to the argument of Teer and Spence is the pollsters' valid claim that between elections and particularly on specific issues, such as the Common Market, polls do create a public opinion. They do serve as a channel of communication between the governed and the government, and they have a role as a formalising force in the political process. Nor does it seem to matter that public opinion may be uninformed and shallow — after all, every adult (with a few minor exceptions) has the vote and yet numerous studies of voting behaviour have shown the widespread lack of knowledge about the most elementary political facts of the day.

We can see that the pollsters have adopted the egalitarian-democratic principle of, 'one man, one vote, one value', and have amended it to read, 'one man, one opinion, one value'. Directly as a result of this egalitarian assumption, the pollsters see public opinion as a negative or limiting influence on governments. This is a vital point to grasp, for it is fundamentally different from the dynamic and positive role attributed to public opinion before the advent of the polls. As Hodder-Williams points out,

> ... this positive public opinion can be recognized as one of the forces that drove Sir Samuel Hoare from office in 1936 and which buoyed up the leader-writers in their support of Neville Chamberlain in 1938. This positive public opinion is usually volunteered and, above all, incalculable, since it is not quite clear who exactly constitutes the informed 'public'. It is in fact a synthesis of one public's views, the opinion-leaders, dependent for its influence more on the status of its holders than on their quantity. [21]

Lord Windlesham also makes this point well:

> Even with the development of the mass media, public opinion today will still usually have a positive role only when it originates from informed elites, some of them inevitably concerned to protect or further special interests. In the sense of popular opinions widely held, public opinion is more of a negative, limiting factor: a way of estimating what the public will stand for rather than an expression of what the public wants. [22]

Teer and Spence do concede that voting in an election may be a different matter from voicing one's opinion on a specific question, often of considerable complexity, and that therefore opinions based on ignorance or misconception may not be a useful guide in deciding the direction of public affairs. They emphasise the negative nature of public opinion, as defined by the pollsters, when they argue that opinion polls serve as a navigational aid for governments: 'The course to be plotted should take account of the information in the chart but the chart does not determine the destination.'[23]

In decision-making, the government would need to consider the state of public knowledge and the relative importance of the issue to the public. Questions following from these considerations would include:

> ... should government action be taken to give effect to the policy commanding majority support, or should the government attempt to educate the holders into a different opinion, or should opinion be ignored because the issue is not in any case of major public concern? [24]

One of the few cases where mass opinion could be said to have led the government to take action was the issue of Commonwealth immigration to Britain in 1968. Presumably, the government decided to introduce stricter control of immigration because they felt that they had to act firmly and quickly, rather than to pursue the risky policy of trying to educate the opinion-holders, particularly since the issue was seen to be of major public concern.

In liberal-democracies, the opinion polls are very useful 'navigational aids'. The parties know that they must present themselves, their policies and their records, to the public at regular intervals. Despite our lack of understanding of the processes which create changes in the popularity of the parties, the parties must operate on the assumption that a policy which seems likely to prove unpopular is unlikely to be beneficial — at the very least, it may tarnish an otherwise good party image. The more important that an issue becomes to the public, the greater the damage that a party may suffer if its policy is not popular. For various reasons, when Macmillan's Conservative government was launching its application for membership of the Common Market, the public did not see Europe as an issue which was of immediate relevance to them. Despite this, Lord Windlesham argues that:

> If at any time in 1961 or 1962 the currents had all begun to run strongly in one direction, then the basis on which the Government's policy rested could have been swept away. It can happen that political opinion can come to be shared by an overwhelming majority of the population, and it can happen quickly. [25]

In agreement with Galtung, we have suggested that the European issue may well become more salient to the publics of the Nine. If this is to be the case, it is worth noting that public opinion, as expressed in the polls, is analogous to the public's participation in elections. At elections,

> ... most of the positive activity in creating policies, influencing leaders and encouraging the faithful is done by a group of experts or vociferous activists with strong views. The mass of the electorate merely records their acceptance, or otherwise, of one set of positive performers. [26]

As regards public opinion, Hodder-Williams argues that,

> Informed and positive activists create the issues and form the initial climate of opinion, but, in the last analysis, the pollsters' variety of public opinion may negate the activities of these leaders by being so

overwhelmingly opposed to a project that the Government, or Opposition for that matter, with an eye on a future general election feels obliged to give way. [27]

In conclusion, he states that, 'The general public's influence is thus negative for the most part for it merely approves or disapproves what is presented to it by the pollsters or the party leaders at election time'. [28]

The levels and dimensions of analysis

We have referred to the problem of defining 'opinion' briefly, and we now need to return to the discussion on the meaning of opinion, since the concepts of 'personality' and 'attitude' also require analysis. In this section, the three different levels of analysis − personality, attitude and opinion − will be examined. A discussion will follow on the social influences which permit changes to occur at any of the three levels of analysis. Also, the three dimensions of our analytic framework will be introduced and explained − these dimensions are the psychological, the sociological and the historical.

Moodie and Studdert-Kennedy tell us that, 'Personality refers to those aspects of an individual's orientation to life that are acquired early and deeply ingrained, a relatively stable compound of genetic endowment and early learning and socialization'. [29] Psychologists do seem able to distinguish characteristics which form clusters or 'personality types'. The pertinent question for our consideration is whether certain personality types have consistent political opinions.

Little research has been conducted on the political opinions of personality types. Indeed, a dilemma exists here − generalisations concerning the political opinions of personality types cannot be made from the few in-depth studies of individuals performed to date, but the sampling of greater numbers means that the necessary in-depth analysis of personal interactions is seriously limited. In *Opinions and Personality*, the authors conducted an intensive study into the opinions and personalities of ten men and presented a detailed study of the 'psychological context that gives its full meaning to the opinion'. [30] Such a detailed study could provide those interested in political opinions to posit reasonable predictions concerning 'their intensity, the extent to which they might be modified by, or determine the reactions to fresh information and new experiences'. [31]

Herbert McClosky claims that the link between personality and a person's view on foreign policy seems particularly strong.[32] First, the public is not well informed on foreign policy, being less aware of the complexity of the issues and generally not perceiving the issues as salient. Secondly, there seems to be great scope for the role of personality in views on foreign affairs — fears, anxieties, and so on. In his study of isolationism in America, McClosky concluded that 'isolationism was found to be part of a network of attitudes that are related to common underlying personality dispositions'.[33] Similarly, Verba's study of American opinion poll data on the Vietnam war, in which two groups of respondents were distinguished, 'worriers' and 'nonworriers', came to similar conclusions.[34] Indeed, the inference of a general disposition to worry was unrelated to party or any identifiable group membership, but there seemed to be a slight tendency on the part of 'worriers' to favour de-escalation.

Whether the issues relating to the European Community are to be regarded as foreign or domestic policy, or even *sui generis,* is a question we shall discuss later in this chapter. But certainly, David Nias argues that personality is very much involved in shaping public attitudes towards European integration.[35] Quoting research in social psychology, he introduces a dimension 'that underlies attitudes or opinions on almost all areas of social controversy. This is the dimension of "conservatism", which is closely associated with various other concepts such as authoritarianism, rigidity and dogmatism.'[36] Nias seeks to test the proposition that since conservatism reflects a preference for order, familiarity, security, the status quo, and so on, an anti-Market attitude would also appear to fall into this general category.

Nias found that those who are ethnocentric, introverted, in low status jobs, feel they know little about the Common Market, and think life in Britain is changing for the worse, tended to be both conservative in personality and opposed to joining. Social class also clearly had an effect on attitudes toward the Common Market — a preference for the Labour Party, high scores on conservatism, realism, ethnocentrism and neuroticism, and a perceived lack of knowledge about the Common Market, plus a feeling that life in Britain is deteriorating, are all related to low occupational status and to an anti-Market attitude.

We can see that certain psychological factors do seem to play a vital role in shaping attitudes and opinions toward the Common Market, and Nias is able to assert that his research, 'in demonstrating a strong link between anti-market attitudes and personality dynamics, suggests that certain personality types are unlikely to be happy even if the hoped for economic advantages do eventuate'.[37] But the psychological dimension of analysis alone is inadequate. As McClosky observes, stands on international relations are determined by far more than personality alone — time, geography, social circumstances, and the configuration of forces within which the personality factor is embedded are all vital. Equally the psychological level of analysis is not to be ignored. As McClosky states,

> While isolationism is obviously a political attitude influenced by political circumstances, reference groups, demographic factors, and other such determinants, it is also shaped to a considerable extent by a complex set of personality variables, primarily of an aversive nature. Such personality states as misanthropy, psychological inflexibility, manifest anxiety, and low self-esteem have a powerful influence on the attitudes one adopts toward other nations and toward foreign policy. [38]

At the second level of analysis are 'attitudes', which are 'relatively stable predispositions and beliefs, but these are less part of the basic psychological structure of the individual'. [39] Thus, not only are attitudes 'more vulnerable to the impact of fresh experience', but they are also 'more specifically attached to various stimuli' — for instance, towards students, policemen, apartheid, or the Common Market. [40] But to draw a clear line between personality and attitudes is impossible — the latter may be indirect expressions of the former. Nonetheless, an individual's attitudes may be shaped by his reference groups and yet because these attitudes conflict with his underlying personality, he may undergo rapid attitude-change 'if he were suddenly to find himself in a very different social environment'. [41]

At the third level of analysis are 'opinions' on issues, 'the level at which the newspaper opinion poll is normally operating'. [42] It is worthwhile recalling the definition of opinion by Hodder-Williams, which we quoted earlier: 'an expression, either actual or potential, on a topic admitting of controversy'. Given consistent opinion poll data on an issue, it is possible to identify underlying attitudes, and to chart the short-term fluctuations and the long-term trends in opinions and attitudes toward a particular issue or set of issues. We shall review the specific problems involved in the use of opinion polls shortly.

We can relate the psychological dimension of our analytical framework with the sociological dimension by a consideration of the social influences which are active in the formation of personality, attitudes and opinions. Herbert Kelman provides us with a set of distinctions which are roughly congruent to the three levels of analysis defined by McClosky. [43] Kelman's three processes of social influence are compliance, identification and internalisation.

> Compliance can be said to occur when an individual accepts influence from another person or from a group because he hopes to achieve a favourable reaction from the other. [44]

In other words, the individual may well be acting or speaking regardless of his private beliefs.

> Identification can be said to occur when an individual adopts behaviour derived from another person or a group because this behaviour is associated with a satisfying self-defining relationship to this person or group. . . . Accepting influence through identification, then, is a way of establishing or maintaining the desired relationship to the other, and the self-definition that is anchored in this relationship. [45]

Thus, only when the appropriate role is activated will the induced opinions be expressed and, as a result, opinions adopted through identification remain dependent on social support.

> Internalization can be said to occur when an individual accepts influence because the induced behaviour is congruent with his value system. It is the content of the induced behaviour that is intrinsically rewarding here. The individual adopts it . . . because he perceives it as inherently conducive to the maximization of his values. [46]

Thus, behaviour adopted through internalisation is in some way part of a personal system as opposed to a system of social-role expectations, and gradually such behaviour can become independent of the external source.

Kelman presents the probability of each of the three processes of social influence 'as a function of the same three determinants: the importance of the induction for the individual's goal achievement, the power of the influencing agent, and the pre-potency of the induced response'. [47] Similarly, the consequents of each process can be predicted, as a function of three further determinants. These distinct sets of antecedents and consequents are summarised in Table 1.1.

Clearly, sociological factors are central to any analysis of public opinion. While the newspaper opinion polls are largely limited to providing 'detailed evidence of what it is we want to explain (attitudes, opinions, forms of behaviour)', more detailed surveys have been undertaken on the issue of the Common Market in an effort to ascertain the likely determinants of the attitudes and opinions. [49] Also, the reputable opinion polling organisations do include variables of age, class, party and region when conducting a poll. We shall examine these variables in more detail in Chapter Nine.

Table 1.1

Summary of the distinction between the three processes of social influence[48]

	Compliance	Identification	Internalisation
Antecedents:			
1 Basis for the *importance of the induction*	Concern with social effect of behaviour	Concern with social anchorage of behaviour	Concern with value congruence of behaviour
2 Source of *power of the influencing agent*	Means control	Attractiveness	Credibility
3 Manner of achieving *prepotency of the induced response*	Limitation of choice behaviour	Delineation of role requirements	Reorganisation of means–ends framework
Consequents:			
1 Conditions of performance of induced response	Surveillance by influencing agent	Salience of relationships to agent	Relevance of values to issue
2 Conditions of change and extinction of induced response	Changed perception of conditions for social rewards	Changed perception of conditions for satisfying self-defining relationships	Changed perception of conditions for value maximisation
3 Type of behaviour system in which induced response is embedded	External demands of a specific setting	Expectations defining a specific role	Person's value system

However, we can agree with Moodie and Studdert-Kennedy that 'a more explanatory kind of analysis raises other problems'. [50] Descriptions can give clues to the workings of the processes of social influence, but explanations demand that a new dimension be added to the analytic framework, namely the historical dimension. The significance of its role is illustrated by reference to the work of Butler and Stokes on the familiar correlation between trade-union membership and support for the Labour Party. To quote Butler and Stokes: 'as is so often the case in social analysis, the key to interpreting the correlation of union membership and party support lies in reaching a reasonable view of their temporal or causal sequence'. [51] Moodie and Studdert-Kennedy spell out the result:

> . . . they produce a case for reversing what is generally assumed to be the direction of the causal sequence. Contrary to a common assumption, it is more frequently true that party support leads to union membership than the other way round. [52]

In short, 'any serious and systematic analysis of public opinion and attitudes must be sensitive to this historical context'. [53] It is quite meaningless to seek to analyse man's adaptation to and action on a social environment unless that social environment is itself discussed. A particular social environment has developed as a result of past actions and events, chances and decisions, and forms the social context which sustains an individual's view of 'reality'. This 'social reality' is thus based on facts which are very different to the facts which are the basis for our understanding of natural phenomena, but what is man-made is reified and is merged in our vision of the natural world, 'out there'. Therefore, what is of great significance, despite the public's lack of knowledge of detailed issues, are the more general orientations towards political institutions and activities. The role of the historical dimension has been demonstrated in Runciman's study on relative deprivation and also in the searching analysis of voting behaviour in Britain by Butler and Stokes. [54] Neither of these classic works could be termed 'deterministic' in any sense of the word. It is because of the significance of this historical dimension that a brief historical survey of European integration will be presented in Chapter Two.

Some problems of the polls

We need not claim, along with Robert Mellish, that an opinion poll is 'phoney', to raise some of the very real problems which do exist in the use made of public opinion poll data.[55] Whereas pre-pollster notions of public opinion were incalculable and purely subjective, the pollsters' problems arise precisely because they seek to measure public opinion objectively, to make calculable and quantitative what was once incalculable and qualitive. By interviewing the 'man-in-the-street' in his thousands, pollsters have to face severe problems. Suppose the interviewee will not or, indeed, cannot reply? What if the respondents are not telling the truth? In fact, most polling organisations have devised methods to counter the first problem, while it seems fair to assume that few members of the public are so Machiavellian as to tell deliberate lies — the few that are liars would probably cancel each other out.

A more serious problem for the pollster is his wording of the questions he wishes to ask. Does the wording give rise to a bias in the replies? Hodder-Williams quotes a good example of bias from a Gallup Poll. [56] The first question read: 'If the Government decided not to apply for membership of the Common Market, would you approve or disapprove of this decision?' 39 per cent said they would approve of not joining, while 32 per cent disapproved. The second question read: 'If the Government were to decide that Britain's interest would best be served by joining the European Common Market, would you approve or disapprove?' 43 per cent said that they would be in favour of the decision to enter, while only 30 per cent would disapprove.

All the major polling organisations now give considerable attention to the wording of their questions, and they aim for simple language which is unambiguous and devoid of leading words. Bias could creep in through the human element of the interviewer, but again the polls take care to minimise this influence.

The actual timing of the questions is also crucial — specific events could influence the individual's reply, even if the question is concerned with a general and wide-reaching issue. Some distortion of this kind does seem particularly likely in opinion poll data, since questions on any issue can never be the same as a referendum which occurs following a lengthy campaign in which the major points are crystallised and put before the electorate. However, if a specific event highlights an aspect of the issue which is salient to the individual, there is no reason to discount his opinion — elections can be tilted by trade figures or governmental scandals which may not seem so relevant in the long term. There is evidence that public opinion does react quickly to immediate political events — for instance, each of the parties in Britain enjoys a surge in its popularity immediately following its annual conference.

Because opinion polls are presenting static pictures of public opinion on issues which have not been fully 'crystallised', the data seem likely to be prone to short-term fluctuations. However, opinion polls can be conducted very frequently over a long time series, and thus, over a long time-span the pollsters can provide us with an extremely interesting and useful chart of opinion on a particular issue. In fact, this is the major form of the public opinion poll data which has been utilised for this study.

We can see that opinion polls do enable us to chart patterns and trends in public opinion on various issues over time, and in this way they provide a real channel of communication for the mass public. Since extensive research has shown that only a minority of the public participate in parties and pressure group activity in states which are said to be pluralistic, the opinion poll performs a unique function in liberal-democracies. However, the significance of that function would seem to be minimised to the extent that some replies, which are duly expressed as explicit opinions, may well be meaningless. The very act of being interviewed or completing a questionnaire assumes that the respondent has an opinion which he wishes to offer. All the evidence points to a low level of public awareness of most issues, and although the open-ended question enables an assessment of the individual's knowledge on the issue, this technique is rarely used because of its cost and the great complexity of sifting the replies.

It is all very well to extend the notion of 'one man, one vote, one value' to read 'one man, one opinion, one value', but there does appear to be a real difference between the nature of party identification and views on issues. For the majority of the population, politics is a remote and marginal activity. Their level of involvement in most political issues is low, involvement only increasing with the perceived salience of the issue to their 'valued goals' in life. Thus, issues concerning wages and prices are more easily seen to be relevant than issues concerning foreign policy.

Although charting the trends in public opinion can tell us a good deal on an issue like the Common Market, we must remember that essentially we are comparing a mass of snapshots whose clarity of focus is not at all clear. To quote Bogart, people, on any given topic, 'hold a variety of opinions, articulated or vague, public shading into private'.[57] Hodder-Williams states that, 'Thus, on a general question about entry into the European Community . . . a person may actually hold several views, some favourable, some unfavourable. The economic arguments may be clearly articulated, the emotional and patriotic ones not so.'[58] He continues by indicating that the response will be determined by the particular role played by the respondent at the time of the interview, the perception of the question — which may vary from person to person — and other miscellaneous factors. It is for these sorts of reasons that opinion poll data may sometimes produce contradictory results.

16

Since the respondent may be expressing only one part of his views on an issue, if he has even formulated any meaningful opinions, it seems questionable to attribute the value of one to each 'opinion' expressed to the pollsters. However, Hodder-Williams concludes a searching critique of the opinion polls by stating that,

> We all know that the question, 'For which party would you vote if there was a general election tomorrow?' is readily comprehensible; this does not mean that the answering is necessarily a very simple matter. But the question, 'Are you in favour of Britain entering the Common Market?' is also readily understood, even if all the implications of the question may be totally incomprehensible to the respondent. A gut reaction against entering the Common Market is a gut reaction against entering the Common Market. In a society which claims to be democratic, it is important to know the reactions of the public to political issues, however subjective, emotional, and irrational they may be. The weight to be attached to such opinions is another matter. [59]

Hodder-Williams sums up the argument succinctly: 'the pollsters' definition is seen to be not merely convenient but also morally correct, since it reflects the practices of those symbols of democracy, the polling booth and the referendum'. [60]

Still further questions about the use of polling data arise from the methods used to select the issues on which people are polled. The main criterion for the newspaper opinion polls is, of course, the newsworthiness of the issue. Seemingly it is the editorial groups of the press, radio and television who judge this. Recent research in this area has demonstrated how the mass media can 'manufacture' news, and this is perturbing in view of the great use made of opinion polls by the mass media. [61] Again, we can minimise the impact of fluctuating coverage of integration in the press and so on by the use of long time series and cross-national comparisons of opinion poll data.

A feature of public opinion toward issues which most newspaper opinion polls fail to detect is the existence of cross-currents of opinion change, which are taking place beneath the surface, so to speak, of apparently stable attitudes. Nowhere is the significance of this more clearly illustrated than in the 'panel surveys' of the type conducted by Butler and Stokes. The use of panel surveys conducted over time has become increasingly popular, since an individual's opinions can be charted over time and in this way changes of attitude are detected and analysed while the more typical opinion poll samples would fail to detect any cross-currents which happened to cancel each other out.

The extent of this fluidity is summed up in the following extract from *Political Change in Britain:*

> On the issue of Britain's entry into Europe, for example, fully half of our sample conceded either at the interview in the summer of 1963 or at the interview in the autumn of 1964 that they had no opinion. The views of those who did offer an opinion at both interviews proved quite unstable. Less than four-fifths of this group and therefore less than two-fifths of the whole sample voiced the *same* opinion at both points in time. A highly fluid pattern of individual replies was found beneath the surface of an overall division of opinion that was almost unchanged between the summer of 1963 and the autumn of 1964. [62]

Butler and Stokes continue:

> . . . movements in both directions were found in each party, as well as in each class, and in every other category for which an hypothesis as to the direction of change suggested itself. The most reasonable interpretation of the remarkable instability of responses is that Britain's policy towards the Common Market was in 1963–4 a matter on which the mass public had formed attitudes to only a very limited degree. [63]

Butler and Stokes also examine the fluidity of opinion on a policy which has been at the centre of the party debate for years — nationalisation. They found that, 'only 50 per cent were consistent in either supporting or opposing further nationalisation over the three interviews'. Among those who expressed a view on the issue of nationalisation, there was little doubt as to which party favoured more nationalisation, but this contrasted sharply with the changeability of attitudes towards the merits of nationalisation. [64]

However, the findings of Butler and Stokes show that under certain conditions, political issues become of great significance to the public. In short, we should focus on the content of issues, since it is clearly this that can come to matter to people — it would be incorrect to assume that issues never count. For an issue to count, as far as an individual is concerned, it must come to be salient to him — he must perceive its relevance to his life, his well-being. In addition, the issue must come to creates strongly-held opinions or attitudes, which often occurs through a perceived correlation with an individual's 'valued goals', and this usually leads to greater consistency in opinion poll data. Indeed, the considerations of salience and of the strength and consistency of opinions recur throughout our examination of opinion poll data.

Community policy as an issue area

Our examination of public opinion on the issue of European integration will be facilitated by an understanding of the concept of an 'issue area', as defined by James N. Rosenau. [65] Issue areas are 'categories of issues that affect a political process in sufficiently similar ways to justify being clustered together', and Rosenau distinguishes the 'domestic policy' and 'foreign policy' issue areas. [66] A particular issue area can be said to consist of:

> (1) a cluster of values, the allocation or potential allocation of which (2) leads the affected or potentially affected actors to differ so greatly over (a) the way in which the values should be allocated or (b) the horizontal levels at which the values should be allocated that (3) they engage in distinctive behaviour designed to mobilize support for the attainment of their particular values. [67]

In distinguishing between the foreign policy and domestic policy issue areas, Rosenau makes three distinctions – the types of motivation found in each, the numbers and types of political roles pertaining to each, and their respective patterns of interaction. As Pentland shows, a review of these three distinctions points to the existence of a third issue area, namely that of 'community policy'. [68]

Let us examine the main conclusions of Pentland's analysis. First, the general public is ill-informed and little interested in foreign policy, and consequently this issue area is more likely to be the subject of intense and clear-cut motivation for the mass, in contrast to the visibly more complex and salient issue area of domestic policy. This is not the case for the decision-making elite, since their intensity of motivation is low and they are aware of the extensive nature of foreign policy issues – hence a 'motivational gap' can be said to exist between elite and mass. Community policy seems to be different from either of the above issue areas. Pentland argues,

> What 'motivation gap' can be said to exist, seems to be based not only on immediacy and levels of information, but on perceptions of the relations of specific issues to the integrative process. Among the general public, in the first place, most issues are perceived and acted

upon as domestic issues, whatever meaning observers and elites might place on them for the progress of integration. [69]

Pentland continues by showing that within the elite, community policy issues are treated by some as domestic, others 'attempt to make diplomatic gains from the interdependence of states' economic and political systems', while a third group 'tends to see such issues as opportunities to increase the level of integration in the system as a whole'. [70]

With reference to Rosenau's second major distinction, the domestic policy issue area is typified by a very high degree of structural differentiation — there are numerous, specific roles — whereas in foreign policy the roles are few, and those that do exist are often multi-faceted. In community policy, the latter type of role predominates, but increasingly actors playing traditionally domestic roles (e.g. interest group leaders) are becoming involved.

Thirdly, the patterns of interaction in foreign policy are, 'largely hierarchical, or "executive", while those of domestic policy are horizontal or "legislative".[71] Again, community policy cannot be conceived in the traditional foreign policy model — as the states have become more closely integrated, there is 'increasing fragmentation and internal conflict', and although this development is now universal in foreign policy issue areas the world over, it occurs to a much more exaggerated degree in the community policy issue area. [72]

In Pentland's view, it is correct to talk of a community policy issue area and, exercising great caution, he proceeds to outline three major categories of influences on a state's behaviour toward its colleagues in an integrating system. These are:

> (a) needs and constraints arising in the general non-political environment of the state's decision-makers — that is from geographical, economic, technological and cultural sources;
> (b) influences arising in political systems formally external to the state, including the global and regional international systems, the integrating system, and the domestic systems of other states; and
> (c) influences arising in the state's domestic political and social system. [73]

These three major categories of influences on the community policy of a state puts the role of public opinion in the process of integration more clearly in focus. But the exact nature of this role is a subject of much debate among integration theorists, and it is this discussion which is reviewed fully in Chapter Three. The basic definitions of integration given by the various theorists are analysed in Chapter Two, which also seeks to complete our analytical framework by presenting a brief survey of European integration, thus forming the historical dimension to our study.

Notes

[1] Johann Galtung, *The European Community: A Superpower in the Making,* Geo. Allen and Unwin, 1973, pp. 160–1.

[2] For an illuminating article on the debate about sovereignty in Britain, see J.E.S. Fawcett, 'The issue of parliamentary sovereignty' in *The World Today* vol. 27, no. 4, April 1971, pp. 139–43.

[3] Andrew Shonfield, *Europe: Journey to an Unknown Destination,* Pelican, 1973.

[4] J. Galtung, op. cit., p. 160.

[5] V.O. Key, Jr., *Public Opinion and American Democracy,* Alfred A. Knopf, 1961, p. 14.

[6] R. Hodder-Williams, *Public Opinion Polls and British Politics,* Routledge and Kegan Paul, 1970, p. 5.

[7] Lord Windlesham, *Communication and Political Power,* Jonathan Cape, 1966, p. 155.

[8] Ian Gilmour, *The Body Politic,* Hutchinson, 1971, p. 413.

[9] A.L. Lowell, *Public Opinion and Popular Government,* Longmans, 1919, pp. 15–16.

[10] R. Hodder-Williams, op. cit., p. 6.

[11] This distinction is discussed fully by S.E. Finer, *Anonymous Empire,* Pall Mall Press, 1966, pp. 107–11.

[12] Ibid., p. 109.

[13] Ibid., p. 109.

[14] Ibid., p. 109.

[15] Ibid., p. 110.

[16] Henry Durant, 'Public opinion, polls and foreign policy' in *British Journal of Sociology,* 1955, pp. 149–58. Cited in R. Hodder-Williams, op. cit., p. 7.

[17] R. Hodder-Williams, op. cit., p. 7.

[18] See R.J. Pranger, *The Eclipse of Citizenship, Power and Participation in Contemporary Politics,* Holt, Rinehart and Winston, 1968.

[19] E.E. Schattschneider, *The Semisovereign People,* Holt, 1960, p.141.

[20] F. Teer and J.D. Spence, *Political Opinion Polls,* Hutchinson University Library, 1973, p. 11.

[21] R. Hodder-Williams, op. cit., pp. 7–8.

[22] Windlesham, op. cit., p. 155.

[23] F. Teer and J.D. Spence, op. cit., p. 12.

[24] Ibid., p. 12.

[25] Windlesham, op. cit., p. 160.

[26] R. Hodder-Williams, op. cit., p. 74.

[27] Ibid., p. 74.

[28] Ibid., p. 75.

[29] G.C. Moodie and G. Studdert-Kennedy, *Opinions, Publics and Pressure Groups: an Essay on Vox Populi and Representative Government,* George Allen and Unwin, 1970, p. 28.

[30] M. Brewster Smith, Jerome S. Bruner and Robert W. White, *Opinions and Personality,* Wiley, 1956. Cited in Moodie and Studdert-Kennedy, op. cit., pp. 24–7.

[31] Ibid., pp. 25–6.

[32] Herbert McClosky, *Political Inquiry,* Collier-Macmillian, 1969. Cited in Moodie and Studdert-Kennedy, op. cit., pp. 27–31.

[33] Herbert McClosky, 'Personality and attitude correlates of foreign policy orientation' in James N. Rosenau (ed.), *Domestic Sources of Foreign Policy,* The Free Press, 1967, p. 106.

[34] S. Verba *et al.,* 'Public opinion and the war in Vietnam' in *American Political Science Review* vol. 61, no. 2, June 1967, pp. 317–33. Cited in Moodie and Studdert-Kennedy, op. cit., p. 29.

[35] David Nias, 'Psychology and the EEC' in *New Society,* 8 March 1973, pp. 529–31.

[36] Ibid., p. 529.

[37] Ibid., p. 531.

[38] H. McClosky, op. cit., 1967, p. 106.

[39] G.C. Moodie and G. Studdert-Kennedy, op. cit., p. 29.

[40] Ibid., p. 29.

[41] Ibid., pp. 29–30.

[42] Ibid., p. 30.

[43] Herbert C. Kelman, 'Three processes of social influence' in M. Jahoda and N. Warren (eds.), *Attitudes: Selected Readings,* Penguin, 1966, p. 151–9.

[44] Ibid., p. 152.

[45] Ibid., p. 153.

[46] Ibid., p. 155.

[47] Ibid., p. 157.

[48] Ibid., p. 157.

[49] G.C. Moodie and G. Studdert-Kennedy, op. cit., p. 32.

[50] Ibid., p. 33.

[51] D. Butler and D. Stokes, *Political Change in Britain,* Pelican, 1971. Cited in Moodie and Studdert Kennedy, op. cit., p. 33.

[52] G.C. Moodie and G. Studdert-Kennedy, op. cit., p. 33.

[53] Ibid., p. 37.

[54] G. Runciman, *Relative Deprivation and Social Justice,* University of California, 1962, and D. Butler and D. Stokes, op. cit.

[55] Robert Mellish, Chief Whip in the Labour Government, 1974, is reported to have termed an Opinion Research Centre poll on voting intentions in July 1974, as 'phoney' *(The Times,* July 1974).

[56] R. Hodder-Williams, op. cit., pp. 24–5.

[57] L. Bogart, 'No opinion, don't know and maybe no answer' in *Public Opinion Quarterly,* 1967, pp. 331–45. Cited in R. Hodder-Williams, op. cit., p. 61.

[58] R. Hodder-Williams, op. cit., p. 61.

[59] Ibid., p. 63.

[60] Ibid., p. 72.

[61] Paul Rock, *Deviant Behaviour,* Hutchinson University Library, 1973, pp. 37–47.

[62] D. Butler and D. Stokes, op. cit., p. 221.

[63] Ibid., p. 221.

[64] Ibid., p. 224.

[65] James N. Rosenau, 'Foreign policy as an issue area' in J.N. Rosenau (ed.), *Domestic Sources of Foreign Policy,* The Free Press, 1967, pp. 11–50.

[66] Ibid., p. 15.

[67] James N. Rosenau, 'Pre-theories and theories of foreign policy' in R.B. Farrell (ed.), *Approaches to Comparative and International Politics,* Evanston, 1966, p. 81. Cited in Charles Pentland, *International Theory and European Integration,* Faber and Faber, 1973, p. 220.

[68] C. Pentland, op. cit., pp. 220–1.

[69] Ibid., p. 221.

[70] Ibid., p. 221.

[71] Ibid., p. 223.

[72] Ibid., p. 223–4.

[73] Ibid., p. 225.

2 European Integration: the Historical Dimension

It is not enough to present a chronology of events in Europe since 1945. We must consider the relevance of these events to the process of European integration in a way which will facilitate a more satisfactory description of the public's attitudes and opinions and which may enable us to offer sound explanations of those mass attitudes and opinions. For this reason, we must review the significant post-war events from the standpoints of the various theorists of integration.

An immediate problem which occurs with this approach is that theorists offer quite different definitions of integration. A 'lowest common denominator' definition therefore seems necessary, and this is offered by Charles Pentland, who states that 'international political integration is *a process whereby a group of people, organized initially in two or more independent nation-states, come to constitute a political whole which can in some sense be described as a community'.*[1]

This very general definition is not particularly enlightening, but Pentland points out that, 'even at this level of generality, it is possible to ask two fairly concrete questions', which are: 'First, to what sort of political whole or community is this process of change expected to lead? And secondly, what are the major conditions which bring the process about?' Pentland concludes that 'on the basis of their answers to these two questions, it is possible to group most of the important writers on international integration into four general approaches'.[2]

In their views of the end-product of the process of integration, two groups of theorists — the federalists and the neofunctionalists — envisage some form of supranationality. The political community resulting from integration is in keeping with a 'state-model', since the creation of new supranational institutions is central to federalist and neofunctionalist thought. For the federalists in particular, integration involves a real loss of sovereign powers by the participant nation-states. In contrast, the two groups of theorists comprising the functionalist and the pluralist schools place more emphasis on the character of the relationships between peoples. The establishment of institutions is seen to be secondary to the development of common habits, loyalties and values. Their view of integration therefore approximates a 'community-model', which is a more minimal definition than that found in federalist or neofunctionalist writing.

The other major dichotomy within integration theory concerns the contrasting views held on the role of independent variables in the process of integration. The federalists and the pluralists lay stress on the significance of political, or the 'direct', independent variables, by which they mean the 'problems concerning the power, responsiveness and control of political elites, and ... the political habits of the general public'. Moreover, 'much of the analysis is pitched at the level of the states', since it is held that integration can only proceed with the states' support.[3] On the other hand, the functionalists and the neofunctionalists focus on the more indirect independent variables, which consist of economic, social and technological forces. It is said that these forces can bring about political change incrementally. If the functionalists and neofunctionalists are 'deterministic', the federalists and pluralists are 'dramatic'.

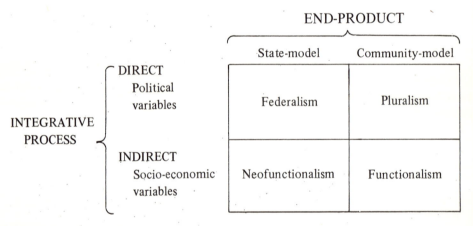

Fig. 2.1   Four approaches within integration theory

Source: C. Pentland, *International Theory and European Integration*, p. 23

These four approaches within integration theory, identified by their differing responses to Pentland's two questions, are shown diagrammatically in Figure 2.1. Pentland elaborates,

In each cell there is a core of values and assumptions, a concept of the purpose and product of integration, an explanation of the process of change, and an identifiable community of scholars whose ideas and exchanges constitute the nucleus around which the approach is centred.[4]

We shall concentrate on the theorists' views of the role of public opinion in the integrative process in Chapter Three, but firstly we shall examine the notions of the end-product in more detail by way of a review of the development of European integration since 1945.

It may not seem surprising that the earliest post-war developments in European integration consisted of the creation of co-ordinating agencies, lacking supranational powers. Yet this notion, despite its apparent factual validity, does not do justice to the active groups who favoured European unity of a federal type when peace had been achieved. Often with their roots in the Resistance, active federalist groups existed in most European countries by the end of the war, notably the Anglo-American Federal Union, the French Committee for European Federation, and the Italian Movimento Federalista Europeo. In 1947 most of these groups coalesced to form the Union of European Federalists (UEF), but many other groups at this time also favoured unity on a federal basis.

Although federalists possessed militant membership and popular support (the latter, at least, in large parts of Europe), they lacked access to those whose decisions shaped post-war Europe, while they found themselves overpowered by the force of events. It was the Allies who dictated the terms of Europe's recovery. Of the Europeans, the Scandinavians were not keen on European federalism — they shared Britain's preference for functionalist forms of integration which lacked any supranational agencies. Belgium, Luxembourg and the Netherlands had agreed, in 1944, to form a customs union, taking effect from October 1947, and although this now seems to have been a prophetic move the 'Benelux' countries were too small to influence the rebuilding of Europe. Italy possessed many federalist politicians and writers, but had been ruled by the Fascists from 1922 and finally had suffered German and Allied invasion and occupation: as a result of their economic and political plight, the Italians could contribute little in those crucial, early post-war years. The Soviet presence prevented participation in the reconstruction by the East European federalist groups, and Germany, of course, was under occupation by East and West. France's was the only European government with any real chance of influencing Europe's future, but de Gaulle was not a federalist and it was his foreign policy, the 'French thesis', that was advanced by French Foreign Ministers until the Moscow Conference of 1947.

Churchill favoured the political unification of Europe for much the same reasons as the Americans, but the British Government's attitude in these crucial years was that Britain was not to be a party to the union. The reasoning seemed obvious then, albeit antiquated now. Britain was still thought to be a world-power, one of the 'Big Three', sharing a special relationship with the USA and still possessing an empire, together with close ties with the Dominions. Her traditional policy towards Europe had been non-involvement (better known in Britain as 'splendid isolation'), opting for intervention only when events on the Continent appeared to threaten British interests.

Intervention, not integration, was the essence of Britain's European policy after the war. According to Kitzinger, those few Britons who preached integration were considered by their compatriots to be 'cranky', and were certainly unrepresentative.[5] It was in keeping with the traditional British foreign policy and despite strong American opposition that Churchill, in November 1944, had decided to support de Gaulle's demands for French participation in the invasion and occupation of Germany. Later Churchill wrote,

> The French pressed very strongly to have a share in the occupation of Germany, not merely as a sub-participation under British or American command, but as a French command. I expressed my sympathy with this, knowing well that there will be a time when the American armies will go home and when the British will have great difficulty in maintaining large forces overseas.[6]

The French did achieve participation in the invasion and occupation of Germany, thus gaining a voice in the reconstruction of Europe and laying claim to the great-power status which de Gaulle sought. In effect, the French voice at this time was de Gaulle's. His *de facto* position of leader of the free French dated from his assertion of 18 June 1940: 'Whatever happens, the flame of French resistance must not, and shall not, go out.'[7] Four years later, installed in the Premiership of Liberated France, de Gaulle claimed that, 'To decide without France anything that concerns Europe would be a grave error.'[8] His vision of Europe was similar to the federalist notion, in that its role would be that of a third power, balancing 'the Soviet and Anglo-Saxon camps'. But this vision was in the far-distant future. In the meantime the German question took precedence over all other European issues, and this question was, above all, a French concern. In 1945 de Gaulle stated, 'Germany was amputated in the east but not in the west. The current of German vitality is thus turned westwards. One day German aggressiveness might well face westwards too.

There must therefore be in the west a settlement counterbalancing that in the east.'[9]

De Gaulle resigned in January 1946, and his 'French thesis' was abandoned in March 1947, when the French Foreign Minister, Bidault, had his proposals for a decentralised German state and the internationalisation of the Ruhr vetoed by Molotov. F. Roy Willis notes the consequences:

> Molotov's rejection of the French thesis helped persuade France to throw in its lot with the West. On May 4, 1947, the Communists were forced out of Paul Ramadier's cabinet, and the French government reconciled itself to a solution to the German problem that would take into account Cold War realities. The creation of an independent West German state followed directly from the rejection of the French thesis at the Moscow Conference.[10]

With the intensification of the Cold War, a fully European federal union had become impossible. Not until the prospect of East–West *détente* became more feasible was the United Nations Economic Commission for Europe able to develop even trade and economic co-operation across the Iron Curtain. But in the late 1940s, Western Europe was faced with a real and clearly perceived threat from without, a situation which some federalists compared with that of the American colonies immediately prior to the formation of the USA. Hopes of the formation of a West European 'United States of Europe', were raised further by changes in the composition of the French and Italian Governments. De Gaulle's departure, followed by that of the Communists just over a year later, meant that the main anti-integration forces had been removed from office. Moreover, except for the four weeks of the Blum Government, the French Foreign Ministry was headed from October 1944 to June 1954 by a member of the Mouvement Republicain Populaire (MRP), France's most 'European' party. The Communists and Socialists had been ousted from the Italian Government too, resulting in a series of centre-based cabinets dominated by the 'European'-minded de Gasperi, whose party, the Christian Democrats, shared the Catholic philosophy and European sentiments of the MRP. It also became clear that in any newly created West German state, the European-minded Christian Democrats would constitute a strong political force.

Despite the increasingly federalist sympathies of these Western European governments, the attitudes of the British and Scandinavian governments remained a stumbling block to unification. The aims of American financial aid to Western Europe (the Marshall Plan), announced in June 1947, were to promote economic recovery and to encourage political unification to meet the perceived Soviet threat. The Organisation for European Economic Co-operation was created to realise the prior agreement and co-operation upon which the Americans insisted, but French and 'Benelux' pleas failed to persuade the British to allow OEEC any supranational power. Similarly, the North Atlantic Treaty Organisation, formed in 1948 in response to a perceived military threat to Western European security, failed to realise its potential supranational status because of the opposition of those member-governments who had retained a pluralist view of international co-operation. [11]

This clash between federalist and pluralist views of international organisation was illustrated most clearly in the debates at the Hague Congress of May 1948, which had been organised by the International Committee of the Movement for European Unity. [12] In the last analysis, the pluralist view prevailed, supporting traditional forms of co-operation among European states. Although the federalists had demonstrated their strength, none of their demands survived the long negotiations which followed the Congress to find substance in the Council of Europe, which was created in May 1949. Moreover, those federalists who were active in the Council's Assembly, which was drawn from the national parliaments, were soon attracted to the idea of a more gradualist approach to unification, since the setbacks of the late 1940s had confirmed the revival of the nation-state in Western Europe.

In a shock announcement on 9 May 1950, the French Foreign Minister, Robert Schuman, capitalised on the growing support for the more gradualist approach. He proposed a plan 'to place all Franco-German coal and steel production under a common High Authority, in an organization open to the participation of the other countries of Europe'. Schuman gave a succinct summary of the functionalist approach when he stated that this would mean 'the immediate establishment of common bases of industrial production, which is the first step toward European Federation and will change the destiny of regions that have long been devoted to the production of war armaments of which they themselves have been the constant victims'. [13] F. Roy Willis concludes, 'The primary motive, however, was not economic, but political: "to end Franco-German hostility once and for all", as Schuman wrote later.' [14]

The Schuman Plan had been drafted in secrecy by Jean Monnet and his staff at the offices of the Commissariat du Plan de Modernisation et d'Équipement, Monnet believing that 'secrecy and speed were essential, that surprise would permit an appeal over the heads of governments to European citizens anxious for some positive step toward integration'. [15]

30

Furthermore, individuals and organisations favouring European unification were advocating economic integration as the first step. By 1949 there was the threat of imminent overproduction in the two basic industries of coal and steel, and although the Schuman Plan was designed to overcome this problem, Monnet's choice of these industries stemmed from their role as the basis of war production and their resultant psychological importance.

Not surprisingly, the British Government rejected the invitation to participate in the creation of a supranational agency, leaving the representatives of six states to draft the ECSC Treaty. 'The Six', as they became known, were Belgium, France, Italy, Luxembourg, the Netherlands, and the newly formed West Germany. The reaction within these states to the Schuman Plan was generally favourable, although in West Germany a fierce party debate did rage, with the Social Democrat (SPD) leader, Schumacher, succeeding 'in mobilising all the irritations of the German man in the street' against a plan which, it was claimed, posed a threat to German unity and would prevent Germans from determining ownership of their industries. [16] But Schuman's trump card was that although the ECSC would involve some loss of national sovereignty, its creation would hasten the end of occupation, since this could be achieved only with French approval.

In France, the opinion polls reported a generally favourable attitude toward the Plan, but, again, Monnet's claim of appealing 'over the heads of governments to European citizens' implies a popular demand which did not exist. F. Roy Willis can state that 'the debate over the Schuman Plan hardly affected the French people', whose attitude reflected 'only a vague, uninformed benevolence'. [17] None of the six countries directly consulted their people on the ECSC issue, the debate being restricted in the main to the various national interest groups and parliamentary parties.

Seven weeks after Schuman's original announcement, North Korean troops crossed the 38th parallel, precipitating European rearmament and removing fears of overproduction in coal and steel. Already the Six were discussing the creation of the ECSC, and for the federalists the issue of rearmament 'seemed to offer a fortuitous combination of the "sector approach" with that common control of the armed forces of member-states which federalism traditionally stressed'. [18] Schuman would have preferred the ECSC to prepare the way for the gradual extension of integration, but the American demand for the arming of ten German divisions led the French Premier, Pleven, to suggest the creation of an integrated European army which would include small German units.

The Pleven Plan recognised the need for German rearmament, but by creating the European Defence Community (EDC) the new German divisions would be subjected to supranational control. The major snag was that the EDC proposal was forced on the French too quickly, for in July 1949 Robert Schuman stated to the National Assembly that 'Germany still has no peace treaty. It has no army, and it must not have one. It has no weapons, and it will have none.'[19] By May 1952, the EDC Treaty terms had been settled by the Six, but they still proved unpopular in France. The Government hoped to clinch ratification of the Treaty in the French National Assembly by stressing the importance of the EDC to European unification.

In the bitter and divisive debate which broke out in France, the Communists and the conservatives played on natural French fears of German rearmament, stressing the prospect of German hegemony within an integrated Europe. The Gaullists exploited the doubts that existed concerning the future of the French nation-state. As time passed, the Government's position became increasingly weak. Firstly, Schuman admitted that the Government's hand had been forced on the EDC issue by the Americans. In addition, the future of the Saar, which had bedevilled Franco-German relations, remained uncertain, while the ECSC did not become operational until early 1953 and therefore could not even attempt to produce the predicted benefits with which the 'Europeans' could have bolstered their arguments. Colonial problems in Indo-China and Tunisia created further complications, and with the departure of the Socialists from office in 1952 instability increased, while the Gaullists also regained influence in the Government.

Ratification proved to be an easier process for the West German Government, although the opinion polls showed that a majority of Germans opposed rearmament. The SPD exploited popular opposition with election successes in 1950 and 1951, but Chancellor Adenauer was certain of victory since the EDC was coupled with an end to occupation. Adenauer argued that rearmament was a necessary step towards regaining German sovereignty, that the Germans had a duty to contribute to their own defence, and that the EDC was good for European integration and Franco-German relations. To the SPD charge that only a reunited Germany should be rearmed, he asserted that reunification could only be won from a position of strength. The EDC Treaty was ratified by the *Bundestag* in February 1952, but several qualifying clauses were added which angered the Americans. [20]

In an effort to guarantee ratification, successive French governments tried to negotiate 'prerequisites' to the EDC, which usually amounted to preserving as much autonomy for the French army as seemed possible.

From the outset, federalists had felt that the EDC Treaty was a union of 'little Europe', or 'the Six', rather than all Western Europe, and it placed military integration before political integration.[21] French manoeuvres over 'prerequisites' lost the Government still more support from federalists, who were now lobbying for the creation of a European Political Community (EPC). The EPC had been a federalist brainchild, and in September 1952, at the instigation of Schuman and de Gasperi, the ECSC Council of Ministers agreed to allow the ECSC Common Assembly to draw up a draft EPC Treaty.[22] This draft treaty was approved by the Assembly in March 1953 by a 50:0 vote, but it was not as far reaching as some federalists had wished. Indeed, the controversy over the exact powers of the EPC served to weaken still further federalist commitment to the EDC.

On 17 June 1954, Mendès-France became French Premier, committed to securing political unity and economic recovery for France, which he felt demanded a speedy solution of French problems in the colonies and regarding the EDC. The other member-states of the Six vetoed the prerequisites demanded by Mendès-France, who proceeded to put the EDC Treaty to the National Assembly for ratification and did not make the vote a matter of confidence. Ratification was not achieved, and within four months Reynaud's prophecy that the defeat of the EDC would lead to the creation of an independent German army was proved correct.[23]

The EPC died with the EDC. On the initiative of the British, and also the French, who had now joined the British in opposition to supranationality in vital political areas, the Brussels Treaty of 1948 was revised. West Germany and Italy thus became members of the Western European Union (WEU), which was 'in the classic mould of pluralist organizations'.[24] Pentland continues, 'It had two main functions: a military one, dealing with arms control and problems of Western European defence in relation to NATO, and a political one, in providing a regular meeting place for Britain and the Six.'[25] In its military role the WEU fulfilled the pluralist conception of aiding security 'without compromising its members' autonomy', while in its political role it 'has served primarily as a channel of "elite communication" for its seven members', any attempts at strengthening its framework having been blocked by the French.[26]

The pluralist ascendancy seemed complete. The ECSC had not yet lived up to its predicted performance, Franco-German relations had been damaged by the French veto of the EDC, and in October 1955, contrary to expectations, the Saarlanders voted against the Europeanisation of their territory and in favour of union with West Germany. The federalist movement was thrown into disarray, which developed into a split when faced with the *rélance Européenne,* marked by the Messina Conference of 1955. In March 1956, a group of mainly Belgian, French and Italian social democratic federalists, including Spinelli, left the Union of European Federalists to form the Mouvement Fédéraliste Européen (MFE). The aim of the MFE was to launch a propaganda campaign culminating in the formation of European institutions 'over the heads' of the apparently inevitable conservatism of the national leaders. The influence of the MFE faded, and the gradualist or functionalist federalists, comprising mainly Dutch and German and some French organisations, which formed the Action Européen Fédéraliste (AEF), became increasingly significant. The AEF was prepared to work with existing national forces, and it was this collaboration which found its expression in the 'community method' of the emergent European Economic Community (EEC), thus introducing a new theoretical approach to integration termed 'neofunctionalism'. [27]

In 1955 the tide began to turn in favour of the integration movements. The economic benefits of the ECSC at last began to be felt, helping to create an economic boom from the time of the Messina Conference to the signing of the Rome Treaty. There were also signs that the federalist campaigns for unity throughout post-war Western Europe were producing the desired public support for integration. [28] Against this favourable backcloth, and on the initiative of the Benelux and Italian Foreign Ministers, the Messina Conference of the Foreign Ministers of the Six were able to agree on the principle of further integration in energy and in the economic sphere in general. An Intergovernmental Committee co-ordinated by Paul-Henri Spaak was established to prepare more detailed proposals, and, after many prior consultations, the so-called Spaak Report was presented to the Six on 21 April 1956.

The essence of the Spaak Report was that Europe

> ... could not continue its progress and sustain by itself the present rhythm of expansion with its present economic organization. ... None of our countries is large enough to support the extensive research and basic investments that will give impetus to the technical revolution which the atomic era promises. [29]

In the first section of the Report, the creation of a European Common Market was deemed necessary, and its object was defined as the creation of, 'a vast area with a common economic policy, which would form a powerful productive unit, and which would make possible continuous expansion, increased stability, a rapid rise in the standard of living, and development of harmonious relations between member-states'. [30] A common European approach toward the development of atomic energy was urged in the second part of the Report. In May 1956, the Foreign Ministers of the Six decided to base two treaties on the Report, one treaty creating the EEC and the other creating Euratom.

In negotiations over the treaties, the main reservations were expressed by the French Government, but their caution was practical rather than reflecting any obstructive opposition, since the Socialist Premier, Mollet, favoured integration and had the backing of his cabinet on this issue, following Gaullist defeats in the election of January 1956. The French surrendered their right to secede from the EEC Treaty in return for the inclusion of an agricultural policy and the satisfactory settlement of terms for French overseas territories. In the West German Government, the negotiations revealed a disagreement between Adenauer and his Finance Minister, Erhard. The latter opposed the proposal for an EEC external tariff, since he feared the effects on German trade – instead, he advocated European free trade. But Adenauer overruled Erhard, since he placed more emphasis on the prospect of long-term political unity in the EEC than he placed on short-term economic problems. [31]

Despite the political intentions of the Treaty of Rome, with its reference to 'an ever closer union', the mass publics were not mobilised to the same extent as they had been in the ECSC and EDC debates. Not only were civil servants and politicians familiarised with the workings of European institutions by 1956, but the EEC negotiations thrashed out the conflicts between different interests before the EEC began work, with the French in particular involving agriculturalists', employers' and workers' representatives directly in the talks before the final terms of the Treaty were settled. The role of the Action Committee for the United States of Europe, founded in October 1955 at the instigation of Jean Monnet, was also vital, since the Committee included politicians of various persuasions and trade unionists, who were able to influence the debate in their own countries. Monnet himself placed great store on the need for Euratom, and he did much to overcome a revival of many of the fears voiced in the EDC debates when he stated that a European Atomic authority would be concerned with only the peaceful exploitation of atomic energy. With the ECSC creating a more favourable image in the Six – which played a large part in the conversion of the SPD to the cause of integration – and swinging the advantage to the 'Europeans' still further, F. Roy Willis has written that,

... neither in parliament nor in public did the debate over ratification develop the polemical features that had characterized the debates over ECSC and EDC. In France and in Germany the argument was pursued with greater knowledge and moderation; and the understanding of the treaties' political and economic consequences was more realistic. [32]

The Treaty of Rome came into effect on 1 January 1958, creating the EEC and Euratom on the same institutional pattern as the ECSC, with a supreme Council of Ministers, an executive in the form of the Commission (the High Authority in ECSC), a Court of Justice, and an Assembly common to all three communities but far from being a European Parliament. By 1960, seven countries that had not been able to support this supranational pattern had formed the European Free Trade Association. Although this pluralist alternative to the EEC enjoyed some success, it was unable to stand comparison with the achievements of the Six in the late 1950s and 1960s, and those states that were neither 'neutral' nor ruled by a dictatorship soon approached the EEC with requests for full membership. [33]

Neofunctionalism, a synthesis of federalism and functionalism, had become the unofficial ideology of the Six by 1962. [34] Its plausibility was to be weakened by de Gaulle's veto of the British application for entry in January 1963, but the EEC's achievements remained impressive. Economic growth soared throughout the Six, rapid progress was made toward a customs union, the Common Agricultural Policy had been agreed, and Franco-German relations had never been better. [35] The doubts for integration voiced when de Gaulle seized power in France in June 1958 seemed ill-founded.

Until 1962, de Gaulle was preoccupied with the Algerian problem, but when this was settled he knew that he had secured a firm power base in France from which he could enunciate and endeavour to realise his world-view. His aim was to end the bipolar world and create in the process a special role for Europe and for France. Thus, on the one hand, the French policy was to encourage the East to move toward liberalisation and *détente,* while on the other hand Europe should become independent of the United States. [36] This led to the development of the French *force de frappe* (independent nuclear deterrent), the French departure from NATO in 1967, a preference for gold reserves rather than the dollar, and European unity which remained confederal. De Gaulle opposed British entry, therefore, for three major reasons: the particular problems British entry would create for French agriculture; the ensuing shift in the 'balance' of the EEC, away from a Bonn–Paris axis, and away from any possibility of it developing into a 'Mediterranean community'; and the greatly increased influence which the USA would gain in European affairs through the Anglo-American 'special relationship'. [37]

De Gaulle's veto imperilled Franco-German relations, since he had presented Adenauer, who favoured British entry, with a *fait accompli* – it seemed that the Germans were not seen as equals to the French in the EEC. Yet Adenauer signed the Franco-German Treaty on 22 January 1963, thus 'putting the final seal on Franco-German *rapprochement*'.[38] Like Monnet, Adenauer felt that a European confederation would ultimately result in a federal union. But Adenauer's domestic power base had been weakened at the very moment that de Gaulle's had been secured: the *Spiegel* affair, resulting in the dismissal of Defence Minister Strauss for trying to muzzle an anti-Gaullist editor, precipitated a rebellion by the *Atlantiker* majority within Adenauer's own CDU–CSU party. In April, the Christian Democrats chose Erhard as successor to Adenauer, who had to serve out his remaining months as Chancellor under notice to an Atlanticist whose world-view was almost totally at odds with that of de Gaulle. The ineffectual Adenauer could secure parliamentary ratification of the Franco-German Treaty only by accepting a preamble which stated the aims of West German foreign policy and which amounted to a declaration that West Germany had no intention of adopting French foreign policy. [39]

During Erhard's three-year Chancellorship, Franco-German relations grew predictably worse. With support for Adenauer's conciliatory policy limited to the minority of CDU *Gaullisten,* and with the opinion polls plotting the decline in de Gaulle's popularity in Germany in 1964, many Frenchmen began to fear that Gaullist nationalism could revive German nationalism. [40] By late 1964, Erhard concluded that the only solution to the French problem was to press for political unification of the Six. Consequently, the Germans conceded to French demands for a lower common cereal price for the CAP than then existed on the German market, encouraged by French concessions on the terms of the forth-coming Kennedy Round talks. [41]

But in March 1965, the French Government was enraged by a Commission proposal which would have transformed the institutions of the EEC into a supranational political authority. French anger was particularly aroused by the announcement of this proposal to the press and the European Parliament, with no prior notification to the member-governments. The President of the Commission, Hallstein, saw that the growing demands on de Gaulle by the French agricultural lobby were causing the French Government to make further demands in the CAP talks. Hallstein felt that the Commission's chance had come to win more supranational powers in return for CAP concessions to the French. F. Roy Willis summarises the implications of the Commission's proposals:

> Had they been accepted, the proposals would have converted the Commission into a genuine supranational executive with a very large income independent of the member-states' control, and the European Parliament into a legislature with real powers over a Community budget. [42]

Also, as envisaged in the Treaty of Rome, the Council of Ministers would move from unanimity voting (i.e. each state holding the power of veto) to weighted-majority voting, which would mean that France would lose her right to veto.

These proposals had caused much debate within the Commission during their formulation, and it soon became clear that Hallstein had under-estimated the extent of Gaullist intransigence. On the night of 30 June–1 July 1965, when the deadline set for the conclusion of the CAP talks was reached, the French Foreign Minister, Couve de Murville, announced that 'a community whose partners do not abide by their agreements has ceased to be a community'. [43] Within a week the French permanent representative to the Communities had been ordered to return to Paris and French participation was limited to the day-to-day matters of the Communities.

The French boycott, or so-called 'empty-seat' policy, caused a great constitutional crisis in the Communities. De Gaulle's intention had been to defend his notion of *L'Europe des patries* by demonstrating the dependence of the Communities on France. In the event he was largely successful, but de Gaulle also came to realise the large degree of French dependence on the Communities. His position was weakened by the forthcoming Presidential election in December 1965, since de Gaulle knew that he could not afford to lose the 'European' vote. To complicate matters still further, he found that the agricultural unions, whose demands he had been advancing in the talks on CAP, were leading the campaign for an end to the boycott. Business interests and the trade unions also pointed to the damage that the boycott would inflict on the French economy and on the integration movement. De Gaulle's major Presidential rivals, Lecanuet (MRP) and Mitterand (Left-wing coalition), emphasised their commitment to European integration, with the result that in the first-round ballot of 5 December de Gaulle's percentage of the vote was only 43·97. In the ensuing run-off, de Gaulle was re-elected with 55 per cent of the vote, but Mitterand's share of 45 per cent seemed to show that the public wanted an end to the 'empty chair' policy. [44] Meanwhile, in the

West German parliamentary elections of 19 September, all the major parties had opposed the Gaullist European policy, thereby strengthening Erhard's hand in Brussels. [45]

The talks, between the governments of the Six, that began in January 1966, in an effort to end the deadlock, were held in Luxembourg at the insistence of the French. At the outset, Couve de Murville presented ten demands which one correspondent believed to represent an effort to reassert 'French hegemony'. Following lengthy talks at a second meeting of Foreign Ministers in Luxembourg, a decision was reached on the voting system in the Council of Ministers:

> When, in the case of decisions that may be made by majority vote on a proposal of the Commission, very important interests of one or more partners are at stake, the Members of the Council will endeavour, within a reasonable time, to reach solutions that can be adopted by all the members of the Council. ... The French delegation considers that when very important issues are at stake, the discussion must be continued until unanimous agreement is reached. The six delegations note that there is a divergence of views on what should be done in the event of failure to reach complete agreement. The six delegations nevertheless consider that this divergence does not prevent the Community's work being resumed in accordance with normal procedure. [46]

On the role of the Commission, 'the French insistence on depriving the Commission of all the attributes of an independent government' were met, but the Commission's powers of initiative were retained. [47] F. Roy Willis concludes, 'Both in the rule on majority voting and in preserving the Commission's powers of initiative, the Five hoped to have saved the nucleus of a supranational state to be created when the Gaullist regime in France came to an end.'[48]

In fact, the Luxembourg settlement preserved the Gaullist notion of *L'Europe des patries,* leading de Gaulle to reiterate his plans for 'political union' by the creation of a Council of Heads of State or Government whose decisions would require unanimity. This cornerstone of French European policy was further developed by Couve de Murville in 1967:

> It is obvious that the economic union which is being established among the Six and which operates satisfactorily must be followed by progress toward political union, that is, toward a *rapprochement* among the Six in the political field, not to be too ambitious. [49]

Charles Pentland spells out the Gaullist thesis:

> Not being 'too ambitious' in this case clearly means understanding 'political union' not in the Monnet—Hallstein sense as the culmination of economic integration in a United States of Europe, but in the pluralist sense of a 'community of states' co-operating over the inherently political subjects of defence and foreign policy. [50]

The purity of the Gaullist notion of Europe was maintained in 1967 by de Gaulle's second rejection of British entry to the EEC, a rejection which the new Kiesinger Government in West Germany felt unable to challenge for fear of antagonising the French at a time when the Americans were heavily committed in the Far East. Similarly, there was little German opposition to the premature departure of Hallstein from the Presidency of the Commission in objection to the Commission's loss of autonomy *vis-à-vis* the Council, following the Luxembourg settlement. [51]

By the late 1960s, neofunctionalism or 'gradual federalism' seemed a far less plausible theory of integration than it had seemed in the early 1960s, the heyday of the EEC. First, the neofunctionalist emphasis on the 'cumulative logic of integration', whereby economic integration led inevitably to political integration, ignored the apparent differences between issues of 'low' and 'high' politics, or the distinction between 'negative integration' and 'positive integration'. [52] Without detracting from the considerable achievements of the EEC, these were mainly examples of 'negative integration', or 'the removal of obstacles to free exchange between the states'. [53] The European customs union was achieved on 1 July 1968, a year ahead of the original timetable, but it seems dubious to claim that the 'community method' could achieve comparable success in the field of positive integration, where detailed common policies and institutions capable of performing a much more interventionist role have to be developed.

Secondly, the European Community appears to have reached a watershed: if further progress toward unification is to be made, a policy of positive integration is essential, since the immediate aims of the Treaty of Rome had been achieved by 1969. But in 1970, at a time when neofunctionalism faced its most severe test, the Six institutionalised the Gaullist, or pluralist, concept of 'political union', by accepting the Davignon Report's recommendation for twice-yearly ministerial meetings on political co-operation. These recommendations followed the decision made by the Six at the Hague Summit of December 1969 to complete, enlarge and strengthen the Community.

The Davignon Report and the decision by de Gaulle's successor,

Pompidou, to support enlargement of the Community have raised further problems for neofunctionalism. De Gaulle's claim that his opposition to supranational agencies enabled other leaders to pay lip-service to federalist ideals, secure in the knowledge that France would veto any such move, seems to have gained at least some credibility. [54] The other major Community power, West Germany, pursued a policy of *rapprochement* with France during Adenauer's time, and there has been a good deal of emphasis on the role of European integration as a means to the more fundamental goal of reunification. Pentland continues:

> It has become increasingly clear in the early 1970s that the West German government, especially since the Hague 'summit' of December 1969, shares the French view on the importance of co-operation and harmonization in foreign policy, although it is careful to place this in the long-run perspective of gradual elimination of 'sovereign elements'. [55]

With the entry of Britain, by tradition the most 'pluralist' state in terms of Western European integration, the view that enlargement would lead to a new dynamism in the Community seems dubious. Indeed, the sheer size of the enlarged Community has made it even less likely that the 'community method' can achieve any progress towards 'positive integration'. The Paris Summit of the Nine in October 1973 prepared a blueprint for the future development of the Community in which the Nine reaffirmed their intention, which had first been declared at the Hague, of clinching Economic and Monetary Union (EMU) by 1980. Some observers felt that this new long-term commitment, together with 'the tying-in of such issues as short-term currency stability (France's major concern), central banking control (Germany's interest), structural change and regional development (Italy's interest)', would reactivate the 'community method'. [56] But the type of issues involved here are politically very contentious, involving differing national and ideological views of economic planning, the distribution of wealth, and so on. The contrast between this 'positive integration' and the earlier, pre-1969, 'negative integration' is clear.

It is partly because of this contrast between the two stages of integration in the Community that we can agree with Galtung that the role of public opinion is likely to become more important in the future. Referenda on entry into the Community were held in Denmark, Eire, and Norway — and a referendum on renegotiated terms has subsequently been demanded by the Labour Party in Britain — because of the different nature of the Community's policies since 1969. This factor is combined with the growing support for forms of more direct democracy in Western European liberal democracies. Affluence, disillusionment with parliamentary and bureaucratic institutions and the increasing popularity of egalitarian ideals are also powerful forces which have led to the emergence of a populist strand in the politics of the Community.

We have presented the historical dimension to our study, and we shall relate the detailed analysis of public opinion poll data to this historical context. However, any analysis of public opinion poll data demands that we examine critically the role which the various integration theorists believe public opinion plays in the process of integration. From a discussion of integration theories we are able to generate six propositions which can be tested against the evidence from the polls in the remainder of the study. It is to this task that we turn in Chapter Three.

Notes

[1] C. Pentland, *International Theory and European Integration,* op. cit., p. 21.

[2] Ibid., p. 21.

[3] Ibid., p. 22.

[4] Ibid., p. 23.

[5] Uwe Kitzinger, *Diplomacy and Persuasion,* op. cit., p. 20.

[6] Winston S. Churchill, *The Second World War,* Boston 1948–53, p. 252. Cited in F. Roy Willis, *France, Germany and the New Europe, 1945–1967,* Oxford UP, 1968, p. 11. Much of the information for this section, 'European Integration; Theory and Practice', is drawn from the splendid account given by Willis.

[7] Charles de Gaulle, *Mémoires de Guerre* vol. 1, Paris 1954–59, pp. 267–8. Cited in F. Roy Willis, op. cit., p. 7.

[8] C. de Gaulle, op. cit., vol. 3, p. 305. Cited ibid., p. 8.

[9] *The Times*, London, 10 September 1945. Cited ibid., p. 15.

[10] Ibid., p. 19.

[11] C. Pentland, op. cit., pp. 52–4.

[12] Ibid., p. 178.

[13] Pierre Gerbet, 'La genèse du Plan Schuman: dès origine à la declaration du 9 mai 1950' in *Revue française de science politique,* July–September 1956, pp. 525–53. Cited in F. Roy Willis, op. cit., p. 80.

[14] Ibid., p. 80.

[15] Ibid., p. 83–4.

[16] Ibid., p. 127.

[17] Ibid., p. 98.

18 Ibid., p. 130.
19 France, Assemblée nationale, *Debats,* 15 July 1949, pp. 5227–31. Cited ibid., p. 130.
20 Ibid., pp. 154–6.
21 Ibid., p. 158.
22 Ibid., pp. 158–9.
23 Ibid., p. 184.
24 C. Pentland, op. cit., p. 55.
25 Ibid., p. 55.
26 Ibid., p. 56.
27 Ibid., pp. 181–2.
28 F. Roy Willis, op. cit., pp. 227–42.
29 Ibid., p. 245.
30 Ibid., p. 245.
31 Ibid., p. 265.
32 Ibid., p. 251.
33 Those states with a 'neutral' foreign policy – therefore prevented from joining the potential federal union of the EEC – were Austria, Sweden and Switzerland (Finland was only an associate of EFTA). The dictatorship was Portugal. Applications for membership of the EEC were made by Britain, Denmark and Norway.
34 C. Pentland, op. cit., pp. 131–2.
35 F. Roy Willis, op. cit., pp. 281–3.
36 Ibid., pp. 323–4.
37 Ibid., p. 303.
38 Ibid., p. 310.
39 Ibid., pp. 312–7.
40 Ibid., pp. 330–2.
41 Ibid., p. 334.
42 Ibid., p. 343.
43 *L'Année Politique,* Paris 1965, pp. 270–4. Cited ibid., p. 344.
44 Ibid., pp. 345–7.
45 Ibid., p. 348.
46 Ibid., pp. 349–50.
47 Ibid., p. 350.
48 Ibid., p. 350.
49 Ambassade de France à Londres, Service de Presse et d'Information, 'Excerpt from the Press Conference given by General de Gaulle', Paris, 21 February 1966, p. 1. See also 'Press Conference' of 28 October 1966 and television 'Interview' of M. Couve de Murville, 12 November 1967, p. 5. Cited in C. Pentland, op. cit., p. 57.

[50] Ibid., p. 57.

[51] F. Roy Willis, op. cit., pp. 360–2.

[52] For a fuller critique of neofunctionalist theory, see Chapter Two. The terms 'negative' and 'positive' integration are from J. Pinder, 'Positive integration and negative integration: some problems of economic union in the EEC' in *World Today* vol. 24, no. 3, 1968, pp. 90–1 and p. 97.

[53] C. Pentland, op. cit., p. 136.

[54] Ibid., p. 58.

[55] Ibid., p. 58.

[56] Ibid., p. 141.

3 Theories of Integration and the Role of Public Opinion

It has been argued that public opinion is of much less weight than the actions of economic and political elites in making progress towards a more united Europe. For instance, one leading theorist, Ernst B. Haas, modifies the idea of an emerging international consensus on economic and social questions leading to the reinforcement of international organisations whose decisions would thereby come to hold sway over those made by nation-states.[1] This was the essence of the older 'functionalist' view, and Haas is stating the 'neofunctionalist' case when he asserts that there can be no 'common good', 'other than that perceived through the interest-tinted lenses worn by the actors'.[2]

It follows that the neofunctionalist view of integration emphasises the role of 'interest-politics', played out within international institutions. Functionalism, which is identified with the work of David Mitrany, stresses the development of a socio-psychological community, a feeling of mutual affection, identity and loyalty as a precondition for integration.[3] The neofunctionalists place more weight on the prior development of supranational institutions, which make policy decisions and with which the various interest groups can bargain, thereby hastening still further integration.

Because economic problems are interconnected, the neofunctionalists argue that the solution of one problem by joint action through supranational institutions would necessarily lead to joint action on other related problems. As it becomes clear that the supranational agencies are the true problem-solving bodies, the leaders of the relevant interest groups and even members of the national bureaucracies would shift their attentions, and ultimately their loyalties, from the nation-state. As regards the attitudes held by the general public, the formation of any socio-psychological community ('consensus') is not a necessary element in the neofunctionalist theory of integration.

'The cumulative logic of integration' is thus central to the neofunctionalist theory. The outcome is that, like the federalists, who are concerned with the management of interests within a single political framework, the neofunctionalists tend to focus on institutional developments. For them the main dynamic of integration within the European Community lies in the interrelationship between national governments and the European Commission. It is the Commission which proposes any new Community-level measures to the Council of Ministers. As a result of the interdependence of economic problems in modern societies, the transfer of formal powers to the Commission enables it to increase its capacity through the process of 'spillover'.

The core of the neofunctionalist thesis is revealed in the following statement by Haas and Schmitter:

> Integration can be conceived as involving the gradual politicization of the actors' purposes which were initially considered 'technical' or 'non-controversial'. Politicization implies that the actors, in response to the initial purposes, agree to widen the spectrum of means considered appropriate to attain them. This tends to increase the controversial component, i.e. those additional fields of action which require political choices concerning how much national autonomy to delegate to the union. Politicization implies that the actors seek to resolve their problems so as to upgrade common interests and, in the process, delegate more authority to the center.[4]

Haas and Schmitter add that, 'Industrial society is the setting in which supranationality and a lively spillover process are able to flourish'.[5]

The functionalists see a more circular set of interactions taking place — a view shared in the European Community by the 'nationalists', such as de Gaulle, who intended to prevent the full logical development of this 'functionalist' pattern. Paul Taylor, who isolates the differences between functionalists and neofunctionalists succinctly, provides a neat diagrammatic summary of their views of the process of integration (see Figure 3.1).[6]

Figure 3.1 shows that the essence of functionalism 'is to be found in a complex set of assumptions about the linkages between international collaboration and the political attitudes of individuals'.[7] Pentland shows that the process of attitude change through international co-operation operates in two phases. In the first phase, only individuals participating directly in the international venture are placed in a 'learning situation', but, in the second phase, education, the media, and also the increasing scope of the international agencies mean that the general public have some experience of international co-operation. The idea that experience can develop into the existence of a socio-psychological community, and thus meaningful integration, is derived from the functionalists' view that men's basic loyalties focus naturally on those institutions which gratify their basic material and social needs.[8]

46

(a)   Neofunctionalist view (generally shared by the federalists, who actively support any signs of the 'United States of Europe')

(b)   Functionalist view (shared by de Gaulle and other nationalists, integration being a development they seek to frustrate)

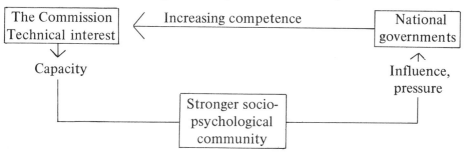

Fig. 3.1 The neofunctionalist and functionalist views of the process of integration

Source: P. Taylor, 'The concept of community and the European integration process' in *Journal of Common Market Studies* vol. 7, no. 2, 1968

The neofunctionalist concept of 'the cumulative logic of integration' taken to its conclusion demonstrates the emergence of a supranational authority as more and more powers are taken away from the nation-state. The gist of this thesis is that the economic and political elites (viz. Jean Monnet, Robert Schuman, and others) can initiate plans for integration in one sector of the economy (viz. the European Coal and Steel Community), which inevitably leads to integration of all sectors of the economy (viz. the European Economic Community) and, ultimately, to a full-blooded political unification (viz. the United States of Europe).

But the work of Haas is very much a product of its time. His thesis was first fully expounded in *The Uniting of Europe,* published in 1958, and his later work, *Beyond the Nation State,* appeared in 1964. The European

Communities did not receive their first serious setback until the veto on British entry by de Gaulle in early 1963. Haas's thesis, reflecting a seemingly inevitable transition from a simple Coal and Steel Community to a full economic union, and ultimately to a full political union, was a thesis which appeared viable and, of course, attractive to the optimists in the European movement.

By the mid 1960s the critics of neofunctionalism were able to quote the growing disappointments and setbacks suffered by the Six. As Hansen argues, however, much of this criticism 'analyses *what* has happened rather than *why* it happened, thereby contributing little to a better understanding of the integration process in industrially and politically developed regions'.[9] Yet new insights were made by some members of the neofunctionalist school, most notably by Leon Lindberg and Stuart Scheingold, who in 1970 published a 'mid-term' report on European integration entitled *Europe's Would-be Polity*.[10] As we shall see, this study placed new emphasis on the role of public support for integration.

Yet some fundamental criticisms were made of the neofunctionalist approach. For instance, Stanley Hoffmann launched a biting attack on the notion of a 'cumulative logic of integration'.[11] He argued that although it may seem regrettable, the nation-state has not been superseded in Western Europe, nor is it likely to be, for several basic reasons. The kernel of his case is that,

> Political unification could have succeeded if on the one hand, these nations had not been caught in the whirlpool of different concerns, as a result of both profoundly different internal circumstances and of outside legacies, and if, on the other hand, they had been able to and obliged to concentrate on 'community-building' to the exclusion of all other problems situated either outside this area or within each of them.[12]

According to Hoffmann, political unification has not developed because of the 'logic of diversity' — each country has its own domestic features, a unique geo-historical situation and its own 'outside' aims, all of which are buttressed by the strongly embedded 'nationalist' content of all political debates and processes. Moreover, there is, in Hoffmann's, view, a lack of specifically West European problems — today's problems are either global or local. Finally, other world powers could, if they so wished, check any signs of political unification in Western Europe.

These last two points would seem to be supported by international developments in 1973 and 1974. The third Arab-Israeli war sparked off a series of events which led to President Nixon's threat to reduce American forces in Western Europe. The West European countries would then have had to make a choice. Their first option would have amounted to accepting an even graver imbalance of troops between West and East Europe than already exists and thereby being effectively 'Finlandised' by the Soviet Union. The other course of action would be a commitment to spending more on defence, with the aim of minimising the troop imbalance.

The public relations exercises conducted by Mr Brezhnev in the West in recent years, aimed at demonstrating his country's sole concern for peaceful co-existence, would appear to show that at least the Soviet leadership recognises the significance of public sentiment in Europe. It may well suit the Soviet Union for the Americans to remain in Europe, since the East enjoys a favourable imbalance and the West finds it hard to achieve real unity. But American troop reductions could have the effect of uniting Western Europe on defence policy – presumably it is this development which Brezhnev seeks to prevent, should the Americans decide to withdraw. Hoffmann's observation that Europe's future rests in the hands of the super-powers is thus only a part of the truth. At least one super-power is paying great attention to the role of the West European public in the future of Europe, thereby giving support to the arguments of those who stress the internal sources of foreign policy as opposed to the more traditionalistic interest in external factors.

Hoffmann appears to be far nearer to the truth when he demonstrates how the logic of diversity sets limits to the extent to which there can be 'spillover':

> It [the logic of diversity] restricts the domain in which the logic of functional integration operates to the area of welfare; indeed, to the extent that discrepancies over the other areas begin to prevail over the laborious harmonization in welfare, even issues belonging to the latter sphere may become infected by the disharmony which reigns in those other areas. [13]

For Hoffmann, the logic of integration is equivalent to a 'blender' which crushes the most diverse products and produces, presumably, a most delicious juice. The ambiguity inherent in the neofunctionalist view of integration appears to help – each ingredient can hope that its tastes will prevail in the end. Hoffmann's point is telling, in contrast to the 'woolly' neofunctionalist view of a natural continuum between economic integration and political unity. Hoffmann argues that in areas of key importance to the national interest, nations prefer the certainty, or the self-contained uncertainty, of national self-reliance, to the uncontrolled uncertainty of the untested blender. On matters of vital interest, nations will not be prepared to suffer losses and merely gain 'compensation' in another area. Thus, the ambiguities of integration, far from being creative and guaranteeing satisfaction, can be destructive. Hoffmann claims that the cost of unfulfilled expectations on the part of supranational organisations could well be a resurgence of nationalism.

Haas's response to Hoffmann's critique fails to produce the necessary theoretical refinement. In 'The uniting of Europe and the uniting of Latin America', Haas endeavours to incorporate the French boycott of the Communities into his conceptual framework.[14] In deference to de Gaulle's refusal to allow the Council of Ministers to adopt the majority voting method in place of the unanimity rule, and thereby allowing it to become a fully political supranational institution, Haas allows for the interference of a 'dramatic-political' actor. But Haas is still assuming that integration is in some way automatic, given a congruence of aims among the statesmen and 'the non-governmental elite' (i.e. businessmen and interest group leaders). He is continuing to dodge the issue. Hoffmann's point remains that some areas may continue to be classified as 'high politics' and no amount of economic integration will change this.

We have seen that the earlier neofunctionalist model expects too much to stem from integration at the level of 'low politics'. As Hansen argues, the neofunctionalists fail to relate the process of regional integration to factors in the surrounding international system; they tend to deny rather than to investigate the discontinuity between 'high' (national interest) politics and 'low' (welfare) politics, proclaimed by Hoffmann and other traditionalists, such as Aron;[15] and finally they fail 'to recognize that sizeable (and equitably distributed) economic gains would result from a common market *co-ordinated* by sovereign states rather than managed by ceaselessly expanding supranational authorities'.[16]

Yet the traditionalists fail to clarify their use of the terms 'national interest', 'national will', and so on. Indeed, Hoffmann fails to perceive that statements asserting the irreducibility and overriding importance of the nation assume the existence of an objectively discernible national interest. This would seem to provide an excellent example of an author's 'domain assumptions' causing him to reach a predictable conclusion.[17] The traditionalist conviction of the ongoing reality of nationalism has led them to underestimate the significance of conflicting interests and public attitudes *within* nations which are members of a supranational organisation.

As Pentland claims, the neofunctionalists have made a great advance compared with traditional international theory by recognising that the nation-state is composed of groups who are likely to possess conflicting interests and values. [18] The nation-state is thus far from the virtual monolith portrayed by traditionalists. When the neofunctionalist liberal-democratic view of the nation-state is coupled with the distinctiveness of 'community-policy' as opposed to foreign policy, which we analysed in Chapter One, we can see that although the traditionalists have exposed certain neofunctionalist weaknesses, their own approach is of little value to the student of European integration. Above all, there is no room in Hoffmann's critique for the growth of significant pro-European loyalties.

The federalist theorists share some of the assumptions of the traditionalists. First, they stress the non-deterministic nature of integration and thus attack both functionalists and neofunctionalists. [19] Secondly, the federalists also assume that the governmental elites embody the 'national will'. Pentland isolates these assumptions clearly when he states that federalists assume that '. . . elites can often act independently of the political and economic forces in their societies', and that '. . . elites are relatively unfettered, free from serious pushes and pulls from transnational interest groups or public opinion and subject only to pressures from their counterparts in other states'. [20] Yet there is a strong 'populist' element within federalism which is reflected in Etzioni's work, when he writes of the need to gain legitimacy for integration by cultivating a 'popular-will'. [21] By and large those federalists who, like Etzioni, take a sociological perspective do see the growth of a 'federal consensus' amongst the public, since they put great store by 'the effects of institutions and power on political attitudes'. To quote Pentland further: 'The political attitudes of individuals, then, are held to have a structure congruent with that of their political community.'[22] Since, in a federal system, political power is not centralised, it follows that federalists assume the possibility of the public developing 'multiple loyalties'.

At this point it is particularly valuable for us to refer to a more recent neofunctionalist study which we have already mentioned briefly above – the work of Lindberg and Scheingold. Their study of integration up to 1970 utilises David Easton's notion of 'inputs' into a political system. [23] To Easton, inputs comprise demands by the members of a political system, and also the support given to a system by its members. Thus, Lindberg and Scheingold examine the effectiveness of the Communities' institutions in meeting the various demands made of them, and, of more significance, in a discussion of the role of public opinion in European integration, the authors examine the nature of the support for the European Communities. Thus, they face problems which Haas evaded – first, the timing of attitude-change in relation to institutional change, and, secondly, the mechanisms of change assumed to be involved. Although their conclusion was that the socio-political environment was becoming increasingly favourable for integration, in the last analysis they emphasise that, whereas the amount of support that is available for any system establishes the 'parameters' of the decision-making process, it is the supranational institutions that are the real engines of the Community and of the process of integration.

However, Lindberg and Scheingold do develop a matrix of support which facilitates a systematic and comprehensive investigation of the Community's socio-political context (see Figure 3.2). [24]

			Basis of response	
			Utilitarian	Affective
Levels of interaction	Identitive			
	Systemic	Community		
		Regime		

Fig. 3.2 Matrix of support for integration

Source: L. Lindberg and S. Scheingold, *Europe's Would-be Polity,* p. 61.

The identitive level of interaction refers to the perceived links among the peoples of the Community, while systemic interaction refers to links between the public and the system itself. Thus, a systemic community response refers to opinions expressed concerning questions on the scope of the Community, while the systemic regime response refers to the actual nature of Community institutions. Questions relating to the need for a Common Defence Policy would thus be reflected in the former response, questions covering direct elections to the European Parliament would be reflected in the latter.

The matrix further distinguishes such responses into those of an affective nature, and those which are utilitarian. In this case, the former would represent some diffuse and perhaps emotional response, for instance, some recognition of a common European identity, while the latter represents support based on some perceived economic or political interest, such as higher living standards or security from invasion.

The conclusion reached by Lindberg and Scheingold was that the strongest basis of support for the Community was utilitarian. This finding, they argue, gives credence to the neofunctionalist thesis of the 'logic of integration', whereby a community can develop from the pursuit of basically economic interests. Evidence of affective support was weaker — in the 1960s, most West Europeans referred to the United States as 'the most trusted ally' — but there was evidence that the Community generated a little affective support. Consequent upon these conclusions, Lindberg and Scheingold posit the existence of a 'permissive consensus' for the Community amongst the public of the Six. However, incremental moves toward integration were accepted in the economic sphere, but diplomatic or military integrative still lacked any real support.

A further improvement made by Lindberg and Scheingold, in comparison with the more limited approach of Haas, is their development of a five-point scale, which they use to measure the degree of integration in any particular sphere, although we have seen in Chapter Two that, in keeping with their neofunctionalist approach, 'integration' is limited to the dimension of decision-making. Their scale stretches from 'nation-states make all fundamental political choices by a purely internal process of decision-making', at one end of the scale, to 'all choices are subject to European-level decisions', at the other end. [25]

Using this scale, the conclusions of Lindberg and Scheingold concur with those reached by Yondorf, who argues that the European Community comprises a curiously ambiguous system.[26] In brief, the Community divides responsibility for conflict resolution and other normal governmental functions among national and supranational authorities, thereby precluding the existence of any single, supreme decision-making body. The several Community authorities would resemble a jagged mountain range rather than the typical pyramid-pattern of unified nation-state authorities. To quote Yondorf, 'The peaks would identify the culminating points of national and supranational decision-making systems, and differences in height and mass would represent differences in competence and power.'[27]

Despite these insights, *Europe's Would-be Polity* remains very much a mid-term report on European integration. The progress toward European-level decision-making is analysed by reference to the four 'mechanisms' which are said to induce integration. These are as follows: (a) functional spillover, which refers to the spread of the area covered by European decision-making institutions, at the expense of national institutions; (b) side-payments and log-rolling, which refer to the deals made by decision-makers to achieve benefits in one sector at the expense of sacrifices elsewhere; (c) actor socialisation, referring to the inculcation of the elites, governmental and non-governmental, into the supranational approach; and (d) feedback, which refers to the development of support for integration among the member-states' populations. [28]

Clearly, the crux is to know by what means and under what conditions the above mechanisms will function. The factors of leadership and of demands made upon the Community are vital to the neofunctionalist model in this respect. It is correct to emphasise that if demands are to be reconciled and a consensus evolved in any policy in the Council of Ministers, a political system requires leadership. Again, however, the flaws in neofunctionalism become evident. First, the 'inevitable' logic of integration is again subject to the whims of the politician. Secondly, and of particular significance for our purposes, the dimension of feedback is relegated to the status of a passive influence, rather than being considered as an active mechanism of integration. Lindberg and Scheingold, despite introducing a useful framework in the analysis of public opinion, remain too restrictive — for them, public opinion defines the parameters of the decisions to be made, but it must always lack a decisive impact.

In order to gain a more detailed and productive analysis of the relevance of public opinion to integration, we must look to the work of Karl W. Deutsch, Ronald Inglehart and Donald J. Puchala. As we saw in Chapter Two, Deutsch can be termed a 'pluralist' in integration theory since he does not consider that the development of supranational authorities is a necessary condition of integration. For Deutsch, it is enough that previously warring states are at peace and that war between these states has become an impossibility, but this does not preclude Deutschian views on public opinion from our discussion. [29]

According to Deutsch, a prerequisite of interstate interaction is a 'sense of community', by which he means that the populations who are the potential participants should share feelings of 'mutual relevance' and 'mutual responsiveness' — i.e. they should see each other as being relevant to each other's interests and responsive to each other's demands. [30] The crucial factor is not the institutional framework, since Deutsch argues that an analysis of integration in the past, such as the formation of the United States, or the unsuccessful unification of Norway and Sweden, does not prove conclusively that the early development of common institutions either helps or hinders integration. Instead, he is concerned with the 'sense of community', which, he feels, can only develop by means of mutual transactions.

Indeed, at times Deutsch has tended to place more emphasis on the behavioural component of 'support' — i.e. transactions between states —

54

than on the attitudinal component. The reason for his concern with the behavioural component is that mutual transactions provide for 'social learning', and, since social learning 'made' nations, 'the same processes which made nationalism probable may soon come to turn against it'. [31] Thus, when Deutsch argued in 1966 that the spectacular development of formal European treaties and institutions since 1950 had not been matched by any correspondingly deeper integration of behaviour, he was talking in terms of 'an end to integration'. [32] His main source of data was figures for foreign trade between countries, flows of mail, exchange of students, holidays abroad and so on.

The emphasis on behavioural or transactional measures of support, which Deutsch favours, is open to criticism on several grounds. In a review of Deutsch's *Arms Control and the Atlantic Alliance,* and his *France, Germany and the Western Alliance,* Inglehart, commenting on the purely empirical side of Deutsch's works, argues that the criteria employed by Deutsch merely serve to determine the conclusions already reached by Deutsch that integration after 1958 was lagging. [33] According to Inglehart, had Deutsch used more valid criteria, he would have found an increase of about 100 per cent in the level of transactions during the period of his research, which would have indicated fuller integration than that found by Deutsch.

Moreover, Deutsch's entire line of reasoning is based on 'zero-sum' assumptions. In other words, trade between member-states of the European Community can increase only at the expense of trade with other *non*-member nations. He is overlooking the fact that trade can increase multilaterally. As he measures trade, increased European integration requires less transactions with the rest of the world. To quote Inglehart, 'relative isolation, autarky, and even relative hostility are requisites of his concept of integration'. [34]

Further criticisms of Deutsch's approach can be made on theoretical grounds. Basically, Deutsch has taken the concept of transactional integration and projects it directly onto the political scene, without specifying how given levels of given transactions may relate to the development of an integrated political system. Although he has undertaken to chart the political outlook for a decade, his model is not predictive. The transaction statistics are of little value since they do not indicate in themselves whether given political effects are likely to occur. Inglehart shows that the levels of trade between the Six increased between 1956 and 1967, but it is not clear that these levels of trade flow must continue to increase in order to constitute a pressure for political integration. [35] For instance, British people today buy an increased number of Japanese goods compared with even a few years ago, but no one has contrived to interpret this particular rise in trade as a precursor of political ties with the Japanese. Of all Deutsch's transactional indices, tourism and educational exchange possibly do more to enhance the likelihood of closer ties than increased trade, which arises quite simply from a desire for mutual economic gains and not for any possible cultural factors, thereby permitting little opportunity for 'social learning'.

In short, we can agree with Inglehart that Deutsch has been too concerned with trade flows, interchange of mail, and so on, rather than with public attitudes. Just as the neofunctionalists put too much emphasis on institutional factors, Deutsch has overrated the role of 'structural' integration. It is not made clear whether transactions are thought to have any impact on government policy-making, or if they are seen merely as indicators of changes in public attitudes.

Opinion polls are more reliable indicators, as we shall see, and, according to Inglehart, they may possess a predictive element. Indeed, public opinion polls come nearest to meeting the demands made by Deutsch himself when discussing the problems of analysing international co-operation and integration. In *France, Germany and the Western Alliance,* he was concerned to answer these questions: (a) are nation-states and national policies in West Europe being superseded by supranational loyalties, interests and institutions?; (b) what are the implications of recent nationalistic and/or supranational currents in European politics?; (c) what are the most important trends in domestic politics, especially with regard to the continued stability of governments, and how do these trends impinge upon foreign policy? In particular, when examining the underlying currents of West European politics, Deutsch was concerned to answer the question: 'Is general sentiment toward unification so great among Europeans that it can outlast disagreements over individual problems such as agriculture?' [36]

We can agree with Inglehart that public opinion survey data is relevant to the study of integration chiefly in so far that it gives an indication of the influence of the public on the decisions of respective national governments, and also the impact of policy on mass attitudes. [37] Our initial consideration must be to establish the relevance of public opinion to community-policy decision-makers. In his study of governmental decision-making, Deutsch recognises the very real significance of 'feedback' on the decision-makers. [38] By 'feedback' he means the public's response to government policy. Policies are reinforced when the public reacts favourably, agreeing with the decision that has been made: this is termed 'positive' feedback. 'Negative' feedback describes a disagreeable reaction by the public, which may limit the decision-makers in their subsequent actions.

In a later work, Deutsch provides a useful framework which identifies the different aims of integration, thus enabling a more realistic assessment of the role of feedback. Deutsch writes: 'The main tasks of integration can be conveniently recalled under four headings: (1) maintaining peace; (2) attaining greater multi-purpose capabilities; (3) accomplishing some specific task; and (4) gaining a new self-image and role identity.'[39]

We must realise that public opinion, including feedback, is not merely a yardstick of the fourth task, but is also a factor which will play a central part in achieving any of the aims of integration. Opinions, and feedback, are themselves 'inputs' of a political system which have to be considered by the decision-makers. Deutsch argues that:

> As a political process, integration has a *take off point* in time, when it is no longer a matter of a few prophets or scattered and powerless supporters, but turns into a larger and more co-ordinated movement with some significant power behind it. Before take off a proposal for integration is a theory; after take off it is a force. [40]

Whatever the task that the integrationists have set themselves, historic cases appear to show that 'the basic issue of integration must become salient to substantial interest-groups and to large numbers of people'. [41] Salience, in Deutsch's view, develops with a new and attractive way of life which engenders common expectations of more good things to come throughout the potential partners in integration. Also, some external challenge seems required to create any joint, supranational response, while the arrival on the political scene of a new generation which takes the earlier degree of common interests and outlook for granted is also a condition of integration.

Even when these conditions have been met and there exists a large degree of popular support for integration, the movement is likely to suffer setbacks and failures. Richard Merritt's study of the unification of the American colonies, which suggests that mass support for integration rises and then declines again during the process of integration, provides a means to assess the significance of these peaks and troughs of support. [42] These peaks and troughs resemble a 'learning curve', but if the learning process is successful each peak and each trough on the curve will be higher than its corresponding predecessor, until some critical threshold is crossed and full integration becomes a major demand. The people will have come 'to connect all or most of their important political concerns and issues with the issue of unification'. [43]

Inglehart provides us with a neat set of three factors which condition the relevance of the public response to integration into any particular political system. [44] In the first place, can the structure of the national decision-making process be termed 'pluralistic' or 'monolithic'? West European countries can usually be termed 'pluralistic' in the sense that their institutions allow a very large share of the various opinions within the country a chance to influence policy. They are not 'monolithic' because one point of view is not adhered to at the expense of all others. As we shall see later, it is preferable to conceive these categories as the end-points on a continuum which would stretch from 'monolithic' to 'pluralistic'.

Secondly, the distribution of political skills within the community is vital. For instance, Italian surveys consistently illustrate the relatively low political skills of many Italians – there are always far more 'don't knows' or 'no opinions' than in other European countries on any question relating to European affairs. [45] However, in most European countries, political skills are not monopolised by the elites. Finally, we must assess the degree to which a particular issue may relate to deep-seated values among the public, or may evoke only relatively superficial feelings. On issues which are often defined as 'low politics' – e.g. food prices – opinions can shift quite easily, whereas in the sphere of 'high politics' – e.g. national sovereignty – attitudes tend to be much more deep-seated. Clearly, there will be many issues which are not of passing interest to an unmobilised public.

The last two of Inglehart's conditions – level of information and degree of intensity of opinions – relate to some of the problems of the study of mass attitudes and opinions, which we have discussed in Chapter One. Also, the notion of 'monolithic'–'pluralistic' decision-making institutions presents us with problems of definition. For years de Gaulle was able to minimise the role of French public opinion toward European integration, but by reference to Inglehart's first condition we can see that the case of de Gaulle would appear to illustrate more about the nature of the French political system between 1958 and the mid-1960s, rather than serving to disprove any proposition concerning the significance of public opinion as an input of West European political systems. Indeed, to quote Pentland, 'In the French presidential elections of 1966 and 1969, however, there is clear evidence that the European issue intruded forcefully.'[46] Willis claims that the 1966 result led de Gaulle to adjust French Community-policy, in particular to resolve the impasse over agricultural policy and majority voting.[47] And, 'In 1969, M. Pompidou was more careful than his predecessor to appeal to the "European" as well as the nationalist wings of the potential Gaullist vote.'[48]

As we have seen, Lindberg and Scheingold talk of an emergent, 'permissive consensus' toward unification amongst the public in Western Europe, but Inglehart argues that the role of public opinion will become increasingly significant for European unification. Inglehart's thesis stems from a changing balance of political skills and also the entry into the political system of new, successive post-war generations. With the spread of literacy, more people are informed and can take part in reasoned discussion. With the favourable environment towards European integration created by the media since 1945 (bar a few notable exceptions), Inglehart feels that a process of 'cognitive mobilisation' has worked to the advantage of a united Europe, fostering a pro-European attitude among the public. [49] Puchala shares this view, laying stress on the importance of the coming to political maturity, and eventually to power, of age cohorts socialised in the era of peace and integration in Western Europe. [50]

Finally, we should reconsider the question of the intensity of favourable attitudes toward integration. Despite the relatively long history of opinion polls containing responses on questions relating to European integration which provide useful and continuous data, their validity is doubted since the degree of favourability or hostility is said to have depended on the issue most salient at any one time. Inglehart argues that 'what is needed is a more continuous effort with greater attention to achieving comparability in the data gathered, together with a clear knowledge of the degree to which given survey items tap relatively basic attitudes'.[51]

In an attempt to comply with Inglehart's rigorous demands, the present study examines six key propositions selected from the host of works published on European integration. Each proposition concentrates on the definition of the nature of public opinion toward European integration. The problem of short-term salient issues giving a false impression of the support for unification is minimised by studying surveys over long time spans, and also by undertaking cross-national comparisons. The major limitation is that we have to utilise other people's questions, often asked in differing order over time and across national boundaries.

The following six propositions will be studied in detail in the remainder of the book:

1   When the public in a nation-state view other nation-states favourably, policies supporting regional integration are also more likely to receive the public's endorsement.
2   Utilitarian support for the European Community is more marked than affective support.

3   Support for supranational institutions or policies is more marked than feelings of a European identity.
4   In any region following the creation of supranational institutions, there is a stronger public commitment to further integration.
5   Public opinion is 'moody' or unstable with respect to both desire for further integration and feelings of mutual sympathy and loyalty or identity.
6   Class and party loyalty correlate closely with opinions toward European integration.

The analysis of these propositions will proceed by (a) a discussion of their source in integration theory and their relevance to various theories; (b) a full examination of the evidence from the polls; and (c) an interpretation of the evidence, thereby seeking to reach some plausible conclusions on the nature of public opinion toward European integration.

Notes

[1]   Ernst B. Haas, *The Uniting of Europe,* Stanford University Press, 1958.
[2]   Ernst B. Haas, *Beyond the Nation State,* Stanford University Press, 1964, p. 35.
[3]   David Mitrany, *A Working Peace System,* Quadrangle Books, 1966.
[4]   E. Haas and P. Schmitter, 'Economics and differential patterns of political integration: projects about unity in Latin America' in W.P. Davison (ed.), *International Political Communities,* Praeger, 1966, pp. 261−2.
[5]   Ibid., pp. 284−5.
[6]   Paul Taylor, 'The concept of community and the European integration process' in *Journal of Common Market Studies* vol. 7, no. 2, 1968, pp. 83−101.
[7]   Charles Pentland, *International Theory and European Integration,* Faber and Faber, 1973, p. 84.
[8]   Ibid., pp. 84−5.
[9]   Roger Hansen, 'Regional integration: reflections on a decade of theoretical efforts' in M. Hodges (ed.), *European Integration,* Penguin, 1972, p. 188.
[10]   Leon Lindberg and Stuart Scheingold, *Europe's Would-be Polity,* Prentice-Hall, 1970.
[11]   Stanley Hoffmann, 'The fate of the nation-state, in *Daedalus,* Summer 1966, pp. 862−915.

[12] Ibid.

[13] Ibid.

[14] Ernst. B. Haas, 'The uniting of Europe and the uniting of Latin America' in *Journal of Common Market Studies* vol. 5, 1965, pp. 315–43.

[15] Raymond Aron, *Peace and War,* New York 1966.

[16] R. Hansen, op. cit., p. 198.

[17] For an excellent discussion of 'domain assumptions' in social science, see Alvin W. Gouldner, *The Coming Crisis of Western Sociology,* Heinemann Educational Books, 1971, pp. 29–37.

[18] C. Pentland, op. cit., p. 122.

[19] See, for example, A. Spinelli, *The Eurocrats,* Johns Hopkins Press, 1966, pp. 110 and 117.

[20] C. Pentland, op. cit., p. 167.

[21] Amitai Etzioni, *Political Unification,* New York, 1965.

[22] C. Pentland, op. cit., p. 174.

[23] David Easton, *A Systems Analysis of Political Life,* Wiley, 1967.

[24] L. Lindberg and S. Scheingold, op. cit., 1970, pp. 38–45.

[25] Ibid., pp. 68–9.

[26] Cited in ibid., p. 307.

[27] Ibid., p. 308.

[28] Ibid., pp. 117–21.

[29] Karl W. Deutsch, *The Analysis of International Relations,* Prentice-Hall, 1968. In particular, pp. 191–202.

[30] Karl. W. Deutsch *et al., Political Community and the North Atlantic Area: International Organization in the Light of Historical Experience,* Princeton University Press, 1957.

[31] Karl. W. Deutsch, *Nationalism and Social Communication,* Technology Press of Massachusetts Institute of Technology, 1966, pp. 190 ff.

[32] Karl. W. Deutsch, 'Integration and arms control in the European political environment: a summary report' in *American Political Science Review* vol. 60, 1966.

[33] Ronald Inglehart, 'Trends and non-trends in the Western Alliance: a review' in *Journal of Conflict Resolution* vol. 12, no. 1, 1968.

[34] Ibid., p. 122.

[35] Ibid., p. 122.

[36] Karl. W. Deutsch, *France, Germany and the Western Alliance:* A *Study of Elite Attitudes on European Integration and World Politics,* Scribner and Sons, 1967, p. vii.

[37] Ronald Inglehart, 'Public opinion and regional integration' in *International Organization* vol. 24, no. 4, 1970, pp. 764–95.

[38] Karl W. Deutsch, *The Nerves of Government,* Free Press of Glencoe, 1963.

[39] Karl W. Deutsch, 'Attaining and maintaining integration' in M. Hodges, op. cit., 1972, p. 108.

[40] Ibid., p. 117.

[41] Ibid., p. 117.

[42] Cited in ibid., p. 119.

[43] Ibid., p. 119.

[44] R. Inglehart, 'Public opinion and regional integration'.

[45] Ibid., p. 772.

[46] C. Pentland, op. cit., p. 257.

[47] Cited in ibid., p. 257.

[48] Ibid., p. 257.

[49] Ronald Inglehart, 'Cognitive mobilization and European integration' in *Comparative Politics,* 1970.

[50] Donald J. Puchala, 'The Common Market and political federation in Western European public opinion' in *International Studies Quarterly,* vol. 14, 1970.

[51] R. Inglehart, 'Public opinion and regional integration', p. 772.

4 Demands for Action and Desires for Affection

Proposition 1: When the public in a nation-state view other nation-states favourably, policies supporting regional integration are also more likely to receive the public's endorsement.

Introductory discussion

We have seen that integration theorists have analysed the role of public opinion in political integration according to their views of (a) the end-product of integration, and (b) the major conditions which determine the integrative process. The federalists and neofunctionalists conceptualise a 'state-model' end-product, whereas the pluralists and functionalists envisage a 'community-model' end-product. Yet the functionalists and neofunctionalists agree that the end-product is brought about by indirect, socio-economic variables, while the federalists and pluralists agree that direct, political variables are the principal causal factors. Reflecting these divisions of opinion within integration theory is the varying significance attached to the different components which comprise public opinion toward international relations and the interrelationship of these components.

The nature of these different 'attitudinal components' is described most clearly by Karl W. Deutsch, although the neofunctionalists also refer to them.[1] Deutsch gives a very minimal definition of international political integration, claiming that integration has taken place when previously warring states are at peace, and war between these states has become an impossibility. The end-product in Deutsch's minimal definition is termed a 'pluralistic-security-community', an example being Norway and Sweden today.

Although Deutsch is termed a pluralist in the sense that his minimal definition of political integration does not require any loss of national sovereignty to supranational institutions, he is very much concerned with the development of 'state-model' political communities, examples of these being the USA and the United Kingdom. He terms these political unions 'amalgamated-security-communities' arguing that,

> To promote political amalgamation, all the usual political methods have been used, but not all have been equally effective. By far the most effective method, in terms of the relative frequency with which it was followed by success, was the enlistment of broad popular participation and support. Among the cases studied, every amalgamation movement that won [such] popular participation was eventually successful.[2]

Deutsch's thesis is that popular participation and support for political amalgamation is enlisted when 'the relevant elites and populations have to learn to connect all or most of their important political concerns and issues with the issue of unification'.[3]

For the amalgamated-security-community to be successful, it is not enough that there is a growth of 'mutual sympathies and loyalties' or 'positive affect' between peoples. There must also be popular support for policies which create political integration – the public must be committed to 'positive action'. Thus, both the affective and the action components of public opinion toward international integration must be positive if an amalgamated-security-community is to succeed. Amalgamation which takes place without popular participation or support, or which follows a military conquest, is, historically, far less likely to be successful.

Our first proposition reflects the fact that pluralistic-security-communities can develop into amalgamated-security-communities, as the sense of 'we-feeling' or community, which has made war within the community impossible, is supplemented by the growth of support for political unification. In addition to the development of a psychological 'no war' community, there are several other characteristics of the integrative process which are particularly relevant to the experience of Western Europe. First, integration often begins around a 'core-area', comprising developed and attractive political units. Also, the growth of mutually cross-cutting divisions within the emergent community weakens national boundaries – the neofunctionalists term this 'mutual heterogeneity'. Finally, Deutsch notes the role of cross-regional political movements which are innovatory, notable examples being provided by liberalism and liberals in the nineteenth-century unifications of Switzerland, Italy and Germany, or the federalists and Democratic-Republicans in American unification. These characteristics, combined with an increase in transactions and communications, can generate the 'action component' of public support for amalgamation, following the creation of a 'no-war' community.

Functionalist theory shares Deutsch's views that the end-product of integration need not be a 'state-model' community and that 'social learning' by the public plays a vital role in the integrative process. However, a very real difference is to be found in the emphasis which pluralism and functionalism place on the two attitudinal components of support for integration. To the functionalist, political attitudes are primarily rational and instrumental, and therefore to change men's loyalties really means to change their expectations as to where material satisfaction is to be found.

According to Pentland, functionalism assumes that international collaboration becomes essential as a result of economic and technological change creating new 'functional needs' which nation-states are ill-equipped to satisfy.[4] National leaders often create international agencies which can provide material-welfare benefits, for the sake of the short-term political benefits they reap from them. But the publics come to realise that international collaboration is more effective at meeting their needs than the competitive and destructive urges of nationalism. Consequently, the leaders' hopes for short-term gain is transformed into a permanent loss of political power, and the affective and action components of support for integration develop. For functionalists, *prior* positive affect is thus not a prerequisite for international collaboration, although the affective component becomes vital in the creation of the 'socio-psychological community' which may enhance further inter-state co-operation.

Early neofunctionalists, notably Haas, paid little direct attention to the mass public's support for integration, but the writings of Lindberg, Scheingold and Inglehart reflect a realisation within the neofunctionalist school that political variables can play a crucial role in the integrative process.[5] Moreover, the efforts of the late 1960s and early 1970s to move from 'negative integration' to 'positive integration' would appear to make public opinion even more relevant.[6] But the neofunctionalists share the basic assumptions of the functionalists about the integrative process, and thus public support is seen to depend upon the mainly material benefits derived from integration. Affective feelings may be developed with successful integration, which also encourages support for further action, which, if realised, in turn can facilitate the generation of greater affection. But the neofunctionalists do not assume that affective support follows automatically.

The faith in the ability of institutions to shape men's attitudes and behaviour is shared by the federalists. Although they share Deutsch's view that the direct, political variables are the vital determinants in the integrative process, the federalists argue that the elites are relatively unfettered in their decision-making, and in the case of agreement among elites there is little need to pay attention to public opinion. However, Etzioni does argue that the elites' actions need legitimation, which can be achieved through education, propaganda, the creation of symbols for the new political community and so on.[7] Etzioni's thesis is the reverse of Deutsch's — the elites favouring integration may mobilise the action component of public support prior to unification, but the affective component is to be mobilised after integration as an effective legitimising ideology.

The evidence and its interpretation

The different roles assigned to the affective and the action components of public support by the various integration theorists are matched by the conflicting evidence which has been presented from the opinion polls and surveys. For instance, in an analysis of the Canadian polls, Scott points to evidence which appears to verify our first proposition, concluding that people who are favourably disposed toward other nations are likely to favour policies promoting regional integration.[8] Likewise, a study of public opinion in West Germany in the early 1950s by Louis Kriesberg indicates a strong positive correlation between the affective and the action components.[9]

However, Deutsch does not perceive any automatic spillover in attitudes from affection to action. His case is only that for an amalgamated-security-community to become a reality there must be prior affection between the publics and a desire for progress toward the closer integration of their states. But the latter does not stem automatically from the former attitudinal component. Our proposition merely states the plausible notion that those people who do share 'mutual sympathies and loyalties' with other peoples are more likely to favour some positive action toward regional integration than people who lack any sense of affection.

Thus, Deutsch's thesis is not invalidated by Beloff's argument that the main reason for the slow pace at which international integration has been proceeding is the discrepancy between the affective and action components.[10] Writing in the early 1960s, Beloff maintained that, in the case of Britain, governmental slowness to participate in European integration reflected a lack of mass support for integration, despite the reciprocal positive affect between Britain and the peoples of Western Europe. His conclusion is quite in keeping with Deutsch's pluralist approach to integration – there is no logical sequence in which affective support generates commitment to positive action towards integration. After all, Deutsch has claimed that the integrative process in Western Europe had reached a 'plateau' by the late 1950s.

It is hardly surprising that there is conflicting evidence on the nature of the interrelationship between attitudinal components which are so complex. In the first place, the concept of affection is particularly difficult to operationalise. Some of the difficulties involved have been stated by Rabier:

> . . . the image people have of each other is a complex phenomenon, made up of very many factors: historical, geographical, political, cultural, etc. . . . Saying that two groups understand each other is like saying that each of them believes that the behaviour of the other is predictable; saying that they have confidence in each other is like saying, in addition, that each expects from the other favourable behaviour towards it. These favourable behaviours may be expected in very different sectors of activity: cultural, economic, and military co-operation, even integration in the same political system. The images – even favourable – that one people has about the others may represent very different things. Moreover, each of these images is the result of images formed in each social group constituting that people. [11]

On the basis of Rabier's expression of caution, we can certainly agree with him that the interpretation of data relating to the affective component is particularly delicate.

Moreover, expressions of support for regional integration are likely to reflect the different meanings which various groups have attributed to 'integration' or 'unification', at different periods in time. For instance, it seems probable that relatively fewer people would have conceived of a supranational federal authority when asked about integration in the early 1950s than would conceive of full-scale political union if asked since the Paris Summit of 1972. Again, we are forced to rely on very imperfect evidence in testing the first proposition, but the historical dimension does alleviate the difficulties considerably, preventing the conclusions from being impossibly tentative.

The evidence is quite clear that during the last years of the war and the immediate post-war years other publics could muster little affection for the German people. In January 1944, 76 per cent of the American people believed that the peace treaty with Germany should be harsher than the Versailles peace, while in September 1945 53 per cent of the British people expressed hostile feelings towards the German people – this figure included 21 per cent who expressed hatred and 14 per cent disgust. [12] Table 4.1 shows that by December 1946, these hostile feelings had abated somewhat in states which were more distant from Germany and had not suffered invasion, but that there was continued strong antipathy towards the Germans from their immediate neighbours.

Table 4.1

Feelings towards the Germans, December 1946 (percentages)

	Sympathy	Antipathy
France	3	56
Netherlands	29	53
Norway	21	44
Great Britain	42	36
Canada	41	28
United States	45	28

Source: Jean Stoetzel, 'The evolution of French opinion' in D. Lerner and R. Aron, *France Defeats the EDC,* Praeger, 1957, p. 75

Yet in these immediate post-war years public support for the idea of European integration was strong. According to an international survey in September 1947, most Frenchmen and most Dutchmen considered the 'United States of Europe' a good idea. [13] Continued hostility towards Germany was evident in both France and the Netherlands, although it remained most intense in the former. To quote Stoetzel, 'Among French respondents eight out of ten included France, Belgium, Switzerland, Great Britain in the European construction; but only six out of ten included Germany, which took last place on a list of 26 countries.'[14] In the Netherlands, seven out of ten favoured German participation in the European construction, but the Dutch were generally more committed to the European idea. However, the Dutch were far less keen on Russian participation in Europe (three out of ten were 'pro-Russian'), whereas fully five out of ten French respondents supported Russian involvement in their view of the Europe of the future. [15]

The Cold War intensified in the late 1940s, and any analysis of public opinions in Europe demands a consideration of the East–West split, since continental Europe formed one of the front-lines in a suddenly bipolar world. East European participation in any moves towards an integrated Europe was no longer viable, but many students of international relations, including Deutsch, have pointed to the importance of a perceived threat from without in encouraging co-operation and unity amongst nations. What evidence is there to suggest that a perceived threat from without led to increased affection and demands for unity within Western Europe?

Between 1952 and 1963, a series of polls were commissioned by the United States Information Agency (USIA) which afford comparisons of feelings of affection and also of the demands for action towards unity within Western Europe. [16] The findings of these surveys in Western Germany, France and Britain are presented in Figures 4.1–4.9, where the findings of the various national polling organisations are also illustrated in a form which enables ready comparisons to be made.

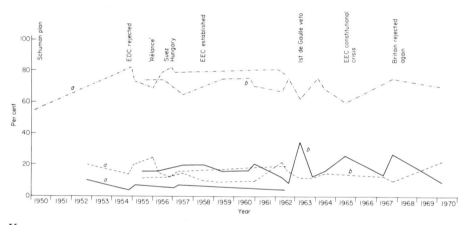

Key:

Lines marked *a* are from tables presented in J.-R. Rabier, *L'Opinion publique et L'Europe*

Lines marked *b* are from tables presented in *EMNID-Information*

—·—·—·— Percentage 'for' European unification

——————— Percentage 'against' European unification

— — — — — Percentage who 'don't know'

Fig. 4.1   Public support for European unification in West Germany, 1950–70

69

In West Germany, public support for European unification has been consistently strong and favourable (see Figure 4.1). The percentage expressing support for unification has not fallen below 60 per cent since 1950, when the SPD was actively campaigning against the Schuman Plan. Short-term fluctuations in this general support for unification appear to reflect setbacks suffered by the integration movement – in particular the rejection of the EDC by the French National Assembly in 1954. President de Gaulle's first veto of British entry in early 1963, and the EEC's constitutional crisis of mid-1965 to early 1966. In February 1970 and July 1971, Community-wide polls found that, of West Germans, 87 and 82 per cent respectively favoured the evolution of the Common Market towards a political federation or 'United States of Europe'. Only the Italians (93 and 91 per cent) and the Luxembourgers (94 and 82 per cent) surpassed the Germans in this. [17]

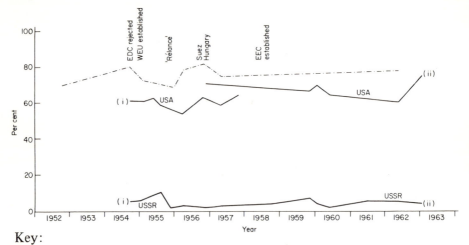

Key:

—·—·—·— Percentage replying 'for' to question: 'Are you in general for or against making efforts toward unifying Western Europe?' [1955, 1956 and 1962 figures include those who favoured British participation]

(i) The question read: 'Please use this card to tell me what your feelings are about various countries. How about [country]?' Response wording = 'Very good, good, fair, bad, very bad'

(ii) Question as above: Response wording = 'Very good, good, neither good nor bad, bad, very bad'

Percentages shown for each country represent 'very good' and 'good' opinions by West German respondents

Fig. 4.2   West German support for European unification and feelings of affection for the USA and the USSR, 1952–63

70

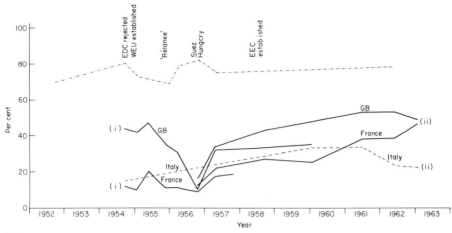

Key:

—·—·—Percentage replying 'for' to question: 'Are you in general for or against making efforts toward uniting Western Europe?' (1955, 1956 and 1962 figures include those who favoured British participation)

(i) The question read: 'Please use this card to tell me what your feelings are about various countries. How about [country]?' Response wording = 'Very good, good, fair, bad, very bad'

(ii) Question as above: Response wording = 'Very good, good, neither good nor bad, bad, very bad'

Percentages shown for each country represent 'very good' and 'good' opinions by West German respondents

Fig. 4.3   West German support for European unification and feelings of affection for France, Italy and Great Britain, 1952—63

Compared with the action component, a glance at the USIA findings (see Figures 4.2 and 4.3) creates an immediate impression that the affective component was much weaker in West Germany. However, several factors must be noted, and their consideration points to a stronger link between support for integration and the development of 'mutual sympathies and loyalties' than we would otherwise identify. First, Franco-German relations, already poor, were further strained after the French rejection of EDC — note the drop in support for European unification and the even smaller number of respondents holding a good or very good opinion of France. The *rélance* of a united Western Europe from 1955 to 1956 appears to have given a boost to the action component, but 1956 brought Suez and a drop in favourable feelings for

Britain and France, who were seen to be responsible for increased tension in East–West relations. The Germans were particularly aware of the fluctuations in East–West relations because they were directly in the front-line of any confrontations between the USA and the USSR. 1956 was also the year of the Hungarian uprising, and this explains the rise in 'sympathies and loyalties' for the Americans by the Germans, who recognised their dependence on the North Atlantic alliance. Also, 66 per cent of Germans were able to give a general explanation of what NATO meant, compared with only 36 per cent in 1954.

Further evidence of some correlation between the affective and action components is to be found in the conclusions of Louis Kriesberg's study, 'German public opinion and the European Coal and Steel Community'. [18] Kriesberg identifies two sets of determinants which seem to explain the respondents' evaluations of the ECSC. The first set is the influence of others, with the second set comprising 'predispositions'. Predispositions can themselves be subdivided into directly relevant predispositions and those that are indirectly relevant. Thus, Kriesberg maintains that feelings about the French and fear of the Russian menace are directly relevant predispositions as regards German opinions toward the ECSC. He supports his proposition by classifying his respondents, according to their feelings about the ECSC, into the following five groups: (1) those who feel that West Germany fares well in the ECSC and that it was no mistake to join; (2) those who feel that West Germany's progress in the ECSC is fair, but who are not sure if joining was a mistake or not; (3) those who feel that West Germany has fared poorly, but still maintain that it was not wrong to join; (4) those who feel that West Germany has fared poorly, and that it was wrong to join; and (5) those who are undecided on both counts.

Kriesberg's conclusion is that those who believed a lasting under-standing with France was possible were more likely to think that Germany did not fare poorly than those who felt that too much divided the Germans and the French. Among those who thought West Germany fared poorly, those who did not believe an understanding with France was possible tended to think it was a mistake to have joined the ECSC (see Table 4.2).

Similarly, amongst those who believed that West Germany was menaced by the Soviet Union, more were likely to think that Germany fared well in the ECSC than those who felt Germany was not menaced (see Table 4.3).

From 1957 onwards, good and very good opinions of the British and French rise strongly and steadily (see Figure 4.3). This would seem to reflect the early successes of economic integration and the German desire to see Britain joining the Six. The good feelings for Britain in 1954 may

Table 4.2

Evaluation of the ECSC by belief in the possibility of
an understanding with France (figures in percentages)

*'Do you believe in general that it is possible for us to reach a lasting
understanding with France, or do you believe too much divides us?'*

	Evaluation of the ECSC				
	(1) Good	(2) Mildly favourable	(3) Bad, not anti	(4) Bad, anti	(5) Undecided
Possible	23	34	14	14	14
Not possible	19	23	18	25	15
Don't know	10	28	14	9	40

Source: Kriesberg, 1959, p. 33

Table 4.3

Evaluation of the ECSC by belief in a Soviet menace
(figures in percentages)

	Evaluation of the ECSC				
	(1) Good	(2) Mildly favourable	(3) Bad, not anti	(4) Bad, anti	(5) Undecided
Menace	21	33	15	13	17
No menace	21	26	15	26	12
Don't know	12	31	16	9	31

Source: Kriesberg, 1959, p. 33

well have been helped by her participation in the Western European
Union, established that year following the collapse of EDC. Indeed, many
Germans had believed meaningful economic integration to be synonymous
with British participation − certainly, this was the opinion of Erhard and

the so-called *Atlantiker* group in the CDU–CSU majority party. But by mid-1962, there was a growing sense in Germany of the British making excessive demands on the Six in the entry negotiations, an awareness which de Gaulle capitalised on, issuing his veto and signing the Franco-German Friendship Treaty twelve days later. The small further increase in good and very good opinions of the French amongst Germans, and the slight drop in favourable feelings for the British, appears to be related to these events.

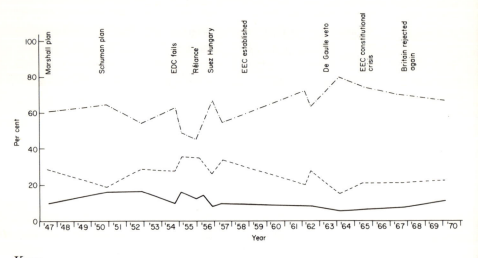

Key:
—·—·—·-Percentage 'for' European unification
————————Percentage 'against' European unification
——————-Percentage who 'don't know'

Fig. 4.4   Public support for European unification in France, 1947–70

Source: *Sondages,* 1947–70.

From the evidence of the German polls and surveys, it seems that Franco-German *rapprochement* is a significant achievement of West European integration, but what light do the French polls shed on this and other post-war trends in mass opinions? As in Germany, public support for moves towards unification is strong and relatively consistent, although less than 50 per cent favoured unification following the collapse of EDC (see Figure 4.4). But it is significant that this fall in support was matched by only a comparatively small increase in the percentage of those opposed to integration – the larger increase occurred in the numbers of 'don't knows', presumably showing that disillusion with unification was not complete.

Although there was a permanent, clear majority in favour of unification, 'There was a great difference between good will on essential purpose (a kind of declaration of intentions) and readiness to overcome specific obstacles, such as the loss of sovereignty which this purpose implied.'[19] It was in the economic sphere, and in particular the coal and steel industries, that the French opposition to any loss of sovereignty seemed to be weakest. In September 1952, 46 per cent of respondents expressed support 'spontaneously' for the Schuman Plan, and after the Plan had been explained to all respondents, fully 60 per cent declared themselves supporters of the ECSC.[20] Moreover, in January 1954, 40 per cent believed that the ECSC was in the interest of all European countries, while only 7·5 per cent felt it was in the interest of Germany – the fears of many producers that it would encourage German economic hegemony seemed ill-founded. By July of that year, 42 per cent were favourable or rather favourable toward the ECSC; 14 per cent gave no opinion. If there was large-scale ignorance of the exact nature of the ECSC, it seems that 'attitudes toward this specific plan were derived from attitudes toward European unification in general', and that, 'on the level of economic co-operation and even at the cost of a certain limitation of sovereignty, French reservations were not irreducible'.[21] Indeed, a third of the respondents in January 1954 favoured the extension of the powers of the ECSC to fields other than coal and steel.

Table 4.4

Fields in which Franco-German co-operation can be achieved, listed in order of facility (July 1954). Figures in percentages

	1st	2nd	3rd	4th	5th and 6th	No opinion
Economic	38	15	10	4	2	31
Cultural	14	15	13	12	13	33
Technical	8	19	17	12	11	33
Political	6	10	7	10	29	38
Military	5	4	4	6	40	41
Financial	2	6	13	20	21	38

Source: Stoetzel, op.cit., p. 85

French attitudes toward military integration were totally different. Great distrust of the Germans could not be overcome by the uncertain security to be gained from any military arrangement which involved German rearmament. Although most Frenchmen favoured unification and many also spoke favourably of a Franco-German *rapprochement*, understanding had to be realised first on the economic level, then on the cultural level, to encourage public acceptance on other levels (see Table 4.4). Stoetzel refers to the emergence of a 'special hypothesis' with regard to EDC – the French army clearly could not prevent an invasion by the Soviet troops, but there was no guarantee that in the immediate future help from other European countries would be any more successful. Thus, the French view of EDC appeared to be that 'its rejection might or not endanger the security of the country', but 'its acceptance clearly did not ensure it'. [22]

Table 4.5

Powers seeking to dominate the world
(figures in percentages)

	February 1946	July 1947	January 1953
There is one nation which tries to dominate the world	68	79	78
It is the USSR	26	36	22
the United States	25	29	15
the USSR and the US	12	13	30

Source: Stoetzel, op. cit., p. 76

The French did feel that two powers were trying to dominate the world (see Table 4.5); but this conflict did not seem directly relevant to many Frenchmen – in October 1954, 39 per cent favoured a neutral position between the East and West camps, while 37 per cent supported membership of the latter. In the case of a war between the super-powers, fully 53 per cent favoured neutrality, with 22 per cent expressing loyalty with the West. Stoetzel has summed up French opinions in the late 1940s and early 1950s as follows:

There is concern about being committed to action for purposes which do not seem very clear. The threat from the East does not appear so blinding as to obliterate the dangers run in the recent past from Germany; and these dangers still exist. Committing itself to the West, the public fears, may increase the risks.[23]

The empty space created in Europe by the destruction of the German forces seemed dangerous to the Americans, the British, and, of course, to the Germans themselves. But the French saw the rearmament of Germany and the existence of German troops, even in EDC, as a real threat to French security. The Pleven Plan, in which the proposals for an EDC were first outlined, did demonstrate that military integration would help unification in general, and thus many Frenchmen expressed support for EDC — 43 per cent supported a European army in June 1953, but 37 per cent also believed that the existence of German troops within the 'Western Army' endangered French security.

It is probably true that a widespread lack of knowledge in France about the EDC allowed the affective component of distrust of Germany to assume dominant proportions in the public's opinions towards the EDC. In May 1953, 21 per cent had never heard anything about the project and 52 per cent did not know if the National Assembly had already ratified the Treaty. [24] With the installation of Mendès-France as Premier in the summer of 1954, EDC became a subject of public debate, and opinions appeared to crystallise (see Table 4.6).

Table 4.6

Attitudes towards the EDC (percentages)

	July 1954	19 August and 8 September 1954
Definitely for	19	15
Slightly for	17	17
Total for	*36*	*32*
Slightly against	11	12
Definitely against	20	21
Total against	*31*	*33*
No opinion	*33*	*35*
Total	100	100

Source: Stoetzel, op. cit., p. 87

That a third of the French public were undecided illustrates the considerable perplexity caused by the EDC debate. Stoetzel concludes:

> The absence of a favourable majority appeared to be the most important fact. And this was not the result of external pressure, or of opposing ideologies and foreign propaganda, but of a conflict between rational attitudes and affective impulses which divided the national conscience. [25]

While it is true that Communist voters were the most strongly opposed to the EDC and that MRP voters expressed strongest support, the views of the various party leaders — particularly those who opposed EDC — would have had less impact if the public had not been ready to receive them. Thus, it is instructive that, in mid-1953, an equal proportion in all parties considered Germany the enemy of their country (see Table 4.7).

Table 4.7

France's enemy, by expressed party preference, June 1953
(percentages)

	Whole sample	PCF (French Communist Party)	SFIO (Socialists)	RGR (Radicals)	MRP (Christian Democrats)	Moderates	RPF (Gaullists)
USSR	17	5	16	23	23	21	32
Germany	16	14	14	20	17	14	19
USA	5	16	3	2	2	2	5

Source: Stoetzel, op. cit., p. 88

The lack of French support for EDC should not be seen as an indication of opposition to European unification. The polls show that despite distrust of Germans, the French favoured unification by stages. In October 1954, 52 per cent felt that the Western European Union, formed to replace the EDC, was a step towards unification. The fact that 35 per cent expressed a preference for WEU, compared with only 8 per cent for EDC, illustrates the French belief that unification must involve Britain. [26] If West Germany had to be included, through its strategic position in Western Europe, French fears could be best allayed by the participation of the British.

In the field of military integration, lack of French affection for Germans proved damaging. However, the surveys sponsored by USIA lead

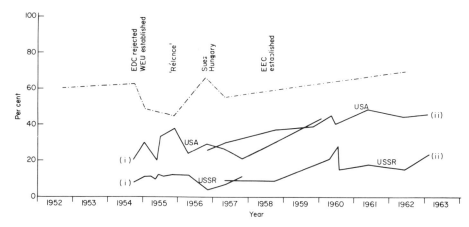

Key:
—·—·—·—Percentage replying 'for' to question: 'Are you in general for or against making efforts toward uniting Western Europe?'
(i) Question read: 'Please use this card to tell me what your feelings are about various countries. How about [country]?' Response wording: 'Very good, good, fair, bad, very bad'
(ii) Question as above: Response wording: 'Very good, good, neither good nor bad, bad, very bad
Percentages shown for each country represent 'very good' or 'good' opinions by French respondents

Fig. 4.5 French support for European unification and feelings of affection for the USA and USSR, 1952–63

to some interesting insights into French attitudes towards the Germans following successes in economic integration in the form of the ECSC and EEC, which the French had been more willing to support (see Figures 4.5 and 4.6). Favourable opinions of the British fluctuated around 40 per cent between 1954 and 1963, but the French have come to see their German neighbours in increasingly good terms, with favourable opinions rising from 9 per cent in 1954 to 37 per cent by 1958, a figure which has been consolidated during the 1960s. It is interesting to quote the commentary to Gallup International's survey of 1962:

> ... the Franco-German problem, such as it existed some years ago, notably at the time when the European Defence Community was being discussed, has now largely disappeared, and ... neither distrust, animosity, nor fear of rivalry between the member countries of the Six, constitutes a serious obstacle to the uniting of Europe. [27]

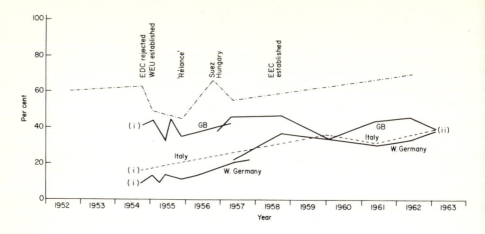

Key:
—·—·—Percentage replying 'for' to question: 'Are you in general for or against making efforts toward uniting Western Europe?'
(i) Question read: 'Please use this card to tell me what your feelings are about various countries. How about [country]?' Response wording: 'Very good, good, fair, very bad, bad'
(ii) Question as above: Response wording: 'Very good, good, neither good nor bad, bad, very bad'
Percentages shown for each country represent 'very good' or 'good' opinions by French respondents

Fig. 4.6 French support for European unification and feelings of affection for West Germany, Italy and Great Britain, 1952–63

From the evidence of the polls it seems that the peaceful solution of Franco-German hostility is one of the major achievements of economic integration. The crises of 1963 and 1965–66 took their toll on the affective components of mass attitudes in France and Germany, but the later polls show that the development of mutual sympathies and loyalties across national boundaries seems able to withstand these temporary setbacks. This is particularly true of France, where growing support for a French foreign policy independent of America can also be identified (see Table 4.8).

The French view of Franco-German relations is indeed indicative of an enormous *volte-face* compared with the attitudes prevalent at the time of the EDC proposals, but these figures convey little of the feelings during the French boycott of the EEC in 1965–66. However, two factors are

80

Table 4.8

Public opinion in France with regard to relations between
France and other countries (figures in percentages)

*'Would you say that relations between France and [name of country]
have improved, stayed the same, or worsened?'*

		November 1964	February 1965	22 December 1966– 4 January 1967
Great Britain:	Improved	9	14	26
	Same	45	40	40
	Worsened	29	19	11
	Don't know	17	27	23
USA:	Improved	5	9	5
	Same	31	36	35
	Worsened	49	27	43
	Don't know	15	28	17
West Germany:	Improved	52	37	31
	Same	30	31	33
	Worsened	7	10	13
	Don't know	11	22	23
USSR:	Improved			77
	Same	NA	NA	7
	Worsened			1
	Don't know			5

Source: *Gallup Political Index* no. 82, February 1967

worth stressing: first, the French public on the whole did not agree with de Gaulle's intransigence, as they demonstrated in the Presidential election of 1965; and, secondly, the French Government's walk-out was precipitated by the Commission rather than by Erhard's stance in the negotiations over CAP – indeed the Germans had made substantial concessions to the French. It is significant that in late 1966 only 13 per cent of Frenchmen felt that Franco-German relations had worsened.

Since it was the French who executed the boycott, it seems more likely that German perceptions of Franco-German relations would have been marked by a feeling of disappointment.

Table 4.9 appears to uphold this notion, with the Germans expressing

81

Table 4.9

German evaluations of Franco-German relations
(figures in percentages)

'Do you think that in the past 12 months, Franco-German relations are rather better, rather worse, or about the same?'

	Better	Same	Worse	No answer
January 1963*	86	1	5	8
April 1965	8	34	45	14
October 1965	5	28	53	14
April 1966	4	20	65	10
October 1966	7	36	43	13
August 1967	17	47	27	9

* In 1963, the question referred to the past decade and not to the previous year only.

Source: *EMNID-Informationen* nos 9–10, 1967, p. 11

greatest pessimism in October 1965 and April 1966. However, the January 1963 result, which shows that 86 per cent of Germans believed that Franco-German relations had improved over the previous decade, is truly remarkable, further demonstrating the growth of positive affect for the French since the defeat of EDC.

Final proof that mutual Franco-German suspicions had been replaced by mutual trust came in 1970, when 58 per cent of Germans felt able to express 'a great confidence or rather great confidence in' the French, and 48 per cent of the French expressed the same feelings for the Germans. [28] In both countries, greater confidence was expressed in the Swiss, the Americans and the British. This indicates the existence of an Atlantic–European pluralistic-security-community, created partly by the Soviet presence, which forms a 'threat from without', and partly – in the case of Franco-German relations – by successful moves towards economic integration. In March 1972, 71 per cent of French respondents stated that Germany was no longer a danger to France; of these, 25 per cent attributed this new-found peaceful relationship to membership of the European Community, 21 per cent to the world situation which necessitates Franco-German peace, and only 16 per cent to a change in German outlook and 6 per cent to the division of Germany into East and

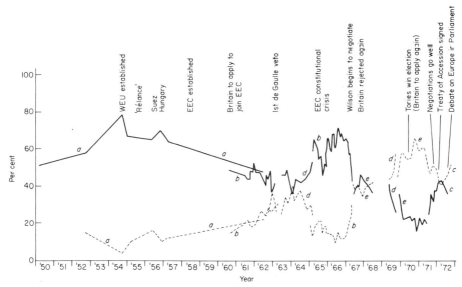

Key:

——— Percentage 'for' integration

– – – – Percentage 'against' integration

Lines *a*   USIA Data (from Merritt and Puchala)

b   'If the Government were to decide that the country's best interests would be served by joining the Common Market, would you agree or disagree?' (Gallup)

c   'On the facts as you know them, are you for or against the Government joining the Common Market?' (Gallup)

d   'If an opportunity occurs for Britain to join the Common Market, would you like to see us join or drop the idea altogether?' (Gallup)

e   'Do you approve or disapprove of the Government applying for membership of the Common Market?' (Gallup)

Fig. 4.7   Public support for European unification in the United Kingdom, 1950–72

West. [29] Clearly, many Frenchmen attribute the growth of affection between themselves and their traditional enemies, the Germans, to economic integration.

Indeed, the significance of economic integration in the growth of Franco-German affection seems to have increased in the era of East–West *détente*. The *détente*, including, in its widest sense, West Germany's

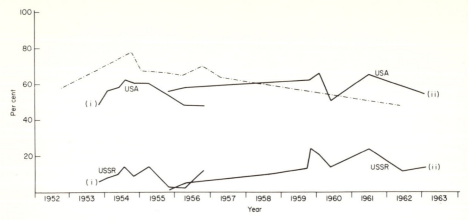

Key:
—·—·— Percentage replying 'for' to question: 'Are you in general for or against making efforts toward uniting Western Europe?'
(i) Question read: 'Please use this card to tell me what your feelings are about various countries. How about [country]?' Response wording: 'Very good, good, fair, bad, very bad'
(ii) Question read as above, Response wording: 'Very good, good, neither good nor bad, bad, very bad'
Percentages shown for each country represent 'very good' and 'good' opinions by British respondents

Fig. 4.8 British support for European unification and feelings of affection for the USA and USSR, 1952–63

Ostpolitik and the Gaullist concept of an independent foreign policy, has served to reduce the perception amongst West Europeans of a Soviet threat-from-without. The West Germans are probably still more aware of the Soviet presence, for obvious geo-political reasons, but evidence from the French polls indicates that, for the French, awareness of an external pressure on Western Europe is now less than it was in the 1950s, although the French have never been as conscious of a Soviet threat as the Germans. In November 1968, despite the Soviet invasion of Czechoslovakia three months previously, only 32 per cent of the French felt that the Soviet Union constituted a political threat to Europe, and 39 per cent a military threat. Yet 44 per cent stated that there was no political threat from the Soviet Union, and 39 per cent that there was no military threat. [30] It is a fascinating proposition that *détente,* by reducing mass perceptions of a clear threat-from-without, may have weakened a potential catalyst of integration.

84

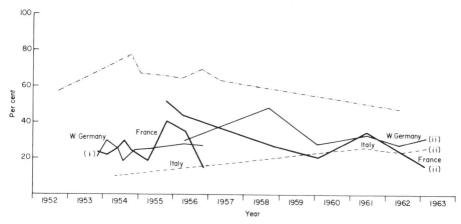

Key:

— · — · — Percentage replying 'for' to question: 'Are you in general for or against making efforts toward uniting Western Europe?'

(i) Question read: 'Please use this card to tell me what your feelings are about various countries. How about [country]?' Response wording: 'Very good, good, fair, bad, very bad'

(ii) Question read as above, Response wording: 'Very good, good, neither good nor bad, bad, very bad'

Percentages shown for each country represent 'very good' and 'good' opinions by British respondents

Fig. 4.9   British support for European unification and feelings of affection for France, Italy and West Germany, 1952–63

In the United Kingdom, the surveys conducted by USIA found that 'bad' or 'very bad' feelings for the Soviet Union exceeded those held by the French for the Russians but were less than those held in West Germany (see Figures 4.2, 4.5 and 4.8). A more significant feature of British attitudes towards other countries is the lack of strong feelings of positive affection for the major members of the European Community (see Figure 4.9). British 'good' or 'very good' feelings for the West Germans did increase between 1952 and 1963, but not by much and not in a steady, or secular, manner. In view of West German participation in the Western Alliance, German support, in 1962–63, for British entry of the Common Market, and the extent of the strong feelings of distrust for the Germans in the early 1950s, the relatively small increase over the decade in affection for the Germans is surprising.

Friendly attitudes toward the French reached a high point during the

85

year before Suez, but with de Gaulle's veto they slumped to 1954 levels. Meanwhile, favourable opinions toward the USA recovered well after Suez to reach new levels of strong, positive affection in the Macmillan—Kennedy era. Even the Russians received greater support than they had done in the mid-1950s, largely because of the thaw in the Cold War. Of the three major members of the Six, the Italians received more favourable comments from the British — they probably gained new-won respect for their role as founder-members of the European Community. But the French and the Germans failed to make any significant impact on the affective feelings of the British, and this seems to indicate some correlation with the action component which was becoming weaker during the late 1950s and early 1960s (see Figure 4.7).

Compared with public support for integration in France and West Germany, British opinions appear to be much more confused. Public support for British participation in the Common Market was clearly positive from the beginning of the 1950s until 1962, and also between 1964 and 1967. In 1962, 1964, 1967 and 1972, the percentage of those in favour of entry equalled the percentage of those who opposed entry. From 1969 until January 1973, when Britain entered the Community, a majority continued to oppose entry, and since entry a majority have felt that their Government was mistaken (see Table 4.10). Only in polls taken immediately after the Treaty of Accession (January 1972) and British entry (January 1973) were small pro-Market majorities recorded.

Table 4.10

Attitudes towards the British Government's decision
to enter the European Community (figures in percentages)

	Right	Wrong	Don't know
1973 January	38	36	26
April	40	42	19
May	36	45	19
July	39	44	17
August	32	52	16
October	34	49	17
1974 February	28	58	14
June	32	53	15

Source: *Gallup Political Index* nos 150, 153, 154, 157, 159, 163, 167

It is instructive to note that public support for British membership was at its greatest in the 1950s and in 1965–66, when the Common Market was not an issue of political debate – in the mid-1960s all three major parties favoured entry. Therefore, it would seem more correct to conclude that in those particular years the opposition to entry was at its weakest, than to speak of strong and positive public support for entry. Also, it should be noted that the swing against entry in 1967 preceded de Gaulle's veto; but his prior public utterances did not suggest that there would be any change of mind since 1963, and during the Wilson Government's negotiations the Common Market became a topic of increasing political debate – indeed, opposition to entry became strongest within the Labour Party and the trade unions.

British attitudes towards the member-states of the Community seem to have suffered a decline in feelings of affection which parallel the falling support for entry (see Table 4.11). In December 1967, the French and Italians were the only member-states of the Six who did not gain support as 'Britain's best friend on the Continent of Europe' – presumably, in the case of the French, Britons knew who was to blame for their two unsuccessful attempts to enter the Common Market. By January 1969, with British opposition to entry greater than support for entry, all of the Six lost support, except Italy and France, which were relatively unpopular in any case.

Since 1959 Britain had been a member of the European Free Trade Association, and although EFTA was not formed with the intention of ultimate political integration, its existence seems to be correlated with some perception of ties of affection. The Danes in particular, but also the Swedes and Norwegians, were seen to be 'friends' of Britain. It does not seem too far-fetched to argue that large-scale sales of 'Danish bacon' are partly responsible for such a notable demonstration of friendliness. The *Board of Trade Journal* has shown that imports from Denmark have consistently exceeded imports from Ireland, Italy and Belgium, and were on a par with imports from Australia and New Zealand during the 1960s. [31]

When asked which other countries throughout the world can be regarded as friends of Britain, the replies showed that most countries lost face in the mid-1960s, but none more so than France (see Table 4.12). Of the other member-states of the Six, the British seemed to recognise West Germany's support of the British case for entry in 1967. The continued dominance of Britain by US 'culture', large-scale investment and membership of the Western Alliance is reflected in the perception of 'mutual relevance' for the Americans by the British public. The

Table 4.11

British attitudes towards European countries
(figures in percentages)

'Which country is Britain's best friend on the continent of Europe?'

Country	July 1963	December 1967	January 1969
Denmark	12	11	10
Holland	11	14	13
Belgium	7	8	5
West Germany	7	18	12
Sweden	5	7	4
France	4	4	5
Switzerland	–	–	8
Norway	4	5	4
Italy	2	1	2
Others	4	3	5

Source: *Gallup Political Index* nos 42, 80, 106

remarkable fact to emerge from British attitudes towards other countries in the late 1960s is the decline in feelings of friendliness for all countries except West Germany. This seems to reflect a growth of isolationism in Britain, a greater sense of apathy towards foreign affairs after 1965. The most plausible explanations would appear to be a recognition of Britain's decline in world politics, the realisation that Commonwealth ties were weaker by 1967, and, finally, another veto by de Gaulle to check any hopes of entering the Common Market.

Whereas the British were reluctant to enter the European Community, and were at times clearly opposed, the publics of the Six were very favourable to British entry. A Community-wide poll in January and February 1970 shows this marked contrast between the opinions of the British and the Six on the enlargement of the EEC (see Table 4.13). Furthermore, this strong action component in the Six seems closely linked with strong affective feelings for Britain – in 1970 Rabier found that the publics of the Six expressed great confidence in the British, who came third to the Swiss and the Americans in all member-states except for Belgium, where confidence in the French exceeded that in the British by only 4 per cent. [32]

Table 4.12

British attitudes towards other countries
(figures in percentages)

'Which other countries do you regard as Britain's friends?'

Country	January 1965	May 1965	December 1967
USA	73	70	57
Australia	57	51	44
Canada	48	45	38
Scandinavia	22	24	14
Holland	17	22	13
France	14	20	5
Switzerland	10	11	6
Belgium	9	9	6
West Germany	9	8	12
India	13	6	3
Austria	3	4	0
Italy	4	4	3
USSR	4	4	5
Others	22	15	17

Source: *Gallup Political Index* nos 60, 93

Conclusions

In general our first proposition has been verified, since most of the evidence from the opinion polls indicates that when the public in a nation-state view other nation-states favourably, policies supporting regional integration are also more likely to receive the public's endorsement. Alternatively, where affection for other nation-states is lacking, policies supporting regional integration do not receive strong public support. However, certain qualifications must be made to these generalisations if mass attitudes to regional integration in Western Europe are to be more fully understood.

All the evidence points to strong public support for integration in Western Europe since 1945. However, this commitment to unification faced a major obstacle in the great distrust felt for the Germans by the

Table 4.13

Attitudes towards British entry, January–February 1970
(figures in percentages)

'Are you for or against the entry of Great Britain into the Common Market?'

	For	Against	No opinion
Belgium	63	8	29
France	66	11	23
Italy	51	9	40
Luxembourg	70	6	24
The Netherlands	79	8	13
West Germany	69	7	24
European Community	64	9	27
Great Britain	19	63	18

Source: *Les Européens: 'Oui a l'Europe',* Commission des Communautés Européenes, Brussels 1970, p. 5

other European publics, and more particularly in the mutual Franco-German distrust. Events dictated that if the publics favoured unification, they would have to accept participation on equal terms by a German state. But the people did favour *rapprochement* with the Germans and gave strongest support to the idea of integration by stages. Thus, the Schuman Plan proved acceptable, albeit gaining rather qualified support, because it limited integration to the coal and steel industries and ensured supranational control of the sector of the economy responsible for the production of the materials of war. As a result, the Germans were denied full sovereignty, but to a large number of Frenchmen the EDC would have nullified this limitation, facilitating the resurgence of Germany's military power. In the event, an independent German army was created, but few Frenchmen now see Germany as a threat and many attribute improved Franco-German relations to integration in the economic sphere.

In the United Kingdom, lack of support for specific moves towards integration seems to be correlated with stronger affective feelings for the United States and the white Commonwealth powers than for the member states of the European Community. There were signs that British loyalties and sympathies lay more with Scandinavia, and seemed to be reinforced by membership of EFTA. It will be interesting to see if membership of the Common Market can create stronger feelings of affection for their fellow member-states on the part of the British. The publics of the Six already possessed affective feelings for the British, also favouring British entry to the Community, but the effects of British renegotiation and possible withdrawal could well damage these feelings of loyalty and sympathy for the British.

If the Western European experience largely validates our first proposition, we are also prompted to ask more questions about the motives of public support for integration. In this chapter, we have limited our discussion to affection in the sense of mutual loyalties and sympathies developing between the publics of nation-states, but we also need to consider the affective feelings which may exist for the idea of Europe itself, for a European identity. There is some evidence that the mass support for European unification, which was so strong in all the major West European states, including the United Kingdom, in the 1950s, may have owed more to the sense of a common European identity than to support for specific policies which would necessitate integration. It is to this more detailed discussion of the bases of support for integration that we turn in Chapter Five.

Notes

[1] Karl W. Deutsch *et al., Political Community and the North Atlantic Area,* Princeton University Press, 1957, p. 36.

[2] Karl W. Deutsch, 'Attaining and maintaining integration' in M. Hodges (ed.), *European Integration,* Penguin, 1972, pp. 119–20.

[3] Ibid., p. 119.

[4] C. Pentland, op.cit., 1973, pp. 64–7.

[5] Leon Lindberg and Stuart Scheingold, *Europe's Would-be Polity,* Prentice-Hall, 1970; Ronald Inglehart, 'Public opinion and regional integration' in *International Organization,* 1970, and 'Cognitive Mobilization and European Integration' in *Comparative Politics,* 1970.

[6] John Pinder, 'Positive integration and negative integration: some problems of economic union in the EEC' in M. Hodges, op.cit., 1972, pp. 124–50.

[7] Amitai Etzioni, *Political Unification,* New York 1965.

[8] Scott, 'Psychological and social correlates of international images' in M. Kelman (ed.), *International Behaviour,* 1965.

[9] Louis Kriesberg, 'German public opinion and the European Coal and

Steel Community' in *Public Opinion Quarterly* vol. 23, 1959.

[10] J. Beloff, 'Britain, Europe and the Atlantic Community' in Wilcox and Haviland, *The Atlantic Community,* Praeger, New York 1963.

[11] J.-R. Rabier, 'Europeans and the unification of Europe' in *Government and Opposition* vol. 6, no. 4, 1971.

[12] J. Stoetzel, 'The evolution of French opinion' in D. Lerner and R. Aron (eds), *France Defeats EDC,* Praeger, 1957, p. 91.

[13] Nederlands Instituut voor de Publieke Opinie (NIPO), *Bericht* no. 152, Amsterdam 1947.

[14] J. Stoetzel, op.cit., 1957, p. 79.

[15] Ibid., p. 79, and NIPO *Bericht* no. 152.

[16] R.L. Merritt and D.J. Puchala (eds.), *Western European Perspectives on International Affairs: Public Opinion Studies and Evaluations,* Praeger, New York 1968.

[17] Commission of the Communities, *L'Opinion des Européens sur les aspects régionaux et agricoles du Marché Commun, l'unification politique de l'Europe et l'information du public,* Brussels, December 1971, p. 50.

[18] L. Kriesberg, op. cit., 1959.

[19] J. Stoetzel, op.cit., 1957, p. 79.

[20] Ibid., p. 94.

[21] Ibid., p. 81.

[22] Ibid., p. 84.

[23] Ibid., p. 78.

[24] Ibid., pp. 85–6.

[25] Ibid., p. 87.

[26] Ibid., p. 101.

[27] Gallup International, 'Public opinion and the European Community', edited and translated by M. Forsyth, in *Journal of Common Market Studies* vol. 2, no. 2, 1963, p. 111.

[28] J.-R. Rabier, op.cit., 1970, p. 481.

[29] L'Institut français de l'Opinion, *Sondages* nos 2–3, 1972, pp. 31–2.

[30] Ibid.

[31] Central Information Office, *Britain: an Official Handbook,* London 1961, 1964, 1968–72.

[32] J.-R. Rabier, 1970, op.cit., p. 481.

5 Utilitarian and Affective Support

Proposition 2: Utilitarian support for supranational institutions is more marked than affective support.

Introductory discussion

Our second proposition is drawn from the schema of political attitudes presented by the neofunctionalists Lindberg and Scheingold in *Europe's Would-be Polity,* which we outlined in Chapter Three. Lindberg and Scheingold use the term 'utilitarian' to refer to support for integration which stems from a recognition of common interests and positive, mutual benefits that will result. The 'affective' basis of support, defined by Deutsch, describes the more diffuse, emotional support which may exist between peoples, and which may also comprise a sense of common identity.[1]

This distinction in the bases of support for integration is also made by Haas. Pentland writes that 'a distinction is drawn between the cognitive and affective components which together make up the total complex of attitudes, or the image'.[2] The cognitive components match the utilitarian basis of support defined by Lindberg and Scheingold. Thus, support for integration which stems from perceived economic or political interests – for example, increased standards of living or a guarantee of peace – is termed cognitive or utilitarian support. Affective support, or the non-rational attitudes of loyalty, sympathy and shared values, may exist between peoples or may reflect attachment to an international community.

In view of the original neofunctionalist belief that the end-product of integration is a 'state-model' supranational political unit, the timing or 'phasing' of attitude change is significant. Formerly, neofunctionalists concentrated almost solely on elite perceptions of integration, but 'the public consensus or apathy which they long took for granted in Europe now seems increasingly problematic'.[3] Thus, neofunctionalists are faced with the prospect of a lag between utilitarian and affective support for integration. Could affective support eventually be generated by the supranational government, rather like the affective support generated by one-party regimes in developing countries? Or could this lack of affective support thwart the creation of authoritative supranational institutions?

Since the European Community has, to date, been concerned with economic integration, it should follow that support will be mainly utilitarian, with economic self-interest predominating over political self-interest. A further distinction to be drawn within the utilitarian basis of support is that between national interest and individual self-interest. This distinction is of crucial significance, since the strength of these types of utilitarian interests will provide some indication of the strength of support for European unification. Support for economic integration which is based on a perception of the national interest clearly has very different implications for further integration, in contrast to support which stems from a perception of personal self-interest.

The evidence and its interpretation

We saw in Chapter Four that public support for European unification was very strong in the late 1940s and throughout the 1950s, but that, certainly in France, distrust for the Germans contributed to the defeat of EDC. The result was that by the 1960s the only supranational authorities to have been established in the cause of European unification were the High Authority of ECSC and the Commission of Euratom and EEC, and their territorial power was limited to only six of the West European nation-states. Bearing in mind this distinction between support for unification and the actual progress made towards integration, let us examine the motives underlying the support for and opposition to the idea of unification and the image and expectations of the supranational organisations which have been created in Western Europe.

In 1962, Gallup International conducted a survey of the Six and Great Britain which sought, amongst other things, to identify the varying bases of support for unification.[4] The reasons given spontaneously by the pro-European respondents to explain why Europe must be united fell into three categories of ideas. First came the theme of security, the desire to ensure peace and to avoid a return to conflicts. It seems reasonable to argue that it is in anyone's self-interest to avoid conflict, and therefore the theme of security reflects a basically utilitarian basis of support. However, the general sense of this theme was that of ensuring peace, removing the possibilities of conflict and of putting an end to quarrels. Only rarely did notions of containing pressure from the East or of forming a third bloc in the world appear in the publics' responses. Thus, it seems fair to conclude that this theme contained a large affective element, a general desire for mutual trust and peace, as opposed to the pure political self-interest of forming a defensive or balancing bloc in the world.

This theme of security did dominate all other motives for unification in West Germany and France, where 23 per cent and 24 per cent respectively of pro-Europeans spoke of the desire to ensure peace and to avoid conflict. That this evidence reflects a degree of affective support by the public is affirmed by the fact that in informal conversations held before the Gallup International survey was conducted, it became clear that support for unification was associated with a geographic entity much larger than the Europe of the Six — indeed, in June 1962, 39 per cent of Frenchmen favoured participation by Eastern European countries, while only 32 per cent opposed this proposal and 29 per cent expressed no opinion. In short, there is evidence of a positive affective-identitive element in public support for European unification.

Yet the theme of security did include utilitarian sentiments. 18 per cent of the Dutch pro-Europeans stressed that no small nation-state could remain viable in modern world conditions, while 15 per cent of West German pro-Europeans expressed a desire 'to contain the East'. 10 per cent of the Belgian and the French pro-Europeans argued the need for a third bloc to check the power of the USA and USSR, but this view was very rarely expressed elsewhere.

Utilitarian sentiment is strongest of all in the second theme to emerge from the 1962 Gallup International survey. This theme is spontaneously expressed by pro-Europeans in either of two forms — in terms of the general economy by developing the prosperity of a country, or in terms of the benefits to the individual by the acquisition of greater comfort and a higher standard of living. The feeling that it is essential to stimulate the national economies and that the construction of Europe provides the necessary stimulus, was expressed frequently (15 per cent of pro-Europeans in Italy and France, 17 per cent in West Germany, and 9 per cent in Belgium). However, it is in Holland that this idea was dominant (32 per cent of pro-Europeans), taking precedence over all other motives. The feeling that Europe must be united so as to improve the standard of living for the individual was the principal motive of the Italian pro-Europeans, but in other countries this idea was significantly less important than the idea of the national interest.

The third category of ideas or motives was the pursuit of progress in the non-materialist sense — intellectual, spiritual and humanist. Although the pro-Europeans who were inspired by this current of thought were found to be in a minority, it is notable that this theme did come a strong third in importance as a motive for support in France and the Netherlands. Indeed, this theme is rarely tapped by the pollsters because their questions are usually directed towards feelings about ECSC or EEC, the very nature and *raison d'être* of which tend to preclude non-materialistic responses on the part of the public.

A good example of a public opinion survey which reveals a strong correlation between the utilitarian motive of individual self-interest and attitudes towards a supranational organisation is Kriesberg's study of mass attitudes in West Germany and the ECSC.[5] As a test of individual self-interest influencing attitudes towards the ECSC, Kriesberg studied the correlation between domestic users of coal and opposition to the ECSC. This study is made particularly interesting by the fact that 90 per cent of domestic heating units in West Germany in the mid-1950s depended on coal, yet the briquettes used were often in short supply and were expensive. Respondents who reported that others obtained the coal or that coal was not used in their household were less likely to think that West Germany fared badly in the ECSC (see Table 5.1). However, among those who felt that West Germany fared badly, those who did not bother with household coal tended to think that it was a mistake to have joined the ECSC. As we shall see later, however, this apparent deviation can be attributed to differing opinions according to the respondents' level of income.

In France too, support for the ECSC appeared to be predominantly utilitarian. In September 1952, 46 per cent expressed spontaneous support, with 17 per cent giving the economic advantage for France as their motive and 11 per cent mentioning the economic advantage for all the participating countries.[6] However, 11 per cent also spoke of the ECSC as the first step towards the United States of Europe, and 9 per cent reasoned that 'unity makes strength'. It is also worth noting that despite strong support in France for European unification in 1954 (see Figure 4.4), fully 26 per cent of Frenchmen in a poll of January 1954 'did not know' the ECSC and a further 29 per cent could express 'no opinion' on the question of extending the powers of the ECSC to fields other than coal and steel.

Similarly, polls on the EEC highlight the utilitarian basis of support, because of the very nature of the Community created by the Treaty of Rome. Thus, in August 1968, West Germans felt that the four main advantages of the Common Market were cheaper, stable prices (29 per cent), a larger economic unit (22 per cent), improved exports (21 per

Table 5.1

Evaluation of the ECSC in West Germany by
concern about household coal (figures in percentages)

'Who in general concerns himself in your household with getting coal?'

	Evaluation of ECSC				
	(1) Good	(2) Mildly favourable	(3) Bad, not anti	(4) Bad, anti	(5) Undecided
Others/Do not use coal	25	28	10	16	21
Respondent and others	17	29	20	17	16
Respondent alone	17	32	17	19	16

Source: Kriesberg, op.cit., 1959, p. 38

cent) and cuts in tariffs (14 per cent).[7] However, 11 per cent saw the EEC as a step toward political unity, but only 5 per cent felt that it helped to create better relations between peoples.

We have already seen in Chapter Four that, after 1969, British public opinion towards joining the Common Market became consistently hostile. We noted an apparent tendency towards isolationism in British attitudes in the late 1960s, but the major motives for the increasing opposition to the European Community which the Gallup polls detected were utilitarian. It is clear from the report on the Gallup Political Index of December 1969 that this utilitarianism was economically motivated rather than possessing a political basis. The report stated that, '. . . the major reason for the change in attitudes is the expectation of higher prices, particularly of food'.[8] On political factors the report continued, 'The effect of British entry on the Commonwealth, once the main reason given for opposition to the Common Market, has declined in importance, although it is still given some weight.' However, the report added that 'if people are asked to choose between close economic and political ties with Europe, or with the USA, more pick Europe and more than half expect Britain to join some day.'[9] The report goes on to talk of an increased willingness on the part of the British public to act in much closer co-operation with European countries on several issues. This seems to indicate a reluctant acceptance of the apparent facts of political life – the Labour Party had only recently applied for membership, and therefore the

Table 5.2

Expected economic effects in Britain of entry
of the Common Market (figures in percentages)

'When we join the Common Market, do you think that in the short/long term these will go up, go down, or remain the same? If go up: a lot or a little?'

| | | Go up | | | Go down | | Same | | Don't know | |
| | | a lot | | a little | | | | | | | |
		1971	1972	1971	1972	1971	1972	1971	1972	1971	1972
(1)	*Food prices*										
	Short term	71	62	23	30	—	—	3	4	3	4
	Long term	57	48	22	30	5	4	11	12	5	6
(2)	*Other prices*										
	Short term	41	35	32	34	7	7	12	16	9	8
	Long term	37	32	31	33	10	10	14	18	8	7
(3)	*Level of*										
	wages										
	Short term	18	23	35	36	6	3	27	25	14	13
	Long term	25	29	37	39	4	2	19	17	15	13
(4)	*Level of*										
	taxation										
	Short term	19	19	26	25	7	8	27	27	21	21
	Long term	20	20	25	27	5	7	27	22	24	24
(5)	*Level of*										
	employment										
	Short term	16	13	21	25	23	20	22	27	19	15
	Long term	20	19	25	26	16	18	17	20	22	17

1971 – September; 1972 – October

Source: *Gallup Political Index* no. 147

major parties seemed likely to reapply for entry, and Britain's links with the Commonwealth and special relationship with the USA were facts of the past, not the future.

In October 1972, when 39 per cent of the British public favoured entry and 41 per cent were against, with 20 per cent saying 'don't know', a special Gallup Poll found that the opposition stemmed largely from fears of the effect on food prices (see Table 5.2). It should be noted that in September 1971 opposition to entry had been stronger (35 per cent), with 47 per cent in favour and 18 per cent 'don't knows'.[10] Table 5.2 shows that a slightly more optimistic view of the effects of entry on prices, wage levels and employment had developed by October 1972, but in view of the swing towards opposition which followed it seems that this was short-lived (see Figure 4.7). Table 5.3 also reflects the movement of opinion towards support for British entry into the Common Market between September 1971 and October 1972. Gallup's report sums up the situation:

> More people think that Britain's membership of the Common Market will benefit her in terms of defence, her position in the world and her voice in international affairs than those who think it will weaken her in these areas. Elsewhere, the main emphasis of opinion is that Britain's relations with the United States and Russia will remain the same, but her relations with the Commonwealth will worsen.[11]

In view of the general movement in favour of entry, it is not unduly surprising that, on all five items in Table 5.3, people have become more optimistic since the same question was asked in September 1971. But the relatively large falls in the percentages of those who felt that Britain's relationships with the Commonwealth and with the USA and Russia would worsen is of particular interest.

The conclusion drawn from Gallup's two-part survey of British opinions in 1971 and 1972 is that 'fears of rising prices on entry into the EEC still dominate the domestic scene, although people do accept that there could be wider benefits'.[12] This raises an interesting question — are there meaningful differences between perceived effects on the nation-state, whether they be economic or political, and perceived effects on the individual, whether economic or political? In other words, is there evidence that the public may be willing to accept personal losses in order that the national economy or political situation can improve through membership, or, alternatively, do considerations of individual gains outweigh any fears of damage to the national economy or political system? If the major utilitarian factor in the basis of support for the

Table 5.3

How the British expected Britain's military and political status
to be affected by entry of the Common Market
(figures in percentages)

*'When Britain joins the Common Market, do you think that things will be
better, worse, or remain the same for . . .?'*

	Better		Worse		Same		Don't know	
	1971	1972	1971	1972	1971	1972	1971	1972
(1) Britain's defence	37	39	11	10	28	31	24	20
(2) Britain's position in the world	37	36	23	21	27	33	13	10
(3) Britain's voice in international affairs	30	35	22	20	28	31	19	14
(4) Britain's relationship with the United States and Russia	15	21	27	17	37	43	23	19
(5) Britain's relationship with the Commonwealth	14	17	54	42	18	29	14	12

Source: *Gallup Political Index* no. 147

Common Market is the national interest rather than individual or personal interests, the notion of a clear progression from economic to political integration is seriously weakened — indeed, federalist critics of the present Community feel that its main achievement has been to strengthen the nation-state in Europe, and not to lay the basis of a 'United States of Europe'.[13]

Some of the most helpful evidence in reviewing perceived effects of integration on nation-state or individual is the data on the expectations and fears of the process of integration expressed by the public. A seemingly paradoxical situation was revealed in Gallup International's survey in 1963 — in the country where public support for unification was strongest, namely the Netherlands, there existed the most acute awareness of the dangers and risks of unification (see Table 5.4).

Table 5.4

Awareness of the dangers and risks of
European unification

	Percentage of public	
	who believe unification presents dangers	in favour of unification
The Netherlands	49	87
France	41	72
Belgium	30	65
Luxembourg	24	27
West Germany	18	81
Italy	9	60

Source: Gallup International, op.cit., 1963, p. 108

But is the belief that unification presents dangers founded on the feeling that one's own country will find itself at a disadvantage? Table 5.4 could be indicative of nationalistic reactions amongst the Six, but Table 5.5 shows that, where national interests were considered, the majority perceived that the Common Market was advantageous to their own country. The French and the West Germans seemed to feel that their countries were at some risk, whereas the Italian and Benelux publics seemed far less cautious.

But we must be careful not to fall into a trap — it could be argued that while many people feel that their country will gain from the Common Market, this is not tantamount to believing that their country will also gain from further integration — indeed, by definition, a member nation-state cannot 'gain' from unification, since the resultant United States of Europe would involve the transfer of national sovereignty to the

Table 5.5

Evaluation of national position in the Common Market

| | Percentage thinking their country | | |
	will gain	no different	will lose
The Netherlands	70	7	7
Italy	55	8	3
Belgium	55	13	9
France	39	17	16
Luxembourg	23	17	11
West Germany	21	51	15

Source: Gallup International, op.cit., 1963, p. 109

new federal authority. But it is quite possible for a nation-state to gain from membership of the EEC while blocking any moves towards political unification by the use of its veto in the Council of Ministers. In this sense, nationalists can accept, and even favour, membership of the EEC – de Gaulle was a case in point.

Any apprehensions and fears expressed by the public of the Six in 1962 when they were asked to think about unification did not spring from nationalist reactions. Nor was there any sense that it would be their country that would have to 'pay the costs' of unification. In fact, those fears which were expressed had several sources, none of which were particularly potent. With percentages varying from country to country throughout the Six, between 1 and 7 per cent feared the risk of conflict with non-European powers; 1 to 7 per cent feared intra-Community conflicts; 1 to 7 per cent were worried by the inequalities between member-states; 1 to 5 per cent found cultural differences within the Six disturbing; and 1 to 3 per cent only feared the loss of national independence. However, 2 to 10 per cent disliked the possibility of economic crises or upheavals; and between 1 and 4 per cent feared a fall in living standards and a disruption of the labour market.[14]

It seems that those fears of unification which did exist in the Six stemmed from individual self-interest rather than from nationalistic feelings, although Gallup International's findings are by no means conclusive. Further discussion of this finding will be undertaken when we review perceptions of which groups in each nation were seen to be most likely to suffer from integration. Also, we shall examine the contrasting conclusions which can be drawn from surveys of publics in countries outside the original Six. But there is some evidence that West German support for European integration came to clash with the West Germans' perception of their national interest in the 1960s. The conflict was between European integration and German reunification. Table 5.6 appears to show that during the 1950s German unity took increasing precedence over the future of Europe.

Table 5.6

German unity or European unity?
(Figures in percentages)

'What do you consider to be the most important? The unity of Germany or a united Europe?'

	United Germany	United Europe	No answer
1951	55	27	18
1953	57	29	14
1954	67	28	5
1955	76	21	3
1956	73	22	5
1957	68	27	5
1958	70	25	5
1959	67	26	7
1960	68	26	6
1965	69	24	7

Source: *EMNID-Informationen,* 1951–65

But the responses presented in Table 5.6 must be seen in the context of a nation-state divided by the arbitrary establishment of frontiers by occupying powers in 1945, rather than as a display of nationalistic sentiment of a type which could threaten progress towards fuller integration in Western Europe. In Table 5.7 we see that, despite the West Germans' desire for national reunification, they have come increasingly to oppose any return to pre-war national independence. But are the West Germans exceptional?

Table 5.7

Independent nation-state or European unity?
(Figures in percentages)

'What would be a better outcome — the restoration of Germany as a fully independent nation-state with its own customs barriers or Germany as an equal member of a united Europe?'

	Independent Nation	United Europe	No answer
June 1949	44	36	20
May 1950	29	48	23
March 1951	32	49	19
May 1952	35	42	23
April 1953	38	43	19
March 1954	44	48	8
September 1955	45	50	5
September 1956	43	51	6
September 1957	39	54	7
April 1958	44	50	6
April 1959	37	52	11
May 1966	23	62	15

Source: *EMNID-Informationen,* 1949—66

Recent Community-wide polls have shown that, in the six founder-member countries, the publics feel that their nation has benefited from the Common Market and that they, personally, have benefited to a lesser extent (see Tables 5.8(a) and 5.8(b)). The marked difference in opinions between the Six and the three new member-states is also noticeable in Table 5.8(b).

There is a general awareness throughout the Nine that the nation-state has benefited from the Common Market more than the individual has. Further evidence from Community-wide polls (see Table 5.9) shows that only a minority — albeit a large minority — is willing to make some personal sacrifice in the cause of European unification. The Belgians and the French seem no more willing than the Danes to make personal sacrifices — indeed the French are almost as unwilling as the British. While Table 5.9 tells us nothing about the intensity of a public's nationalism, it could be argued that those publics who are unwilling to make some

Table 5.8(a)

Evaluation of national position in the Common Market,
September 1973 and May 1974 (figures in percentages)

	Good		Bad		Neither good nor bad		No reply	
	1973	1974	1973	1974	1973	1974	1973	1974
Belgium	57	68	5	3	19	15	19	14
France	61	68	5	5	22	20	12	7
Luxembourg	67	79	3	4	22	12	8	5
Italy	69	77	2	5	15	9	14	9
The Netherlands	63	66	4	4	20	14	13	16
West Germany	63	59	4	8	22	26	11	7
The 'Six'	63	67	4	6	19	18	14	9
Denmark	42	35	30	31	19	24	9	10
Great Britain	31	33	34	39	22	19	13	9
Ireland	56	48	15	25	21	19	8	8
The Community	56	59	11	14	20	18	13	9

Source: Commission of the Communities, *Euro-Barometer* no. 1, Brussels,
July 1974

Table 5.8(b)

Evaluation of personal position in the Common Market,
September 1973 (figures in percentages)

	Good	Bad	Neither good nor bad	No reply
Belgium	46	5	29	20
France	50	6	30	14
Luxembourg	42	6	41	11
Italy	54	2	26	18
The Netherlands	48	6	28	18
West Germany	47	5	33	15
Denmark	32	29	29	10
Great Britain	22	38	28	12
Ireland	41	20	32	7

Source: Commission of the Communities, *Europe as the Europeans See It,*
Brussels, November 1973

Table 5.9

'Would be willing to make some sacrifice in the cause of European unification':
January–February 1970, July 1971, September 1973 (figures in percentages)

	Belgium			France			Luxembourg			Italy			Netherlands			West Germany			Denmark	Great Britain	Ireland
	'70	'71	'73	'70	'71	'73	'70	'71	'73	'70	'71	'73	'70	'71	'73	'70	'71	'73	'73	'73	'73
Very willing	5	5	8	5	6	6	6	9	14	7	12	10	9	8	13	13	13	5	7	4	8
Fairly willing	18	16	19	22	21	23	31	30	28	29	24	39	34	24	28	29	25	42	29	23	32
Not very willing	19	16	22	22	16	19	21	29	20	20	16	20	19	20	23	24	27	26	28	21	22
Not at all willing	47	45	43	41	42	42	29	19	28	34	24	21	32	48	28	27	27	13	30	44	30
Don't know	11	18	8	10	15	10	13	13	10	10	24	10	6		8	7	8	14	6	8	8

Source: Commission of the Communities, *L'Opinion des Européens sur les aspects régionaux et agricoles du Marché Commun, l'unification politique de l'Europe et l'information du public*, Brussels, December 1971, and, *Europe as the Europeans see it*, Brussels, November 1973

personal sacrifice in order to promote unification may be more willing to suffer if they felt that it was in the national interest. Yet in Table 5.10, we can see that in reply to the question of the desirability of the Common Market evolving into a political European union, there is once more a very noticeable difference between the six founder-members and the three newcomers. This does appear to indicate a relatively stronger sense of national loyalty in the newcomer-states and less affective-identitive support for the European idea. In Table 5.11 the difference between the Six and the newcomers in terms of their attachment to the Common Market is again marked. It is instructive that in the founder-member states the publics have become increasingly likely to express great regret in the event of the abandonment of the Common Market. Only in West Germany, between September 1973 and May 1974, did the public show any signs of wavering in their attachment, but this probably reflects the combination of European and national problems, which meant that the West Germans felt that they had been put in a position of 'baling out' the Community at a period when they themselves were facing serious domestic economic troubles. Certainly, this was the impression created by West German representatives during the negotiations over the Community Regional Fund in December 1973 and January 1974. Yet Tables 5.8 and 5.9 show that the West German public has been more willing than several other member-publics of the Six to make some personal sacrifices in the cause of unification, while also supporting the idea of a political European union very strongly indeed.

Clearly, the publics' perceptions of which sectors of the population in the member-states suffer as a result of integration are central to any evaluations of personal position or any expressions of willingness to make some personal sacrifices in the cause of integration. Several polls have been conducted on the publics' views of which groups in society will suffer or have suffered as a result of Common Market policies. In 1962, the poll conducted by Gallup International found that in reply to the question of which group will suffer most from membership of the Common Market, one reply emerged distinctly – 'the farmers will be the victims'. [15] This view was held by 30 per cent of West German respondents, 21 per cent in the Netherlands, 18 per cent in Luxembourg, 16 per cent in France, 12 per cent in Belgium and 4 per cent in Italy. Undoubtedly, these figures reflected the terms of the CAP as it stood in 1962, as well as the social compositions of the member-states of the Common Market. The other replies were spread over quite a large number of themes – for example, in Belgium 7 per cent mentioned the mining industry, in France 4 per cent quoted the car industry, and in

Table 5.10

Opinions on the evolution of the Common Market towards European political union: January–February 1970, July 1971, September 1973 (figures in percentages)

'Are you, yourself, for or against the Common Market developing into a political European union?'

	Belgium			France			Luxembourg			Italy			Netherlands			West Germany			Denmark	Great Britain	Ireland
	'70	'71	'73	'70	'71	'73	'70	'71	'73	'70	'71	'73	'70	'71	'73	'70	'71	'73	'73	'73	'73
For	62	53	58	63	50	57	77	66	69	77	72	65	75	67	55	69	71	70	28	26	35
Against	10	13	12	13	17	12	5	15	13	6	7	12	14	18	23	10	15	12	58	54	41
Don't know	28	34	30	24	33	18	18	19	18	17	21	23	11	15	22	21	14	18	14	20	24

Source: Commission of the Communities, op.cit., 1971 and 1973

Table 5.11

Degree of attachment to the Common Market:

January–February 1970, July 1971, September 1973, May 1974 (figures in percentages)

'If you were told tomorrow that the Common Market had been given up, would you feel great regret, relief, or indifference?'

	Belgium				France				Luxembourg				Italy				Netherlands				West Germany				Denmark		Great Britain		Ireland	
	'70	'71	'73	'74	'70	'71	'73	'74	'70	'71	'73	'74	'70	'71	'73	'74	'70	'71	'73	'74	'70	'71	'73	'74	'73	'74	'73	'74	'73	'74
Great regret*	53	25	39	48	58	31	42	56	57	36	51	73	60	35	41	60	68	40	46	54	68	52	57	53	30	27	20	24	37	38
Relief	3	4	3	2	5	5	2	3	4	6	3	3	3	3	1	4	5	10	4	4	6	7	4	5	29	31	37	40	17	28
Indifference	32	53	44	30	30	52	43	40	28	42	35	17	28	38	44	22	20	35	37	20	16	29	24	28	29	27	33	28	40	27
Don't know	12	18	14	20	7	12	13	11	11	16	11	7	9	24	14	14	7	15	11	22	10	12	15	14	12	15	10	8	6	7

* In 1970, the response wording read 'great regret' *and* 'little regret'; hence the larger percentage who expressed regrets

Source: Commission of the Communities, op.cit., 1971 and 1974; and J.-R. Rabier, op.cit., 1970

Luxembourg 9 per cent designated tradesmen as victims too. In general, 'the small, weak, marginal businesses, those which cannot prepare themselves', and so on, were expected to be the main losers. [16]

Table 5.12

Those feeling that to date the Common Market
has been a good/bad influence on their region,
1967 and 1971 (figures in percentages)

	Belgium		France		Italy		Netherlands		West Germany	
	1967	1971	1967	1971	1967	1971	1967	1971	1967	1971
Very good or quite good influence	53	34	22	27	33	35	56	37	46	55
No influence at all	24	23	31	29	14	23	20	16	17	14
Quite bad or very bad influence	21	9	25	12	9	8	16	15	18	14
No reply	2	34	22	32	44	34	8	32	19	17

Source: Commission of the Communities, op.cit., 1971

Further and more detailed information on the economic sources of opinions on the Common Market is provided in the Community-wide polls sponsored by the Commission of the Communities in 1967 and July 1971. For instance, Table 5.12 shows that by 1971 more people throughout the Six had come to feel that the Common Market had had a beneficial effect on their region, although the Belgians and the Dutch had become far less pleased with the perceived effects on their regions. But in those two countries the percentages of those who perceived a bad effect also decreased slightly, and thus the trend was towards a neutral viewpoint, rather than there being signs of growing dissatisfaction.

In Table 5.13 we can see in which particular sectors of the economy the various publics felt their regions had gained or suffered most from Common Market membership. In every country, industry was seen to have had the most beneficial effect on their regions as a result of the Common Market. This view will be examined in more detail shortly. In West Germany, Italy, France, the Netherlands and Belgium, those who felt their

Table 5.13

Sector in which the Common Market's influence
is mostly perceived, and whether
it is seen as good or bad, July 1973 (figures in percentages)

	Belgium		France		Luxembourg		Italy		Netherlands		West Germany	
	Good	Bad	Good	Bad	Good	Bad	Good	Bad	Good	Bad	Good	Bad
Industry	50	21	35	15	45	24	39	17	37	19	44	8
Agriculture	11	44	18	59	12	24	15	60	16	55	13	75
Tourism	5	–	12	–	7	3	18	2	12	1	8	1
Commerce	22	29	26	18	23	35	17	5	22	16	29	13
Transport and communications	6	1	3	1	7	3	3	–	6	1	4	1
No reply	6	5	6	7	6	11	8	16	7	8	2	2

Source: Commission of the Communities, op.cit., 1971

Table 5.14(a)

Effects of the Common Market on agriculture, July 1971
(figures in percentages)

	Belgium	France	Luxembourg	Italy	Netherlands	West Germany
Good for agriculture in the Six	23	20	43	34	22	22
Bad for agriculture in the Six	9	4	5	4	8	5
To advantage of farmers in respondent's country	5	8	31	5	14	6
To disadvantage of respondent's country	26	20	5	20	34	44
No reply	37	48	16	17	22	23

Table 5.14(b)

Effects of the Common Market on industry
(figures in percentages)

	Belgium	France	Luxembourg	Italy	Netherlands	West Germany
Good for industry in the Six	40	35	52	46	41	46
Bad for industry in the Six	4	3	3	2	3	2
To advantage of industry in respondent's country	13	8	7	9	21	18
To disadvantage of industry in respondent's country	8	11	14	7	11	9
No reply	35	43	24	36	24	25

Source: Commission of the Communities, op.cit., 1971, pp. 37–8

region had fared badly attributed the blame to the agricultural sector — only tiny Luxembourg deviated from this pattern. Feelings were mixed on the influence of commerce in the regions since the Common Market had been created, although a sizeable minority of those who felt that things had gone badly for their region did also mention the industrial sector.

In Tables 5.14(a) and 5.14(b) we can see an interesting contrast between the perceived effects of the Common Market on agriculture and industry, both throughout the Six and within the respondents' own country. Only the public in Luxembourg felt that the farmers in their own country had benefited from the Common Market more than they had suffered, but in the case of the industrial sector slightly larger percentages in Belgium, Italy, the Netherlands and West Germany felt that their industries had gained rather than lost. However, the most striking contrast is between the percentages of respondents who felt that agriculture in the Six had gained, and the much larger percentages who felt that the Common Market had been to the benefit of the Six. Yet it is also clear that although many felt that the farmers in their own country had suffered, few felt that the Common Market had been bad for agriculture as a whole throughout the Six. This is indicative of a view of CAP as a 'necessary evil' — the farmers may suffer but agriculture in the Six gains.

In an effort to gauge the general or 'global' image of the Common Market, the publics in the Community were asked which of five statements they agreed with or disagreed with (see Table 5.15).

Table 5.15

Global image of the Common Market, July 1971
(figures in percentages)

1   'The Common Market stimulates the modernisation of industry in our country'
2   'It helps the sale of our products abroad and also develops our national output'
3   'It allows a better provision of goods for the consumers in our country'
4   'It opens the door to foreign goods which compete with our goods'
5   'It helps the sale of our agricultural goods abroad'

	1	2	3	4	5
Belgium					
Agree with	57	58	60	60	41
No opinion	14	12	11	11	15
Disagree with	5	7	6	7	19
No reply	24	23	23	22	25
France					
Agree with	65	61	60	78	47
No opinion	17	16	16	8	18
Disagree with	7	10	12	5	21
No reply	11	13	12	9	14
Italy					
Agree with	66	66	59	63	53
No opinion	7	7	11	8	7
Disagree with	4	9	7	10	20
No reply	23	18	23	19	20

Table 5.15 continued

	1	2	3	4	5
Luxembourg					
Agree with	71	76	79	64	55
No opinion	9	5	5	7	10
Disagree with	6	6	9	16	17
No reply	14	13	7	13	18
The Netherlands					
Agree with	69	67	70	72	53
No opinion	24	22	20	20	25
Disagree with	7	11	10	8	22
No reply	—	—	—	—	—
West Germany					
Agree with	70	73	75	78	41
No opinion	13	10	11	9	14
Disagree with	10	10	9	8	35
No reply	7	7	5	5	10

Source: Commission of the Communities, op.cit., 1971, pp. 41–3

In all the countries of the Six, except for Italy and Luxembourg, the response which was expressed most often, and which therefore constitutes the dominant element in the image of the Common Market, was that it opened the door to foreign goods which competed with goods produced in the respondent's own country. This response, which seems to display a nationalistic outlook, was strongest of all in France. In Italy, the strongest response was that the Common Market had stimulated industrial modernisation, although the view also seems evident that imports were encouraged as well as exports. In Luxembourg, much stress was placed on the wider choice of goods available to consumers, with slightly greater weight given to the encouragement of exports. The Commission's report observes that, above all (and even in France), the fact that the Common Market helped the sale of agricultural goods abroad was a view held by relatively few respondents.

The Community-wide polls of the Six do demonstrate the strength of the economic motivations in the utilitarian basis of support for the Common Market. Certainly by 1971 most of the publics had come to feel that membership of the Six benefited their region and that their country's industries had gained. The common feelings of the losses suffered by their country's farmers were at least partly offset by a belief that agriculture in the Six had gained from integration. Large majorities in the Six in 1971 were of the opinion that the Common Market had led to the modernisation of their country's industries, better export performances, greater national output and a wider choice of goods in the shops, while much smaller majorities acknowledged the Common Market's role in their country's ability to export agricultural products. But the strongest response of all in the Six reflects nationalistic sentiments — that the Common Market led to an increased flow of 'foreign' goods onto the respective domestic markets.

This ambiguity in the publics' replies seems all the more surprising in view of the large majorities in the Six which have repeatedly been observed to favour European unification and the evolution of the Common Market towards a political European union (see Table 5.10). We have also noted another ambiguity in this apparently overwhelming affective-identitive support for European unification, namely the apparent unwillingness to make personal sacrifices in the cause of European unification that many respondents in the Community, including the publics of the founder-member states, showed in 1973. Indeed, it will be recalled that the evidence in Table 5.8 was exceptional in that the gap in commitment to integration between the Six and the newcomers was not as marked as usual.

However, the opinions expressed in response to four statements about European political unification in the 1971 Community-wide poll do help to shed further light on these ambiguities in the publics' support.

We can see from Table 5.16 that the proposition which received the largest majorities throughout the Six was that 'The peoples of Europe are becoming increasingly aware of their common interests in all spheres.'[17] The Commission's report is probably correct to argue that the support for this statement is indicative of a sense of the seeming inevitability of the unification of Europe, whatever may be the technical problems, political obstacles or the quirks of history. Indeed, almost as much support was expressed for the statement that 'The United States of Europe may perhaps exist one day, but this will take at the very least a score of years.'[18] Although it is not possible to put an exact measure on the number of years in this statement, it is clear that the public felt that political union was a very long-term project. It may be for this reason that there were many people in the Community who were not very willing to make personal sacrifices in the cause of unification. A significant minority were prepared to make sacrifices for this end, but if the prospect of union was certainly very distant — over a lifetime away for most Europeans —

Table 5.16

The ambiguity of the publics' attitude towards the political unification
of Europe, July 1971 (figures in percentages)

1 'The countries of Europe are too different in their size and power to be able to form together a political union.'
2 'The United States of Europe may perhaps exist one day, but this will take at the very least a score of years.'
3 'The peoples of Europe are becoming increasingly aware of their common interests in all spheres.'
4 'In the countries of the Common Market, the public is already prepared to go further towards unification than are the governments.'

	Belgium				France				Italy				Luxembourg				Netherlands				West Germany			
	1	2	3	4	1	2	3	4	1	2	3	4	1	2	3	4	1	2	3	4	1	2	3	4
Agree with	37	51	57	32	42	65	63	36	41	55	60	42	42	62	62	41	49	63	70	38	44	63	72	51
Disagree with	33	16	10	24	32	11	9	21	33	19	12	17	31	15	15	29	35	15	10	27	42	21	14	23
No reply	30	33	33	44	26	24	28	43	26	26	28	41	27	23	23	30	16	22	20	35	14	16	14	26

Source: Commission of the Communities, op.cit., 1971, p. 56

most people felt that they would not live to see the benefits of their own sacrifices. The distant vision of European unity does not seem as capable of mobilising the public to make willing self-sacrifices as political ideologies or religious beliefs – possibly wars alone can mobilise the public in liberal-democracies to make self-sacrifices willingly.

Table 5.16 shows the publics most guarded in their opinions on the statement that, 'In the countries of the Common Market, the public is already prepared to go further towards unification than are the governments.'[19] The reason for the cautious replies is that to disagree with this statement would contradict the agreement with the preceding statement on the awareness of common European interests, which had been expressed by a large majority. Yet to agree that the people were more keen for unification than were the governments would amount to a criticism of the governments of the Six, who, after all, were elected by a majority of their respective electorates. It seems reasonable to argue that the relatively small percentage of 'no reply' responses in West Germany, and the large percentage of those who expressed agreement with the statement, reflects a disillusionment with the other governments of the Six, rather than with the Germans' own, pro-European government of 1971.

Throughout the Six, there is agreement, albeit by only slight majorities, with the statement that 'The countries of Europe are too different in their size and power to be able to form together a political union.'[20] In a way that the other statements in Table 5.16 fail to achieve, this statement reveals the existence of real fears of political unification held amongst the publics of the Six. Indeed, the findings in Table 5.15 confirm those established by Gallup International in 1962 (see Table 5.4) – in 1971, the Dutch again appear to be the most anxious about the dangers of unification, with the French also expressing real fears, as they did in 1962. It is difficult to draw any accurate comparisons from Tables 5.4 and 5.16, but clearly the West Germans seem, on the whole, to be less fearful of unification than most of their counterparts in the Six.

The Commission of the Communities' report on the Community-wide poll of July 1971 suggests that the ambiguity which was found to exist in the general support for unification amongst the publics of the Six stemmed from fears of being dominated or, possibly, of being 'tricked' into some agreement which would benefit other countries or groups at the expense of their own country or group.[21] It is not altogether surprising that fears of unification are found to be even more evident amongst the British and Norwegian publics, since support for entry into the Common Market in these countries has been far from strong or consistent. In the

Table 5.17(a)

British willingness to accept a European Government,
October 1972 (figures in percentages)

'Could you say definitely whether you would or would not accept a European Government, which would be responsible over and above the British Government for a common political policy on foreign affairs, defence and the economy?'

	Total	Conservative	Labour
Would accept	29	36	23
Would not accept	47	42	52
Don't know	24	22	25

Table 5.17(b)

Britain's position in the Common Market (figures in percentages)

'When Britain joins the Common Market, do you think she will become the leader, will she have to take a back seat, or do you see the Common Market as a group in which all countries are equal?'

	September 1971	October 1972
Britain the leader	5	9
Would take a back seat	36	35
All equal	46	46
Don't know	13	9

Source: *Gallup Political Index* no. 147

British case (see Tables 5.2 and 5.3), we have seen that fears of the effects of entry on prices formed the main factor in 1971 and 1972, while there were also some doubts expressed about the effects on Britain's security and her political position. However, Tables 5.17(a) and 5.17(b) show that one of the major fears expressed by the British public has been that of domination.

There seems to be particular resistance to the idea of Britain having to

Table 5.18

Reason for being for or against Norwegian membership
of the European Community (figures in percentages)

	November 1971	February 1972
In favour of membership		
No reason given	21	6
No choice	14	4
Party loyalty	2	1
Economic advantages, secure employment	27	41
A united Europe, peace in Europe	31	48
Social welfare	1	1
Various other answers	5	1
Total	101	102
Opposed to membership		
No reason given	15	7
Doubt, fear, uncertainty, prefer status quo	9	8
'Strangers'	2	1
Party loyalty	–	1
Self-determination, influence, local democracy	27	34
Big capital, control of the establishment of industries	6	6
Employment, standard of living	11	14
Farming and fisheries	40	35
Various other answers	5	4
Total	115	110

Source: Fakta polls. Because of multiple answers, the percentages add up to more than one hundred (respondents were asked for the main reason but sometimes more than one were recorded by the interviewer). Percentage bases: pro-Community 277 (November) and 413 (February); anti-Community, 671 and 640.

adopt policies decided by a European government, or even by a Common Market, in which Britain was likely to be an equal partner or even take a back seat. Also, in 1972, Gallup found that 35 per cent of the British favoured the evolution of the Common Market into a United States of Europe, but 39 per cent were against the idea, and 26 per cent expressed no opinion. Yet 40 per cent felt that membership of the Common Market would be a good thing for Britain, and fully 50 per cent believed that entry would benefit the British economy. [22] However, the optimism for the general economic effects of entry help to confirm our conclusions that fears of rising prices and the risk of domination were substantial factors in the British reluctance to join the Common Market.

In Norway, where, in the referendum of September 1972, the public decided not to enter the Common Market, the two major fears expressed by the public were the effects on the future of the primary sector of the economy (farming and fishing) and the loss of Norwegian autonomy (see Table 5.18). These fears coincide with a basic cleavage in Norwegian society between the 'centre' and the 'periphery', which we shall discuss fully in Chapter Nine. But clearly, for many Norwegians as well as for many of the British, fear of domination or of a loss of self-determination was a very significant factor in creating opposition to entry of the Common Market.

It should now be clear that a crucial determinant in the creation of support for or opposition to the Common Market or a European political union is the image of the supranational Community which is held by the publics. We have seen in this Chapter that the ECSC and the EEC were conceived of as primarily economic unions, which encouraged trade and economic growth. We shall review images of a United States of Europe more fully in Chapter Six, although we have seen that the publics expect political unification to enhance peace and prosperity. But we must also consider the values and goals to which the publics in the European Community attribute most importance.

Opinion surveys concerned with public attitudes towards European integration have paid little direct attention to the goals of the publics under study, but in September 1973 the people of the Nine were given a series of questions about their sense of satisfaction or dissatisfaction with certain aspects of their lives. Questions covered the following aspects:

Housing
Income
Work (as housewife, on job or at school)
Education for children

120

Leisure
Social welfare benefits
Relations with others
Respect accorded by others
Relations between generations
'The kind of society in which we live (in Britain, France, etc.) today'
'The way democracy is functioning (in Britain, France, etc.)'
One's life as a whole [23]

The respondents were also asked whether they felt more satisfied with their lives today than they did five years ago; and whether they expected that their conditions would improve over the next five years or not.

We can see from Table 5.19 that responses to the foregoing items tend to group themselves into three clusters, as indicated by the results of the factor analysis. The first and most important dimension can be termed 'overall life satisfaction'. In Table 5.19, Factor I is an expression of the dimension of 'overall life satisfaction', and it is evident that those who express satisfaction with one domain also tend to be satisfied with other aspects of their lives. As Inglehart points out, the most sensitive indicator of overall satisfaction is satisfaction with one's life as a whole, which is followed usually by satisfaction with one's income and one's work. [24] The second dimension is clearly political in character – throughout the Community, the items concerning satisfaction with 'the kind of society' in which one lives and 'the way democracy is functioning' tend to form a separate cluster. Thirdly, the dimension concerning perceptions of past improvement and expectations of future change illustrates, in Inglehart's view, 'that one's future expectations are, in large part, a projection of recent experience'. [25]

Some interesting cross-national variations in the items contributing most strongly to overall life satisfaction are evident in Table 5.19. In most nations the items contributing most strongly to this general dimension of satisfaction are predominantly socio-economic in content – for example, work and income feature notably in Belgium, Denmark and Ireland, while West Germany also shows a close correlation between socio-economic factors and general satisfaction. In other societies, 'kind of society' seems to be of some considerable weight – for instance, in Britain, Italy, and particularly the Netherlands. In France and Luxembourg both 'kind of society' and 'the democracy we live in' are clearly important to general satisfaction, seeming to indicate a greater concern in those countries for socio-political factors than elsewhere in the Community.

The findings of Table 5.19 are of particular interest in view of data

Table 5.19

Dimensions of subjective satisfaction in the Nine
(loadings above ·300 in conventional factor analysis)

Factor:	Britain			West Germany			Italy			France			Netherlands		
	I	II	III	I	II	III	I	II	III	I	II	III	I	II	III
Life as a whole	·701			·642			·643			·687			·528		
Income	·504			·527			·515			·575			·377		
Work	·527			·486			·507			·455			·431		
Kind of society	·509	·467		·490	·495		·528	·467		·625	·440		·544		·449
Leisure	·481			·456			·420			·480			·413		
Democracy	·503	·437		·422	·547		·500	·507		·574	·425		·426		·443
Relations with others	·476			·515			·434			·333			·477		
Welfare benefits	·475			·527			·385			·431			·436		
Housing	·453			·481			·361	−330		·382			·384		
Education	(·293)			·382			·354			·328			·425		
Relations between generations	·363			·426			·410			·354			·386		
Respect	·364			·369			·351			·426			·358		
Recent improvement	·462		·481	·339		(·290)	·315		·369	·341	−324	·400			
Future expectations	·310		·454			·673			·503			·386			·307

Table 5.19 continued

Factor:	Belgium I	Belgium II	Belgium III	Denmark I	Denmark II	Denmark III	Ireland I	Ireland II	Ireland III	Luxembourg I	Luxembourg II	Luxembourg III
Life as a whole	·640			·619			·596			·616		
Income	·608			·478			·508			·485		
Work	·645			·474			·550			·347		
Kind of society	·555	·481		·472	·568		·466	·413		·690	·371	
Leisure	·577			·491			·493			·412		
Democracy	·483	·562		·389	·452		·405	·503		·516	·474	
Relations with others	·551			·453			·385			·427		
Welfare benefits	·382			·300			·308			·448		
Housing	·433			·373			·403			·407		
Education	·415			·415			·367			·428		
Relations between generations	·402			·391			·324	·358				
Respect	·373			(·296)								
Recent improvement	·325		·527	·307		·435	·525		·591	(·291)		·759
Future expectations			·596			·324	·359		·380			·342

Source: J.-R. Rabier *Satisfaction et insatisfaction quant aux conditions de vie dans les pays membres de la Communauté Européenne*, Brussels, April 1974

presented in Tables 5.4 and 5.16. There we saw that the Dutch and the French expressed most fears in the Six on the effects of unification, and were also (along with the public in Luxembourg) the most inclined to agree with the view that the nation-states of Europe were too dofferent in their size and power to form a successful political union. It seems that in France, Luxembourg and the Netherlands, with the publics placing relatively less emphasis on socio-economic factors in their sense of general satisfaction, they are therefore less likely to be persuaded of the benefits of unification by economic gains.

Rabier and Inglehart also draw our attention to a significant fact to emerge from the study of subjective feelings of general satisfaction, which could not have been predicted *a priori.* [26] It is that the level of general satisfaction is higher amongst the publics of the five smaller member-states — Belgium, Denmark, Ireland, Luxembourg and the Netherlands — than in the four larger member-states — Britain, France, Italy and West Germany. Rabier is very careful to stress that these findings are only provisional and that much more research needs to be completed in this area, but certainly these conclusions are of great interest for our purposes. We shall consider some of the implications more fully in the next chapter.

Conclusions

From the evidence available to us, it is not possible to affirm our second proposition, which stated that utilitarian support for supranational institutions is more marked than affective support. Much of the data relating to opinions on the ECSC or the EEC does indicate strong utilitarian support, but to a certain extent the replies merely mirror the nature of those particular institutions and the subsequent wording of the questions put to the publics. Nonetheless, it does seem that the image of integration to date which is held by the publics of the Six is inextricably linked with their perceptions of economic growth, greater trade and the modernisation of industry, which have been seen to result from the Common Market.

However, within the Six there was also a clear demonstration of the extent of affective support for European unification. Of course there is an element of utilitarian sentiment in the expectations of peace and prosperity, but affective attachment to the idea of Europe was plainly quite considerable. However, the most optimistic and pro-European publics of the Six could not see political unification as being anything but a long-term achievement. This fact, together with a perception of more national gains than benefits for the individual and a residual nationalistic strand amongst the publics, all help to explain the reluctance of many people to be willing to accept some personal sacrifice in the cause of European unification. Perhaps the surprising fact is the size of the large minority in the Six who were willing to make sacrifices and who were therefore showing great attachment to the European idea. Reluctance to make such personal sacrifices was strongest in Britain, where fears of rising prices (despite perceived long-term economic gains) and a fear of domination mirrored the Norwegian fears for the primary sector of the economy and the loss of the right of self-determination.

In order to reach firmer conclusions on the bases of support for integration, we must refer to the remainder of the matrix of support developed by Lindberg and Scheingold.[27] The distinction drawn in the matrix between the identitive and systemic 'levels of interaction' is particularly relevant in view of three vital considerations: first, the existence of widespread fears of the effects of unification even within the Six; secondly, the significance of the socio-political factors in the publics' general satisfaction, which means that the supporters of integration cannot rely merely on the economic performance of the Common Market — considerable thought must be given to the kind of society and the nature of the political system which is to develop in their Europe of the future; and thirdly, the indication that people tend to be most satisfied with their life in the smallest countries of the Community clearly should lead to reflections on the whole notion of a United States of Europe and the nature of its social and political systems. It is to a further assessment of these points that we turn in Chapter Six.

Notes

[1] L. Lindberg and S. Scheingold, *Europe's Would-be Polity,* Prentice-Hall, 1970, pp. 38–45.

[2] C. Pentland, *International Theory and European Integration,* Faber and Faber, 1973, p. 127.

[3] Ibid., p. 129.

[4] Gallup International, 'Public opinion and the European Community', edited and translated by M. Forsyth, in *Journal of Common Market Studies* vol. 2, no. 2, 1963.

[5] Louis Kriesberg, 'German public opinion and the European Coal and Steel Community' in *Public Opinion Quarterly* vol. 23, 1959.

[6] J. Stoetzel, 'The evolution of French opinion' in D. Lerner and R.

Aron (eds), *France Defeats EDC,* Praeger, 1957, pp. 94–5.

[7] *EMNID-Informationen,* 1968.

[8] *Gallup Political Index,* December 1969.

[9] Ibid.

[10] Ibid., September 1971.

[11] *Gallup Political Index* no. 147, October 1972.

[12] Ibid.

[13] Gallup International, op.cit., 1963, pp. 108–11.

[14] Ibid.

[15] Ibid.

[16] Ibid.

[17] Commission of the Communities, *L'Opinion des Européens sur les aspects régionaux et agricoles du Marché Commun, l'unification politique de l'Europe et l'information du public,* Brussels, December 1971, p. 55.

[18] Ibid.

[19] Ibid.

[20] Ibid.

[21] Ibid.

[22] *Gallup Political Index* no. 147.

[23] Commission of the Communities, *Satisfaction et insatisfaction quant aux conditions de vie dans les pays membres de la Communauté Européenne,* Brussels, April 1974, pp. 1–10.

[24] Ronald Inglehart, *The 1973 European Community Public Opinion Surveys: Preliminary Findings,* University of Geneva, May 1974, p. 13.

[25] Ibid.

[26] Ibid., p. 14, and Commission of the Communities, op.cit., June 1974.

[27] L. Lindberg and S. Scheingold, op. cit., p. 61.

6 European Identity and the European Community

Proposition 3: 'Support for supranational institutions or policies is more marked than feelings of a European identity.'

Introductory discussion

Our third proposition completes the 'matrix of support' presented by Lindberg and Scheingold, since it relates to the 'levels of interaction' which comprise the second dimension of their schema of political attitudes.[1] The 'levels of interaction' refer to the perceived links among the peoples of Europe and also to the development of links, on the part of the public, with the supranational institutions themselves. Lindberg and Scheingold use the term 'systemic' to refer to support for the nature and scope of supranational institutions. 'Identitive' support refers to the sense of being members of a community, or 'Europeans'. As we stated earlier, in Chapter Three:

> Thus a systemic community response refers to opinions expressed concerning questions on the scope of the Community, while the systemic regime response refers to the actual nature of Community institutions. Questions relating to the need for a Common Defence Policy would thus be reflected in the former response, questions covering direct elections to the European Parliament would be reflected in the latter.[2]

We shall see later that much of the data utilised to test our third proposition is also relevant to our second proposition. Affective-identitive support thus refers to the types of feelings for other countries outlined in the discussion of our first two propositions and extends to a sense of shared cultural values, a common identity. Utilitarian-identitive support describes the perception of such common interests as military alliances and trading agreements. Utilitarian-systemic support covers favourable attitudes toward common policy-making on a broad range of issues, resulting from a perception of mutual gains. Affective-systemic support defines the ability of the Community institutions to generate any appeal beyond or independent of expected pay-offs.[3]

Systemic support, or support for supranational institutions or policies, is thus concerned with 'vertical' levels of interaction, and identitive support, or a sense of being part of a European community, with 'horizontal' levels of interaction. Again, in view of the predominantly 'economic' nature of European integration, there would appear to be much plausibility in the neofunctionalist proposition that feelings of community and identity would be far less marked than support for Community institutions and policies.

Indeed, it seems likely that because the Community institutions are not truly supranational, they lack the necessary authority to allocate values and create a sense of identity. But identitive support may be stronger than neofunctionalism allows – Deutsch would certainly expect there to be a strong identitive element, judging by the level of communications and transactions in Western Europe, and the federalists would be disappointed if their efforts to create a European identity and to 'sell' the 'European idea' had made no impact on the public.

The evidence and its interpretation

Although the wording of the questions may have varied over the years, various surveys of public opinion have sought to tap the attitudes concerning the scope of existing or proposed European authorities. These surveys provide us with data which enable us to assess the extent of utilitarian-systemic community support for European integration – in other words, how much scope in making common policies do the publics wish the European authorities to possess? Yet we shall also see that utilitarian-identitive support, or support which stems from the perception of mutual gains, is very closely related to any discussion of the scope of European authorities.

The surveys commissioned by Gallup International (February and March 1962) and by *The Reader's Digest* (January and February 1963) sought opinions in the Six and Britain on nine aims which the Common Market had either adopted, or which had been discussed by the various supporters of integration as desirable policies to pursue in the future (for the results of the *Reader's Digest* survey, see Table 6.1). About a year prior to the poll sponsored by *The Reader's Digest*, Gallup International had found very similar opinions, although in most cases they were a few percentage points more positive in favour of common policies. The Gallup

Table 6.1

Opinions in the Six and Britain on nine aims of the
Common Market, January—February 1963 (figures in percentages)

	Belgium	France	Italy	Luxembourg	Netherlands	West Germany	Britain
1 *'Should customs duties be cut? — i.e. make it easier for us to sell products in the Six and also make it easier for the Six's products to be sold here?'*							
For	73	72	72	76	79	71	70
Against	6	6	4	8	9	4	13
Don't know	21	22	24	16	12	25	17
2 *'Use part of the taxes paid by people in each country to help wherever it is needed in the poorer regions in all seven countries?'*							
For	48	43	61	59	70	52	63
Against	28	34	12	23	18	14	22
Don't know	24	23	27	18	12	34	16
3 *'Use part of the taxes paid by people in each country to help African and Asian countries that are associated with any of the seven?'*							
For	39	23	36	52	61	32	37
Against	37	53	27	27	23	31	45
Don't know	24	24	37	21	16	37	18
4 *'Pool all means of scientific research in the seven countries?'*							
For	71	79	55	66	76	56	71
Against	3	3	4	13	9	8	13
Don't know	26	18	41	21	15	36	16
5 *'Make diplomas and other professional qualifications of the same standard in all seven countries?'*							
For	75	77	63	82	76	53	63
Against	3	3	5	5	11	8	16
Don't know	22	20	32	13	13	39	21

Table 6.1 continued

	Belgium	France	Italy	Luxembourg	Netherlands	West Germany	Britain
6 'Have a single foreign policy for all seven countries?'							
For	50	50	48	61	67	60	41
Against	10	12	10	11	15	7	32
Don't know	40	38	42	28	18	33	36
7 'Have a Common Agricultural Policy in all seven countries?'							
For	53	60	55	65	68	53	49
Against	5	7	8	9	14	8	25
Don't know	42	33	37	26	18	39	26
8 'Have equivalent social benefits in the seven countries, covering, for example, holidays with pay, sickness insurance and family allowances?'							
For	76	80	65	85	78	66	71
Against	3	2	2	4	9	5	13
Don't know	21	18	33	11	13	29	15
9 'Allow workers to work where they want to in the seven countries?'							
For	69	57	62	69	76	64	52
Against	14	24	8	14	13	8	34
Don't know	17	19	30	17	11	28	14

Source: *Products and People,* Reader's Digest Association, 1963

International report concluded that:

> ... in the light of these results, it can be asserted that the 'pro-European' declarations of the public in the Six countries are not solely declarations of principle. It is quite extraordinary that such a large proportion of opinion is in favour of measures which break with tradition.[4]

Although Table 6.1 primarily provides us with a measure of utilitarian-systemic community support in Britain and the Six, it is also possible on closer inspection to make some observations on the extent of utilitarian-identitive support. For example, it is generally the case that those aims which may require some sacrifices from the people in the cause of the common European good receive less support than the other aims. In all seven countries, the aim of giving aid to former European colonies is the least popular, and in five countries it is closely followed in unpopularity by the proposal to give aid to the poorer regions within the Community, which would include Britain. It may be significant that support for intra-Community aid was at its greatest in Italy and Britain, the 'poorest' nations of the seven polled here and the main recipients of the Community's Regional Fund, which was introduced in 1974. The Common Agricultural Policy also proved relatively unpopular, though in Luxembourg and France it fared better than several other aims. It is worth recalling that the perceptions of the 'losers' from the CAP were clear. Table 5.14(a) illustrates the favourable image of CAP in Luxembourg, and, as we stressed in Chapter Two, CAP was established largely in order to secure full French participation in the EEC. Finally, the aim of a common foreign policy, which would surely prove popular if there was a public perception of European common needs and interests in the world, also lacks much widespread support. It ranks highest in popularity compared with the other aims in West Germany and France. The fact that the Germans had most cause to be aware of the threat-from-without which faced Western Europe, and also that the French have been the most likely to see the evolution of a 'third force' from an integrated Europe, seems to signify that these two publics did possess some element of utilitarian-identitive support for this aim — they perceived some common European needs and interests.

On the whole we can see that utilitarian-identitive support remained relatively low. This is confirmed by the character of the aims which received most support. The relaxation of customs and the development of equivalent social benefits proved to be the most popular, with pooled scientific research and common educational standards proving to be other popular aims. Clearly, there must be an element of utilitarian-identitive support in the publics' favourable view of these aims, but they are aims which involve little risk of one sector of the public in one European nation having to make some sacrifice or suffer some loss in the interests of another sector of the public in another state in the Six, or in Britain. Support for the removal of customs duties reflects the image of the Community illustrated in Table 5.14, where increased trade, economic growth and industrial modernisation were seen to be the product of the Common Market. But these gains were all seen to strengthen the national economy, and the fact that the most widely held image in July 1971 was that

131

the Common Market had created much greater competition for 'domestic' industries from 'foreign' goods is scarcely indicative of reduced tariffs reflecting identitive sentiments. Similarly, the widespread support for equivalent social benefits throughout the Six and Britain is the publics' response to a question with no reference to any increase in taxation nor to any international payments, and which, moreover, taps a deep-seated sentiment — even a 'consensus' — that has been prevalent in most of Western Europe since the end of the Second World War — namely, the desirability of state welfare.

Over the years several opinion polls conducted within the member-states of the Six or in Britain have posed questions which refer to support for common policies, and their findings appear to give at least tentative confirmation to the conclusions which were drawn from Table 6.1. The poll commissioned by *The Reader's Digest* asked only about a common foreign policy, but both the West German and French publics have been asked for their views on a European defence policy and a European army respectively (see Tables 6.2(a) and 6.2(b)).

Table 6.2(a)

The duty of West Germany in European defence
(figures in percentages)

'In your opinion, has Germany a duty in the defence of Europe?'

	1951	1952	1953	1955	1956	1957	1962	1963	May 1964
Yes	47	44	59	65	64	58	68	74	68
No	24	27	23	25	26	31	7	9	10
No reply	29	29	18	10	10	11	25	17	22

Source: *EMNID-Information—*

It is evident that, by the 1960s, the West Germans had come to recognise that they had a duty in the defence of Europe. This increased recognition does reflect the emergence of greater utilitarian-identitive support, but by the 1960s the idea of a German army had become more acceptable, and, in addition, West Germany's status as a Western power had become fully established. Also, of course, the West Germans do occupy the front-line in Europe in any East–West clash, and this,

Table 6.2(b)

French opinions regarding a European army
(figures in percentages)

'The idea of a European army is broached by various quarters. In such an army, soldiers from various Western countries − French, Belgian, West German, Italian − would serve together under the direction of a European Minister. Are you for or against the idea of a European army?'

	1951	September 1952	April 1953	June 1953	February 1955	May 1965
For	42	45	46	43	43	41
Against	26	26	22	23	22	31
No reply	32	29	32	24	35	28

Source: *Sondages,* nos. 1−2, 1972, p. 128

combined with the other two factors, indicates that there was a large element of national self-interest in the support for a European defence policy. Indeed, with the possibility of an American troop withdrawal, the Germans could not hope to match Warsaw Pact forces without European collaboration.

In May 1969, 52 per cent of Frenchmen favoured a European defence policy as opposed to 20 per cent who advocated a French defence policy and 28 per cent who were undecided. At the same time, only 44 per cent supported a common foreign policy for Europe.[5] No doubt these percentages reflect de Gaulle's expectation that the *force de frappe* would become European, but there is an apparent contradiction with the data presented in Table 6.2(b) in that the French seemed less sure of the merits of a European army. However, all but the most recent figures were recorded at the time when a European army was synonymous with German rearmament. It is therefore all the more striking that, in May 1965, by which time Franco-German relations had become much improved compared with the mid-1950s, only 41 per cent expressed support for a European army and fully 31 per cent opposed the idea.[6] Again, it seems that on particularly 'sensitive' topics there is a particularly strong element of nationalist resistance amongst the French which remains largely hidden on other vaguer or more general issues of European unification.

Table 6.3

Opinions in Britain on the aims of the Common Market
(figures in percentages)

'Here are some issues which will have to be settled between Britain and the members of the European Common Market. Taking each one separately, do you think it will be a good thing or a bad thing for Britain to agree to it?'

	September 1961	February 1963*	November 1966
1 'Pooling our resources to develop atomic energy for peaceful purposes.'			
Good thing	78	71	80
Bad thing	7	13	7
Don't know	15	16	13
2 'To have as the goal achieving a closer political relationship.'			
Good thing	63		68
Bad thing	11	NA	10
Don't know	16		22
3 'Gradual removal of all trade barriers between members.'			
Good thing	66	70	66
Bad thing	12	13	9
Don't know	27	17	25
4 'Unemployment policies and social services to be brought into line with each other.'			
Good thing	53	71	66
Bad thing	13	13	11
Don't know	34	15	23
5 'Removal, eventually, of all subsidies and other protections to industries, like agriculture.'			
Good thing	39	49	39
Bad thing	34	25	33
Don't know	27	26	28

Table 6.3 continued

	September 1961	February 1963*	November 1966

6 *'Inviting workers here from other countries to take up jobs which cannot be filled by our own labour.'*

Good thing	38	52	37
Bad thing	43	34	47
Don't know	19	14	16

* The wording of the question was slightly different, producing a slightly more favourable response than in 1961 or 1966, but the responses do provide a general indication of British feelings in early 1963

Source: *Gallup Political Index* nos 22, 38, 80

Polls of British public opinion seem to show that in their attitudes towards European unification the British are 'more French than the French'. Table 6.3 shows responses on three occasions in the 1960s to questions concerning the aims of the Common Market – it is worth emphasising that in September 1961 and November 1966 there was a large pro-European majority in the country, while in February 1963 there was a smaller majority in favour of entry (see Figure 4.7). The wording of the question in Table 6.3 means that the responses are bound to reflect a concern for the national interest, but it is instructive that there was greatest opposition to proposals for more of a competitive *laissez-faire* economic policy within the Common Market and an influx of European workers. Opposition to these proposals is indicative of relatively weak utilitarian-identitive support. This view is confirmed in the responses to a Gallup poll in October 1972, when 39 per cent favoured British entry, but 41 per cent were against (see Table 6.4).

Table 6.4 reflects generally favourable support of the utilitarian-systemic community type, but on questions of the organisation of higher education – here the British seem particularly proud and confident – and also economic policy and policy on foreign investment, support for a European common policy is not at all strong. Even in the field of commercial negotiations with the Americans and the Russians, the British seem far from being convinced of the merits of a common European

Table 6.4

Opinions in Britain on the responsibilities of a European government
or national government, October 1972 (figures in percentages)

*'The British Government has the final say in many of today's important
problems. Do you think the following problems will be dealt with better
by a European government or better by a British government?'*

	European	British	Same	Don't know
1	*'Commercial negotiations with the Americans and the Russians.'*			
	38	33	9	21
2	*'The fight against water and air pollution.'*			
	45	32	9	14
3	*'The organisation of military defence.'*			
	45	29	7	19
4	*'Scientific research.'*			
	54	23	6	17
5	*'Policy towards foreign investment.'*			
	33	31	7	29
6	*'Organisation of higher education.'*			
	20	55	8	17
7	*'Fight against drugs.'*			
	48	29	8	15
8	*'Economic policy.'*			
	35	33	7	25

Source: *Gallup Political Index* no. 147

approach. Indeed, the strongest support for joint European action is restricted to the technical issues and does not extend to the more political problems. Thus, scientific research, the fight against drugs and pollution, and the organisation of military defence are the areas where there is greatest perception of the benefits of common policies – also, it is worth noting that Lindberg and Scheingold state that utilitarian-identitive support is more likely to exist in matters of defence than in the sphere of economics.[7] Our conclusions that utilitarian-systemic community support is stronger for technical and defence matters than for economic and political matters, and that there is a lack of strong utilitarian-identitive support, are confirmed in Table 5.17(a). This shows that in October 1972 the idea of a European government which would be responsible over and above the British Government for a common political policy on foreign affairs, defence, and the economy was unacceptable to the British people. Admittedly, the mention of 'a European government' brought other considerations into play, which we have reviewed partly in Chapter Five and which we shall discuss at greater length shortly, but the negative response of the British indicates their inability to identify with Europe on anything other than issues of pure technical utilitarianism or defence.

Table 6.5

Willingness in the Six to accept a European government
(figures in percentages)

'Would you be in favour of having, above the government (of your country), a European government responsible for common policies in the fields of foreign affairs, defence and economics?'

	The Six	Belgium	France	Italy	Luxembourg	Netherlands	West Germany
For	58	52	53	67	47	49	56
Against	23	19	28	16	36	37	23
Don't know	19	29	19	17	17	14	21

Source: J.-R. Rabier, op.cit., 1970, p. 485

In early 1970, the people of the Six were asked the same question (see Table 6.5). We can see that the Dutch and the public in Luxembourg seem

Table 6.6

Opinions in the Community on the responsibilities of a European or
a national government, September 1973 (figures in percentages)

*'For each of the problems I am going to mention, would you say they
would be better dealt with by a European government or by a national
government?'*

	Belgium	France	Italy	Luxembourg	Netherlands	West Germany	Denmark	Great Britain	Ireland
1 *'Pollution of the environment.'*									
European	52	54	63	70	75	68	56	40	37
National	42	32	34	27	23	29	42	56	62
2 *'Military defence.'*									
European	61	50	52	78	74	76	44	44	39
National	30	32	31	12	23	18	50	50	60
3 *'Scientific research.'*									
European	74	75	77	85	75	70	78	56	73
National	18	13	19	8	22	24	18	38	26
4 *'Investments by foreign firms in your country.'*									
European	37	38	54	39	27	37	23	29	34
National	54	41	40	52	70	55	73	64	65
5 *'Drug addiction.'*									
European	66	70	72	80	68	61	52	45	33
National	27	17	24	13	30	34	46	51	67
6 *'Economic growth.'*									
European	57	54	62	68	64	49	46	36	43
National	35	31	34	27	34	45	50	58	56
7 *'Major political negotiations with the Americans, the Russians, etc.'*									
European	80	65	79	87	81	70	66	57	74
National	12	19	16	8	16	24	28	37	25

Table 6.6 continued

	Belgium	France	Italy	Luxembourg	Netherlands	West Germany	Denmark	Great Britain	Ireland
8 *'Poverty and unemployment.'*									
European	41	48	55	66	51	59	37	30	33
National	52	39	41	29	48	35	60	66	66
9 *'Aid to underdeveloped countries.'*									
European	75	70	81	86	77	77	56	67	73
National	17	15	15	8	21	16	39	27	27
10 *'Rising prices.'*									
European	46	50	50	69	56	53	46	31	27
National	48	38	47	26	43	44	51	65	73

Source: Commission of the Communities, *Europe as the Europeans see it,* November 1973, Tables 1, 1a

to be the most apprehensive, with the French also expressing considerable caution. The Italians and West Germans appear to be the most ardent supporters of European unity. Indeed, these findings reflect those of early 1963 (see Table 5.4) and July 1971 (see Table 5.16).

In 1973, a Community-wide poll included questions of the sort put to the British in 1972 concerning the responsibilities of a European or of a national government (see Table 6.6). We can see from Table 6.6 that the problems where the publics feel quite clearly that European action would be most effective are overseas aid, drug addiction, pollution, scientific research, military defence, and major political negotiations with the Americans and the Russians. Of the new member-states, the Danes seem particularly keen on European action on pollution, while the Irish are more in favour of a European approach on political negotiations than the French – indeed, only the British are less inclined than the French to favour a common European 'line' in talks with the super-powers. In all nine countries except Italy, larger percentages of people would prefer their national governments to deal with foreign investment in their country – could this indicate resentment of investment by other member-states of the Nine, which would seem to indicate a relatively weak element of identitive support? Also, there is significant support for national as opposed to European action to deal with economic growth,

Table 6.7

Factor analysis: European integration items, 1973
(positive polarity is pro-European)

	Belgium	France	Italy	Luxembourg	Netherlands	West Germany	Denmark	Great Britain	Ireland	Mean
1 For European unification*	·750	·749	·721	·749	·639	·795	·791	·783	·695	·740
2 Accept personal sacrifices*	·465	·541	·478	·542	·563	·583	·650	·624	·531	·543
3 Regret abandoning EEC*	·586	·628	·572	·481	·579	·668	·728	·689	·505	·604
European government to deal with										
economic growth	·482	·505	·544	·489	·453	·447	·499	·554	·362	·482
rising prices	·523	·522	·554	·462	·496	·442	·484	·530	·324	·482
poverty, unemployment	·485	·525	·491	·418	·446	·401	·455	·472	·357	·447
scientific research	·509	·472	·500	·515	·360	·401	·368	·494	·388	·445
foreign policy	·430	·453	·441	·594	·367	·370	·485	·459	·309	·434
defence	·534	·503	·501	·408	·426	·379	·459	·479	·250	·427
pollution	·478	·491	·485	·403	·438	·430	·358	·409	·295	·421
foreign aid	·459	·375	·450	·460	·385	·349	·436	·439	·354	·413
drug addiction	·475	·465	·437	·540	·344	·374	·333	·411	·264	·405
foreign investment	·178	·257	·333	·310	·074	·203	·303	·308	·144	·234
Aid European countries	·366	·390	·305	·326	·305	·475	·514	·584	·387	·486
Lose national identity	·344	·416	·266	·102	·249	·297	·426	·421	·291	·324

* Index of general support for European unification is based on the replies to these three questions

Source: Ronald Inglehart, *The 1973 European Community Public Opinion Surveys, Preliminary Findings*, University of Geneva and University of Michigan, November 1973–April 1974

poverty and unemployment and also rising prices, particularly in the three member-states.

These results, obtained from the Community-wide poll of September 1973, have been subjected to unusually detailed analysis, and the preliminary findings are particularly useful in the discussion on our third proposition. Two indices of support were constructed — in Table 6.7 we present the European support index, which demonstrates, through the use of multivariate analysis, the relative importance of various items in explaining general support for unification. The index of general support was constructed by responses to three key questions:

1 'Are you in favour of the unification of Europe, against it, or are you indifferent?'
2 'Would you, or would you not, be willing to make some personal sacrifice — for example, pay a little more tax — to help bring about the unification of Europe?'
3 'If it was announced tomorrow that the Common Market was to be abandoned, would you feel regret, indifference or relief?'[8]

We can see in Table 6.7 that, naturally enough, the three items in the general support index are the most sensitive indicators of the desire to see a unified Europe. More specifically, our thesis that public support for European action on economic and political problems is likely to be indicative of a commitment to unification is confirmed by the figures in this table. The items which were most likely to indicate support for unification are those items for which it was found that the proposal to pass responsibility for them to a European government consistently received less public support. Yet on issues of foreign policy and defence, and problems of pollution, foreign aid and drug addiction, where the publics were more willing to favour European responsibility, there is less likelihood that support indicates such strong support for European unification. These findings also confirm earlier evidence — utilitarian-systemic community support is weaker in the new member-states.

It is interesting that not only do comparatively few people favour European responsibility for the control of foreign investment in their country, but also Table 6.7 shows that it ranks lowest, of all the ten questions on problems of European or national responsibility, as an indicator of support for European unification. Italy, however, seems to be the exception, since more Italians favour European responsibility in this sphere and also are more likely to relate this issue with support for unification.

In addition to the items concerning European or national responsibility, two other questions which were put to the respondents in September are included in Table 6.7. First, the item entitled, 'Aid European countries' covers the question which is shown in Table 6.8. Certainly, the figures presented in Table 6.8 appear to attest the emergence of a strong sense of European solidarity, particularly within the original Six and Ireland. This is the most convincing evidence that we have seen of the existence of real utilitarian-identitive support — a willingness to help other countries, even at some cost to the public's own country, in the common European good.

Table 6.8

Aid to European countries: opinions in February—March 1970
(figures in percentages)

'If one of the countries of the European Community finds itself in major economic difficulties, do you feel that the other countries, including your country, should help it or not?'

	Yes, should help	No, should not	Don't know
Belgium	78	9	13
France	78	9	13
Italy	88	2	10
Luxembourg	87	8	5
The Netherlands	79	9	12
West Germany	77	7	16
Denmark	62	25	13
Great Britain	59	28	13
Ireland	80	10	10

Source: Commission of the Communities, op.cit., 1970, Table 2

However, in Table 6.7 we can see that the effectiveness of the item 'Aid European countries' as an indicator of desire for unification is not at all strong. In all the members of the Six except West Germany, the public's agreement with the idea of helping out other countries in economic difficulty is a less sensitive indicator of support for unification than all the items of European or national responsibility except for foreign investment. In other words, five of the publics of the member-states are more likely to favour unification if they express support for European action on drug addiction, for example, than if they express support for helping out other countries in economic difficulties. Only in West Germany and the three new member-states does the dimension 'Aid European countries' effectively tap support for unification. In contrast to the other five founder-member countries, this item is the most sensitive indicator of support for unification, apart from the three items constituting the general support index itself. The Irish are exceptional in that they favour aid to other European countries (see Table 6.8), and the sensitivity of this commitment as an indicator of support for unification is comparable to the case with the publics of the original Six, excepting West Germany. However, only scientific research as a European responsibility is a more effective indicator of being pro-European for the Irish.

We should not conclude that the effectiveness of the 'Aid European countries' dimension as a measure of favouring European unification illustrates that the British and the Danes possess strong support of the utilitarian-identitive type. All that the index in Table 6.7 shows is that, in these two new member-states, the respondents who agreed with helping other Community countries in economic difficulty were the most likely (in terms of the other items on the index) to favour unification. It does seem likely that, particularly in these two new member-states, where support for the Community is relatively weak, those people who do agree with the notion of aid to other European countries are very likely to be pro-European.

The case of West Germany seems more perplexing – why should this be the only country of the original Six where public agreement with the idea of aiding other European countries in economic difficulties should be such a sensitive indicator of support for unification? The most plausible explanation would seem to be that by 1973 there was a general awareness that German funds comprised the largest share in any financing of Community projects, and therefore it was seen to be highly probable that the Germans themselves would have to contribute the largest share of any aid to other European countries. In other words, the West German respondents seem to have recognised that they would almost certainly have to dip still further into their pockets, and consequently their large-scale support for aiding other European countries is a particularly sensitive indicator of their commitment to unification. Indeed, our conclusions from Tables 6.7 and 6.8 signify that the Germans possess a stronger element of utilitarian-identitive support than exists amongst any other publics of the Community. It is extremely fortunate for the Nine that their wealthiest member-state consists of a public which is so strongly committed to giving a European government greater scope, and which readily perceives common European needs and interests. Yet, as we saw in Chapter Five, there is evidence that in 1974 even the West German willingness to promote European unification from their own pockets had weakened slightly (see Tables 5.9 and 5.10).

As regards the item in Table 6.7 headed 'Lose national identity', the figures confirm our earlier statements on the varying significance of national loyalty in the Nine. It appears to be relatively stronger in Denmark, Britain and France than in the rest of the Nine, with the people of Luxembourg, the Dutch and Italians appearing the least concerned with national identities. It would seem that, as we indicated in Chapter Five (see Tables 5.4, 5.5 and 5.16), although the Dutch have often expressed fears of the effects of unification, this does not stem from any deep-seated sense of national loyalty, as it seems to in France.

Table 6.7 demonstrated the close relation between support for unification and items which should be dealt with at the European or national level, but these items also are the basis of a second attitudinal dimension which concerns the scope of European authority rather than intensity of support or opposition to European integration. The loadings on this second factor appear in Table 6.9. Inglehart concludes that, 'Across the nine nations, the most sensitive indicators of whether one favoured a broad or a narrow scope for European institutions were one's attitude toward aid to underdeveloped countries and the problems of rising prices, scientific research and economic growth.'[9] Again, there are marked differences between the founder-members and the three new member-states. It is noticeable that the more technical items, or defence and foreign policy items, are the major indicators of support for greater scope for a European government, particularly in the new member-states, whereas the more directly 'political' items are usually weaker elements in this utilitarian-systemic community support.

So far in our discussion we have considered only utilitarian-systemic *community* support — the willingness to accept common policies at the European level. But we also need to examine the publics' willingness to accept supranational institutions if we are discussing the scope of a European government. This willingness to accept supranational institutions is termed utilitarian-systemic *regime* support, and it forms an attitudinal dimension with which several opinion polls and surveys have been concerned.

We can see from Table 5.10 that there were large percentages in the founder-member states who favoured the evolution of political unification, but that there was considerable opposition to this in the three new members, particularly in Britain and Denmark. But what form of political

Table 6.9

European responsibility or national responsibility?
(Loadings above ·300 only)

	Belgium	France	Luxembourg	Italy	Netherlands	West Germany	Denmark	Great Britain	Ireland
Aid to underdeveloped countries	·400	·489	·341	·443	·347	·417	·326	·402	·358
Rising prices	·338	·338	·426	·347	·368	·446	·300		
Scientific research	·443	·468	·377	·405	·371	·330		·339	·468
Economic growth	·374	·358	·332	·372	·307	·439			
Poverty and unemployment	·345	·372	·544	·415	·384	·399	·341		
Drug addiction	·423	·454		·345	·428	·408	·388	·329	
Pollution of environment	·300	·311		·343	·369	·312	·319		·343
Negotiations with Americans, Russians	·422	·352	·335	·369					
Military defence	·336			·329					·368
Foreign investment			·368						

Source: Inglehart, op.cit., 1974, Table 5

145

organisation should a unified Europe adopt in the publics' view? This question was put to the Six in early 1970 and to the Nine in September 1973; the results are set out in Tables 6.10(a) and 6.10(b).

Tables 6.10(a) and 6.10(b) show that there is strongest support in the Six for some form of unification in which the national governments

Table 6.10(a)

Forms of political organisation of a united Europe,
January—February 1970 (figures in percentages)

'Favour one of three types of political unification.'

The Six	Belgium	France	Italy	Luxembourg	Netherlands	West Germany

1 *'There is no government on the European level, but the governments of all the countries meet regularly to decide common policy.'*

| 16 | 14 | 18 | 13 | 19 | 18 | 16 |

2 *'There is a European government which concerns itself with the most important questions, but each country retains a government which concerns itself with its own particular problems.'*

| 56 | 52 | 51 | 62 | 57 | 63 | 58 |

3 *'There is a European government which concerns itself with all these questions, and the member-countries no longer have a national government.'*

| 11 | 15 | 9 | 7 | 10 | 5 | 13 |

4 *'None of these formulas.'*

| 4 | 4 | 6 | 3 | 4 | 1 | 3 |

4 *'Don't know' or did not answer.*

| 13 | 13 | 20 | 10 | 16 | 12 | 8 |

Source: J.-R. Rabier, op.cit., 1970, p. 490

146

Table 6.10(b)

Forms of political organisation of a united Europe, September 1973 (figures in percentages)

'In the future, for the unification of Europe, which of the following formulas are you more in favour of?'

Belgium	France	Italy	Luxembourg	Netherlands	West Germany	Denmark	Great Britain	Ireland

1 *'Maintain the present degree of national independence.'*

| 29 | 26 | 17 | 19 | 27 | 15 | 57 | 46 | 47 |

2 *'Establish closer ties between the member-states of the European Community.'*

| 26 | 25 | 25 | 38 | 31 | 29 | 27 | 23 | 23 |

3 *'Create some sort of European government to which each national government delegates a large part of its powers.'*

| 24 | 30 | 36 | 25 | 30 | 42 | 8 | 16 | 14 |

4 *'No opinion, don't know.'*

| 21 | 19 | 22 | 18 | 12 | 14 | 8 | 15 | 16 |

Source: Commission of the Communities, op.cit., November 1973, Table 9

continue to play an important role. In keeping with the rest of our evidence, the West Germans again appear to be the most committed partisans of the full supranational formula. From the 1973 poll we can also see the much stronger opposition to the supranational model which exists in the three new member-states. But the general conclusion to be drawn is that there is a considerable amount of support amongst the publics of the original Six for greater supranationalism. This is borne out by the figures presented in Tables 6.11 and 6.12.

Again, our findings seem to indicate that the extent of utilitarian-systemic support is considerable within the Six, whether that support exists for common policies or for supranational institutions. Similarly,

Table 6.11

Attitude towards election of a European Parliament
by direct universal suffrage, January—February 1970 and
September 1973 (figures in percentages)

'Are you for or against the election of a European Parliament by direct universal suffrage — that is, a parliament elected by all the citizens of the member-countries?'

| | For | | Against | | Don't know | |
	1970	1973	1970	1973	1970	1973
Belgium	56	52	12	14	32	34
France	59	51	16	18	25	31
Italy	71	64	8	12	21	24
Luxembourg	70	67	11	12	19	21
The Netherlands	60	62	21	16	19	22
West Germany	63	69	11	12	25	19
Denmark	—	36	—	43	—	21
Great Britain	—	33	—	49	—	18
Ireland	—	45	—	31	—	24

* In 1973, the question read: 'Are you for or against the election of a European Parliament by a popular vote of all the citizens in the member-states of the European Community?'

Source: J.-R. Rabier, op.cit., 1970, p. 484; Commission of the Communities, op.cit., November 1974, Table 7

there appears to be a lack of willingness in the new member-states to endorse either common policies or supranational institutions.

There is, however, a major problem with the nature of the questions which have been asked by the pollsters in an effort to determine the willingness of the publics to accept supranational institutions. The snag is that the respondents are asked only to express their opinions on the elections of a European Parliament or a European President, both of which reflect a federalist vision of the Europe of the future rather than approximating to the present institutions of the Community. The outcome of this gap between the vision and the reality is that the proponents of a United States of Europe point to the apparently strong

Table 6.12

Attitude towards election of a European President, January–February 1970 (figures in percentages)

'*In the case of the election of a President of the United States of Europe by universal suffrage, would you or would you not vote for a candidate who was not of your nationality if his personality and his programme corresponded better to your ideas than those of the candidates of your nationality?*'

	Would vote for	Would not	Don't know
Belgium	52	24	24
France	61	22	17
Italy	45	19	36
Luxembourg	67	20	13
The Netherlands	63	18	19
West Germany	69	12	19
Great Britain	39	41	20

Source: Commission of the Communities, op.cit., May 1970, p. 6

support for supranational institutions to bolster their demands for the radical reform of the present institutions and the speedy creation of a European political union.

But there are two major obstacles which block the federalists' path. First, can we be sure that all the publics of the Six do strongly favour the direct election of a European Parliament and a European President? We have seen from Tables 5.4, 5.9 and 5.15 that amongst some publics there are not insignificant fears of the effects of unification, and that many people are not very willing to make personal sacrifices for unification. We have also seen that a large number of people consider unification to be unlikely in view of the different size and power of the member-states of the Community. For these reasons, which create an ambiguous element within the European public's support for unification, it would be naïve of us to accept the federalists' interpretation of Tables 6.11 and 6.12. Is it not plausible that many of the respondents favouring direct elections at the European level also assume that their national Government would still retain considerable power – possibly even the veto in a Council of

Ministers with powers over and above the European Parliament? Certainly Tables 6.10(a) and 6.10(b) indicate that only minorities favour any drastic reduction in the powers of the national governments in any European political union.

It is also vital to emphasise that any radical reform of the Community of the type envisaged by the federalists is extremely unlikely within the foreseeable future. First, there is the evidence of a certain ambiguity within the general public support in the Six for unification. Secondly, there is the present public opposition to unification in Denmark, Britain and, to a lesser extent, Ireland — it is difficult to see unification proceeding as rapidly as the federalists wish while these nations remain in the Community and reflect their current caution. Thirdly, the national leaders are wary of rapid unification — and this includes President Giscard d'Estaing — for a variety of reasons. Certainly one of these reasons is the pragmatic argument on the dangers of a speedy progress to federalism which has been expounded most succinctly by Andrew Shonfield. [10]

Shonfield's case is quite simple. Suppose that in a directly elected European Parliament with extensive legislative powers a majority vote for a particular policy which is likely to be damaging to one member-state of the Community, and that the representatives of this nation-state are in the minority. Also, let us suppose that there is no way that this policy can be vetoed in a Council of Ministers, and yet public feeling is running very high in the nation-state, which feels that its interests have been sacrificed to those of the rest of the Community. The most likely outcome, of course, is a secession, which could wreck the Community. [11]

Shonfield advances the idea of this possibly ruinous series of events in order to check the demands of the federalists, but in so doing he brings our attention to the crucial question: 'Where would the public's loyalty lie — with Europe or with their nation-state?' And this question requires that we investigate the evidence relevant to the two remaining elements of Lindberg's and Scheingold's matrix of support, both of which are concerned with the affective bases of support. Affective-systemic support refers to the ability of the Community's institutions to generate feelings of loyalty, and affective-identitive support, which we have discussed in Chapter Five, refers to the sense of a European identity, of being European. If there is evidence of strong and well-established affective-systemic and affective-identitive support, then, by Shonfield's test, a United States of Europe would be feasible, since loyalty to any federal institutions and the sense of a common identity over and above nationalistic sentiments would presumably prevent the likelihood of a national public feeling constrained to secede.

150

Table 6.13

Assessment of Community action on the two problems considered most important at the present time (May 1974). Figures in percentages

	Belgium			France			Italy			Luxembourg			Netherlands		
	(1)	(2)	(3)	(1)	(2)	(3)	(1)	(2)	(3)	(1)	(2)	(3)	(1)	(2)	(3)
Rising prices	6	82	12	3	85	12	17	61	22	5	91	4	9	72	19
Energy	13	76	11	9	82	9	13	70	17	23	75	2	11	74	15
Protection of nature	3	89	8	4	87	9	18	67	15	8	86	6	9	74	17
Consumer protection	6	85	9	4	84	12	14	65	21	8	81	11	7	67	26
Political unity	8	80	12	6	85	9	22	74	4	8	87	5	13	77	10
European currency	10	74	16	4	85	11	26	62	12	8	80	12	12	72	16
Difference between regions	4	81	15	4	82	14	19	70	11	6	91	3	14	58	18
Jobs, vocational training	11	73	16	2	90	8	17	71	12	18	82	–	10	33	7
Agriculture	7	89	4	7	78	15	25	62	13	33	56	11	20	66	14
Equivalence of qualifications	3	81	16	4	87	9	23	69	8	3	92	5	5	67	28
Aid to underdeveloped countries	10	73	17	2	95	3	19	73	8	4	92	4	10	76	14
Scientific research	–	100	–	13	81	6	16	72	12	8	75	17	17	71	12
None of these problems	–	28	72	10	30	60	–	–	100	–	8	92	4	–	96

Table 6.13 continued

	West Germany			Denmark			Great Britain			Ireland		
	(1)	(2)	(3)	(1)	(2)	(3)	(1)	(2)	(3)	(1)	(2)	(3)
Rising prices	7	80	13	5	72	23	8	75	17	5	91	4
Energy	7	75	18	9	63	28	12	69	19	11	81	8
Protection of nature	17	73	10	5	71	24	6	73	21	7	87	6
Consumer protection	9	78	13	2	71	27	9	69	22	5	88	7
Political unity	6	84	10	13	67	20	6	76	18	19	67	14
European currency	11	73	16	3	75	22	19	71	10	20	67	13
Difference between regions	24	64	12	6	69	25	9	74	17	11	76	13
Jobs, vocational training	17	65	18	–	65	35	13	64	23	11	79	10
Agriculture	15	71	14	14	69	17	11	69	20	15	79	6
Equivalence of qualifications	7	79	14	4	74	22	7	70	23	12	77	11
Aid to underdeveloped countries	23	60	17	–	68	32	5	71	24	13	84	3
Scientific research	20	63	17	11	75	14	7	67	26	23	73	4
None of these problems	–	5	95	11	18	71	–	33	67	–	14	86

Key to column headings: (1) sufficient; (2) not sufficient; (3) no reply

Source: Commission of the Communities, op.cit., June 1974, Tables 4A, 4B and 4C

However, the evidence of affective-systemic support is particularly sketchy, and its interpretation is made extremely difficult by the gap between the present nature of the Community and its institutions and the nature of the union and the institutions to which the federalists aspire. Indeed, in this particular instance, the evidence is such that its interpretation must depend upon one's domain assumptions about European integration. A pluralist could argue that the inability of the Community to generate loyalties which supersede nationalistic sympathies demonstrates the need for a limited form of political unification. A federalist, it seems, could equally argue that nationalistic sentiments cannot be overcome by the affective-systemic support generated by a Community in which the nation-state continues to remain the dominant political unit.

A Community-wide poll conducted in May 1974 appears to give some credence to the federalist thesis.[12] Respondents were asked which problems of those facing the Community they considered to be the most important, and whether or not they felt the Community was taking sufficient action (see Table 6.13). It is clear that a large majority of the public considered Community action to be inadequate, and the public was just as severe in its expectations of Community policy on future problems as it was for those which were considered important in the present.

Three alternative conclusions can be drawn from Table 6.13: first, that public dissatisfaction with Community action could seriously impair any affective-systemic support which exists for the Common Market, reducing still further the likelihood of the evolution of a political union; secondly, that the expression of such dissatisfaction will strengthen demands for speedier progress towards political unification; finally, that Table 6.13 illustrates a critical reply 'stereotype', by which the public expresses the feeling that 'The Government never does enough'.

It is still not yet possible to state which of these three interpretations is the most plausible. As we saw in Table 5.10, support for political unification did increase between September 1973 and May 1974, and therefore the second interpretation, favoured by the federalists, seems to gain credibility. Also, in Table 5.11 we discerned a slight increase during these months in the numbers of those who would express regret if the Common Market was abandoned, except in West Germany and the new member-states. But this evidence is really too tentative to provide sound conclusions on the findings of May 1974. Indeed, the view that Table 6.13 illustrates a critical reply 'stereotype' is given credibility by the onset of serious economic problems in late 1973 and early 1974, most notably the increased cost of oil following the third Arab-Israeli war, and inflation.

Table 6.14

Attachment to national symbols, January—February 1970
(figures in percentages)

'Would you be favourable, opposed or indifferent to the currency of your country being replaced by a European currency, to the team of your country in the next Olympic Games being incorporated into a European team, and to the flag of your country being replaced by a European flag in solemn ceremonies?'

	The Six	Belgium	France	Italy	Luxembourg	Netherlands	West Germany
1 European currency							
Favourable	51	49	51	51	63	47	52
Opposed	23	23	23	21	13	23	26
Indifferent	18	21	18	18	19	27	14
No reply, don't know	8	7	8	10	5	3	8
2 European Olympic Team							
Favourable	27	26	34	24	53	20	25
Opposed	43	36	36	41	20	54	51
Indifferent	22	27	22	25	21	23	18
No reply, don't know	8	11	8	10	6	3	6
3 European flag							
Favourable	27	26	22	24	26	19	35
Opposed	52	48	61	57	57	57	41
Indifferent	15	20	11	11	12	21	18
No reply, don't know	6	6	6	8	5	3	6

Source: J.-R. Rabier, op.cit., 1970, p. 488

Under these conditions, a critical reply is hardly surprising. Whether this critical reply continues, and the consequences of its continuation for the future development of unification, are open to conjecture.

154

We have seen that there is a certain ambiguity in the publics' support for unification, and that a nationalistic element continues to be manifest amongst popular perceptions of European unification. In Chapters Four and Five we found that the affective component of mass attitudes towards integration was strong, both in terms of sympathies and loyalties for other countries and also in the sense of being 'European', and supporting 'the European idea'. But we now need to subject this affective-identitive element of support to a more thorough analysis.

Table 6.15

Main loyalties to geographical entities, July 1971
(figures in percentages)

	Belgium	France	Italy	Luxembourg	Netherlands	West Germany
Town/locality	52	33	36	50	43	59
Province/ department	9	8	6	1	6	2
State/region	9	11	9	27		7
Nation	24	37	37	15	37	21
Europe	5	6	8	3	11	9
Other geographical entities	–	2	2	2	1	1
No reply	1	3	2	2	2	1

Source: Commission of the Communities, op.cit., December 1971, p. 4

In Table 6.14 we can see the results from a question which sought to measure approximately the attachment of the publics in the Six to certain national symbols such as currency, Olympic teams and the flag. From Table 6.14 it is evident that while majorities in the Six favoured a European currency, most people opposed the replacement of national symbols by European symbols. The people of Luxembourg and France were the most willing to support a European Olympic team, and the West Germans gave strongest support (although more West Germans were opposed to the idea) to the proposal for a European flag to replace national flags. Again, these findings indicate an awareness of being European, of sharing a common identity, but not to the extent of erasing basic national loyalties.

Further evidence on the nature of the peoples' basic loyalties is to be found in Table 6.15, which shows the extent of attachment to locality, region, nation, and Europe itself in July 1971.

The most striking fact to emerge from Table 6.15 is the strong loyalty to the locality in all the member-states of the Six, but particularly in West Germany, where there is also a comparatively weak commitment to the nation. The French appear to be the most nationalistic, with the Italians and the Dutch also expressing loyalty to the nation-state most frequently, although they do appear to be slightly more 'European' than do the French.

In conjunction with the evidence which shows consistent support amongst the founder-member publics for political unification, Tables 6.14 and 6.15 indicate that there is a real sense of being 'European' amongst the publics, but that nationalistic loyalties remain paramount. Indeed, these conclusions are consistent with the results of the many opinion polls and surveys which we have reviewed. But if we are to reach some more meaningful conclusions on the development of systemic and identitive support for integration, we must consider the questions of the ability of political institutions to generate support, the stability of mass attitudes, and the significance of varied and changing societal values.

Conclusions

As far as the utilitarian basis of support is concerned, the evidence of the opinion polls confirms our third proposition in the sense that support for supranational institutions or policies is more marked than feelings of shared needs and interests. Certainly, there is considerable support for common policies within the Community, and also the public seemed willing to accept supranational institutions. But a careful analysis of the common policies which receive the greatest support reveals that the publics, even in the pro-European Six, are wary of common policies which may require some form of personal sacrifice in the common 'European' good. Also, those common policies which are most indicative of support for unification appear to be less popular than the more technical policies or defence policy, where common interests are usually more easily perceived.

The utilitarian-systemic support which is manifest amongst the publics of the Six appears to be qualified by the comparatively weaker utilitarian-identitive element of support. The publics of the Six may affirm their willingness to elect a European Parliament and President, but the most favoured form of political unification remains a form where national institutions would continue to play a very important role. In view of this finding it would be quite erroneous to press for the speedy creation of a United States of Europe in which political institutions at the national level would be rapidly superseded – clearly, this would conflict with popular sentiment.

The findings of the opinion polls are far more sketchy for the affective basis of support, but it does seem that our proposition is refuted – there are signs that affective-identitive support is stronger than affective-systemic support. This conclusion is necessarily tentative at this stage, but it seems plausible because of the very nature of the Community's institutions. Admittedly we have seen that majorities in the publics of the Six would express regret were the Common Market to be abandoned 'tomorrow', but such sentiments seem to stem from the perceived benefits of membership and also from a feeling that the Community is a step towards closer unification. In other words, it is not possible for us to conclude that a sense of regret at the abandonment of the Common Market reflects an affective-systemic response – it could just as plausibly reflect utilitarian and identitive responses.

Indeed, the argument that affective-identitive support is more marked than affective-systemic support is based on the evidence of the growth of 'mutual loyalties and sympathies' – at least, between the publics of the Six – which we discussed in Chapter Four. Also the continuing general support for the idea of unification, even amongst the publics of the new members, attests to the awareness of a common identity. Yet the ambiguities in attitudes to political unification which become evident in reply to more specific questions reveals an underlying caution which could well check the development of strong affective-systemic support.

Our analysis of the evidence relating to Lindberg's and Scheingold's matrix of support suggests some interesting conclusions, which must necessarily remain tentative. On the one hand it seems that utilitarian-systemic support is very strong. Also, affective-identitive support seems to be relatively strong. However, utilitarian-identitive and affective-systemic support seem to be weaker, indicating that the publics do not yet conceive of common European interests or needs, and that they are 'attached' to the Common Market only in so far as it provides clearly perceived benefits and accords with an underlying affective-identitive sentiment. In testing our next proposition, we shall review more fully the evidence on the ability of the Community to generate support for further integration.

Notes

[1] L. Lindberg and S. Scheingold, *Europe's Would-be Polity*, Prentice-Hall, 1970, pp. 38–45.

[2] See also ibid.

[3] Ibid.

[4] Gallup International, 'Public opinion and the European Community', edited and translated by M. Forsyth, in *Journal of Common Market Studies* vol. 2, no. 2, 1963, p. 114.

[5] L'Institut français de l'Opinion, *Sondages* nos 1–2, 1972, p. 106.

[6] Ibid., p. 128.

[7] L. Lindberg and S. Scheingold, op.cit., 1970, pp. 49–50.

[8] Commission of the Communities, *L'Europe vue par les Européens: analyse approfondie des items relatifs a l'unification de l'Europe*, Brussels, March 1974, p. 4.

[9] R. Inglehart, *The 1973 European Community Public Opinion Surveys: Preliminary Findings*, University of Geneva, May 1974, p. 6.

[10] Andrew Shonfield, *Europe: Journey to an Unknown Destination*, Pelican, 1973, pp. 70–1.

[11] Ibid.

[12] Commission of the Communities, *Euro-Barometer* no. 1, Brussels, May 1974.

7   'Fait Accompli'?

Proposition 4: 'In any region following the creation of supranational institutions, there is a stronger public commitment to further integration.'

Introductory discussion

Clearly, the above proposition is closely related to our first proposition, which we examined in Chapter Four. The first proposition was concerned with the interrelationship between the action and affection components of public support for integration, and therefore included some discussion of the effects of integration on that support. However, in the examination of our fourth proposition, we shall concentrate on the impact of integration, in the form of institutions which have been created and policies which have been pursued, on the opinions of the mass publics.

In particular, we are concerned in this chapter to test what can be termed 'the *fait accompli* thesis'. This thesis is a particularly notable feature of functionalism and also forms a significant strand in some of the earlier and seemingly more naïve federalist and neofunctionalist approaches to integration, where public opinion is held to have a comparatively weak role as a minor intervening variable in the integrative process. Essentially, the older functionalist view was that with socio-economic and technological forces creating a functional need for international integration in certain spheres, the national decision-making elites would initiate international integration for their own short-term political gain. But the elites would subsequently find that they could reverse the process only at great political cost, because public support had been won over to integration by the resultant material-welfare benefits, which exceeded those the nation-state could provide. With integration being introduced to meet functional needs, its success was guaranteed, and thus a permanent loss of national sovereignty was certain to follow, fully supported by the publics.

To the extent that the early neofunctionalists shared their predecessors' belief in the overriding importance of the indirect, socio-economic variables in the integrative process, they also subscribed to the *fait accompli* thesis. Although Haas did modify the deterministic element in functionalism, he did so mainly by incorporating the elitist perspective of the federalists.[1] Thus, only the active, participant 'publics' mattered in the integrative process. Integration was seen as an 'elite-pull' phenomenon, lacking any 'mass-push' features. Even the elites would succumb to the 'cumulative logic of integration', since participation by political leaders, group spokesmen and civil servants would involve them in a process of socialisation, during which they would come to accept the norms of the emergent institutions and to support further moves toward integration.

Deutsch has been far more wary of adopting any simplistic *fait accompli* thesis.[2] He has been ready to stress that the public's perception of the results of integration is more problematic than that envisaged by the functionalists and neofunctionalists, as a result of their deterministic assumptions. Haas, in his later work, and Lindberg and Scheingold do modify neofunctionalism to allow for 'dramatic political actors' and for setbacks in the integrative process, but in so doing they raise further doubts about the strength of the 'cumulative logic of integration', upon which so much of their approach depends.[3]

We saw in Chapter Three that Deutsch has undertaken an analysis of 'transactions' in Western Europe, concluding that 'European integration has slowed down since the mid-1950s and has stopped or reached a plateau since 1957–8'.[4] Not only has Inglehart challenged Deutsch's methodology, but he has also undertaken a study of support for integration among the 'youth' age-groups in Western Europe.[5] On the basis of this study Inglehart claims that the post-war generations, who have been socialised during an era of unprecedented collaboration and trust, are strongly committed to further integration and are more likely to consider themselves 'Europeans'. Puchala too has taken issue with Deutsch, pointing to evidence that, following the creation of the EEC, there was a strong increase in support for integration.[6]

However, Puchala is not prepared to subscribe to any *fait accompli* thesis without substantial qualifications. He poses two questions – first he refers to the neofunctionalist concept of 'spillover', the mechanism which induces further integration as elites seek to strike bargains within the institutional setting of the European Community, and he asks; 'does a descriptively similar "spillover" of preferences for more comprehensive amalgamation occur at the mass population level during regional integration?'[7] Secondly, 'is it the case that perceptions of success or reward from limited experiments in international amalgamation generate enthusiasm or preferences for more amalgamation?'[8] If the answers to these questions are negative, Puchala feels that community formation and regional identification processes must be much more complex than was once thought. Also, negative answers would indicate that integration was almost totally an 'elite-pull' phenomenon, and not in any sense a 'mass-push' phenomenon.

Puchala also raises some further points concerning 'attitudinal spill-over', which we must consider.[9] First, initial successes in one field of integration may merely lead to greater demands for further integration in that particular field. Secondly, integration in one field may lead to greater awareness of integration without necessarily leading to demands for more integration, except perhaps in the long run. And, finally, successful integration can also increase the hostility of those who oppose integration and those who feel that they have suffered in the process. These three considerations are particularly pertinent in view of the distinction which has been drawn between negative and positive integration, and the fact that European integration in the early 1970s seems to have reached a watershed between these two qualitively different forms of integration. [10]

The evidence and its interpretation

Again, it is Louis Kriesberg's study of West German public opinion towards the ECSC which provides us with some of the earliest available evidence for our proposition that the creation of supranational institutions leads to a stronger public commitment to further integration. [11] Taking the ECSC as a case-study, Kriesberg tested the proposition that, once a law has been enacted, or an institution established, predispositions about authority and habituation to what exists serve to give that law or institution popular support (see Table 7.1).

Thus, Kriesberg was seeking to test what we have termed 'the *fait accompli* thesis' by means of the seemingly trite question shown in Table 7.1, but it is a question which appears to tap the respondents' willingness to obey – or resistance to obeying – the law. Indeed, Table 7.1 shows that those who condemned a minor violation of the law tended to be more in favour of the ECSC, and that those who felt that Germany had fared badly, but the ECSC was not necessarily a bad thing, were also more likely to condemn any smuggling than those respondents who were also opposed to the ECSC.

In his conclusions, Kriesberg points out that, after the establishment of the ECSC, West German approval of it increased. Yet, at the same time, the belief that West Germany fared well under the ECSC declined. These apparently contradictory trends led Kriesberg to argue that the sources of

Table 7.1

Evaluation of the ECSC in West Germany by condemnation
of smuggling (figures in percentages)

*'If someone returned from a trip out of the country and smuggled a
pound jar of coffee through the customs, would you condemn it or not
condemn it?'*

	Evaluation of the ECSC				
	(1) Good	(2) Mildly favourable	(3) Bad, not anti	(4) Bad, anti	(5) Undecided
Condemn	31	31	14	5	18
Not condemn	17	30	6	21	16
Don't know	21	31	5	37	11

Source: Kriesberg, op. cit., 1959, pp. 34–6

increased approval were probably from support for the established law,
together with the transference of feelings about authority and the
sacredness of laws. But experience as consumers (see Table 5.1) led the
West Germans to criticise the ECSC, although their strong desire for
unification probably led to the feeling that, on the whole, it had not been
an error to join the ECSC.

Of particular interest to us is the idea developed in Kriesberg's study
that, at different stages in the process of integration, the importance of
the several attitudinal dimensions varies. For example, before the ECSC
was established, the respondents' predispositions concerning their feelings
of mutual loyalties and sympathies, and particularly the influence of
significant 'others', largely explained mass evaluations of the proposed
ECSC. But, after the ECSC had been established, additional predispositions – in particular the respondents' readiness to accept the law and
institutions as legitimate – and experience of the ECSC became relevant.
Also, at this second stage, the decline in the ECSC as an item on the
agenda of the party political debate reduced the influence of party loyalty
as a determinant of feelings towards the ECSC.

It would be foolish to argue that Kriesberg's study of West German
opinions on the ECSC is sufficient proof to verify our fourth proposition.
Certainly Deutsch has claimed that the evidence of mass attitudes towards

the EEC from 1957 to 1962 contradicts the conclusion reached by Kriesberg. [12] Deutsch's first point is that the surveys conducted during the first five years of the EEC's operation showed persistently greater mass attention to national concerns than to European affairs. But his major illustration of this point was the trend amongst West Germans to place more emphasis on national reunification at the cost of relegating European unification to a low priority ranking. But the evidence which we have presented in Tables 5.5, 5.6 and 6.1 shows that the West Germans have become increasingly opposed to a return to a Europe of independent nation-states, and very much in favour of wide-reaching European policies combined with fully European institutions. Again, we must stress that Germany's unusual and tragic situation − a country divided by the Iron Curtain − has merely been emphasised by the thaw in the Cold War over the years, and this largely explains any West German preoccupation with national reunification. Deutsch's error was to view this preoccupation in 'zero-sum' terms, assuming that a desire for national reunification precluded any growth in public support for European integration. To the contrary, all other data show the West Germans to be in the vanguard of the European movement.

Secondly, Deutsch points to the fact that both France and West Germany have greater feelings of sympathy and loyalty for Britain and the United States than they have for each other. But he fails to assess the very great significance of the marked increases in mutual sympathies and loyalties between the French and the West Germans from the mid-1950s. While it is true that there was a lack of a comparable increase in 'trust' between the two countries in the event of a war, with such 'trust' remaining much greater in both publics for Britain and the United States, these feelings surely mirrored reality in the early 1960s. The EDC had failed because of French opposition to German rearmament, even within a supranational formula. Moreover, the EEC could hardly be expected to 'spill over' to matters of national security in its very early stages. And, finally, the West German forces depended for their existence on NATO, but from the time of de Gaulle's accession to power the French were becoming increasingly independent of NATO.

In the early 1960s, only the Americans and the British of the Western powers possessed nuclear weaponry, and, with the threat of war being greatest from an East−West clash in Europe, it was only natural that the French and West German publics should place most reliance on Angle-American support in a war. That such support was available was demonstrated by the presence of American and British bases on the continent of Europe. But the differing French and German attitudes towards NATO and the Soviet Union, which seemed to have helped to prevent any 'spillover' of integration to foreign affairs, began to converge in the late 1960s. As the French had come to emphasise a European *force de frappe* and a more conciliatory stance towards the Soviet Union, so the West Germans came to recognise a more active role for themselves in the defence of Europe (see Table 6.2(a)) and also began to pursue the objectives of their *Ostpolitik*. Table 6.6 shows that, by 1973, majorities in France and West Germany felt that a common European policy would be desirable in major political negotiations with the Americans and the Russians.

By far the most compelling critique of Deutsch's thesis is advanced by Donald J. Puchala, who presents opinion poll evidence which quite plainly contradicts the findings upon which Deutsch based his argument. [13] Puchala's case rests upon opinion polls conducted throughout the Six in May 1957 and in June 1962. The significance of these dates to our fourth proposition is that the first poll was conducted before the Treaty of Rome was signed and the second poll took place before the intra-Community crises developed. The major items in Puchala's evidence are presented in Tables 7.2 and 7.3

Table 7.2

French, West German and Italian reactions to the
Common Market, May 1957 and June 1962
(figures in percentages)

'Actually the Common Market is an agreement among France, Germany, Italy and the Benelux countries to unify their economies by gradually eliminating customs, tariffs and other controls over the movement of goods, money and labour. So far as [name of country] is concerned, do you in general approve of the Common Market idea?'

Country	Year	Approve	Disapprove	Don't know
France	1957	60	11	29
	1962	76	10	14
West Germany	1957	73	7	20
	1962	85	5	10
Italy	1957	65	6	29
	1962	76	2	22

Source: Puchala, op.cit., 1970, p.38

164

Table 7.3

French, West German and Italian mass support for a
European Federation, May 1957 and June 1962
(figures in percentages)

France		West Germany		Italy	
1957	1962	1957	1962	1957	1962
37	40	46	54	40	44

Source: Puchala, op. cit., 1970, p.50

The figures in Tables 7.2 and 7.3 are confirmed by the evidence, presented graphically in Figures 4.1—4.6, of public support for integration in France and West Germany. We can see from the Figures that, during the intra-Community crises of 1963 and 1965, public support for unification suffered short-term slumps. That these setbacks were short-lived is affirmed by the figures presented in Table 5.10 and 5.11, which show that in general in the early 1970s — the point at which our graphs end — support for European political union and the degree of attachment to the Common Market in the Six remained consistently high.

Indeed, the data which we have been able to utilise in our study is a more reliable test for the *fait accompli* thesis — our fourth proposition — than the data used by Deutsch, Kriesberg, or Puchala. This is because their studies were based on comparisons of polls conducted over a relatively short time-span, and lacked sufficient information on any fluctuations. Our data illustrates mass attitudes towards integration over a 20-year period and also illustrates the inability of serious setbacks in the progress of integration to reduce permanently French and West German support for further unification.

Yet our conclusions cannot be based on the findings of the French and West German polls alone. Although public support for unification does appear to have increased over the years, the majorities expressing 'European' sentiments have always been large in France and West Germany. Therefore, to attribute consistently high percentages in favour of unification to the creation of supranational institutions following treaties in 1950 and 1957 would be to accept the *fait accompli* thesis uncritically. Such unquestioning acceptance equally would be tantamount to subscribing to a view of integration which was purely an 'elite-pull' phenomenon, and in which the public remained totally passive.

We must remember that the 'European experiment' has been remarkably successful to date for the economies of its member-states. Of the original Six, only the Italian economy has suffered a virtual collapse, but the Italians have always been ready to express their support for European integration. The major factor in the decision of the Italian Communist Party to support the Community was their awareness of the economic benefits which membership of the EEC had brought to the Italian working-class. Thus, the Italian economic collapse is unlikely to reduce public support for unification, particularly since their Community colleagues, the West Germans, performed a vital salvage operation on the Italian economy by making a loan of $2,000 million available to the Rumor Government in August 1974.

We saw from Table 5.15 that the image of the EEC in the Six in 1971 was predominantly utilitarian, with a certain nationalistic element remaining quite marked. Indeed, our conclusions to Chapters Five and Six indicated strong utilitarian-systemic support for integration and a consistent affective-identitive response amongst the publics. In the case of Franco-German relations, it seemed that integration had been instrumental in engendering a growth in mutual sympathies and loyalties, but the 'European' sentiment had been strong in both publics from the immediate post-war years. However, we were unable to observe, from the evidence available to us, any signs of consistent or emergent perceptions of truly common European needs (utilitarian-identitive support), and the institutions of the EEC seem to have generated little affective-systemic support.

These conclusions clearly provide the basis for a critique of any simplistic *fait accompli* thesis, but before we return to a fuller exposition of their implications let us turn to the findings of opinion polls conducted in the new member-states of the Community – notably Britain – and also let us review public feelings in Norway, where, in 1972, the people voted to stay outside the Community. Here, of course, we face a major problem in that Denmark, Ireland and Britain became members of the Community as recently as January 1973. Thus we are confronted by the same inability to utilise data over a long time-span that limited the efficacy of Kriesberg's study of the ECSC and the studies by Deutsch and Puchala. Nonetheless, the publics of the new member-states have had to face the prospect of accession to the Treaty of Rome since the early 1960s, and their governments were committed to entry from the early 1970s.

If we are to draw conclusions from studies of public opinion over short periods of time, we need to undertake a very detailed scrutiny of the findings of the polls. In Chapter Twelve of *Diplomacy and Persuasion: How Britain Joined the Common Market* Uwe Kitzinger has endeavoured to present just such a detailed – at times, day-by-day – account of the movements in British public opinion on the subject of entry into the Common Market.[14] He deals with the period from 1970 to 1972, concentrating on the movements in opinion during June and July 1971, when the British Conservative Government's White Paper on entry was published.

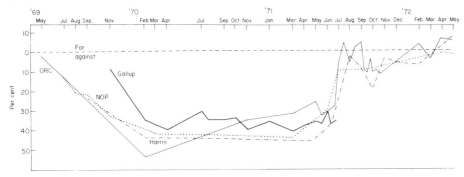

Fig. 7.1   Composite graph of ORC, NOP, Gallup and Harris polls, 1969–72

Source: Kitzinger, *Diplomacy and Persuasion.* Thames and Hudson, 1973, pp. 362–3

In Figure 7.1, we reproduce the curve plotted by Kitzinger, which shows the average swing in Britain as a whole over the period from spring 1969 to spring 1972. It is set out as a single line tracing the difference between the percentage in favour and the percentage against entry in each of four polls (Gallup, ORC, NOP and Harris). Kitzinger writes, 'From a plateau of readings near or below −30 per cent (the minus reading indicates more opposed than favourable to entry) from February until the end of June, all the lines then leapt up suddenly about the beginning of July.'[15] Kitzinger also refers to a National Opinion Polls survey which was in the field from 6 to 12 July and which was subsequently split by the exact date of interview in order to assess any impact which the publication of the White Paper might have had (see Table 7.4)

We can see from Table 7.4 that there was a striking swing in public opinion towards entry, and NOP added, 'This could be a sampling freak, yet in terms of age, class and sex, and voting intention those contacted on Thursday [8 July] or later were not dissimilar to those contacted on

Table 7.4

Approval of entry of the Common Market amongst the
British public (figures in percentages)

'Do you approve or disapprove of Britain joining the Common Market?'

| | | Interviewed on | |
	All	6–7 July	8–12 July
Approve	34	29	39
Disapprove	44	47	41
Don't know	22	24	20

Source: Kitzinger, op. cit., 1973, p. 362

Wednesday or before.'[16] Kitzinger draws our attention to an even more surprising fact, writing that,

> Though it was a Conservative government that was urging entry and a Labour Opposition that was shying away, the percentage of the electors who declared they would vote Conservative dropped from 48 per cent in April to 45 per cent in May, 40 per cent in June and 39 per cent in July (according to ORC). Yet between the end of April and the end of July the percentage in favour of entry (again according to ORC) rose from 30 per cent in late April and 26 per cent in late May, to 45 per cent in late July. In no way therefore can the swing towards the Government's chief foreign policy have been induced by a swing towards the Government as such, on the contrary, the 15 per cent swing towards entry took place in spite of a 10 per cent swing against the government that was advocating it. [17]

Indeed, the picture according to party support is particularly fascinating. In early May 1971, 50 per cent of Conservative supporters opposed entry, with 38 per cent in favour, but by 7–11 July the picture was transformed. This was at and after the publication of the White Paper, but, as Kitzinger emphasises, before the Central Council rally in the Central Hall. The early July findings showed that only 28 per cent of Conservative supporters remained opposed to entry, while 58 per cent were in favour. Two weeks later, only 19 per cent of Tory supporters opposed entry, while a total of 68 per cent of Conservative supporters expressed their commitment to entry. Kitzinger comments that '. . . in just two months at least 30 per

168

cent of Conservatives must have changed their minds'.[18] The fact that Labour supporters in early July swung in the same direction, against the increasingly anti-European stance (on Tory terms, at least) of their party leadership, and by almost half as much as Conservative supporters, indicates that it cannot have been the swing within the Conservative Parliamentary Party alone which influenced that party's supporters. Kitzinger concludes, '. . . most if not all of the swing must have been due to the turn of events, general moods in the country, and the government's appeal over the heads of Members of Parliament direct to the people'.[19]

Kitzinger's analysis of the British opinion polls closes in the spring of 1972, and the evidence of Figure 7.1 leads him to the view that '. . . in spring 1972 people seemed to drift into accommodating themselves, at least temporarily, to their fate, in effect ratifying *ex post* the decision that had been taken by Parliament'.[20] Kitzinger is wise to stress the temporary nature of this 'acquiescence' on the part of the British public. Clearly, the trends in British opinion since spring 1972 show that opposition to entry has been revived following the British experience of the Common Market.

If the *fait accompli* thesis has any relevance to the British experience in the 1970s, it appears to have been limited to three brief periods: first, the publication of the Conservative Government's White Paper in July 1971, when the public appeared to respond to the determined approach of the Heath administration on entry; secondly, at the time of the signing of the Treaty of Accession in January 1972, when the public again appeared to respond to a fresh demonstration of the leadership's commitment; and, thirdly, in January 1973, when Britain entered the Community and 38 per cent felt that the Government was right to enter, while 36 per cent felt that it was a mistaken policy. By April 1973, there was a 2 per cent majority for those holding the latter view (40 per cent said Britain was right to enter, 42 per cent that Britain was wrong).[21] During the later months of 1973, disillusionment had clearly increased – the balance for those who felt Britain was wrong had grown to 15 per cent in October (34 per cent felt Britain was right, 49 per cent said she was wrong).[22]

Things got even worse for the pro-Europeans in 1974 – in February only 28 per cent thought Britain had been right to enter, yet a full 58 per cent thought she had been wrong, which created a balance of 30 percentage points against the Marketeers.[23] This poll coincided with a national election campaign in which Enoch Powell's opposition to entry, despite his allegiance to the Tory party prior to the dissolution of Parliament, made membership of the Common Market a major issue. Powell stepped down from his candidacy for a safe Conservative seat and recommended any anti-Marketeers to vote Labour, since Labour was the only party which appeared to offer the people any chance of having a direct say on British membership of the Common Market. It is instructive that in the West Midlands, where Powell's support is centred, the average swing at the February 1974 General Election was 9 per cent from Conservative to Labour, reaching a peak of 16 per cent in Wolverhampton, the town in which his former constituency is located. By June 1974, with a Labour minority government in the throes of assessing the impact of membership on Britain, the anti-Marketeer majority remained at 21 per cent – 32 per cent thought Britain had been right to enter, 53 per cent felt she had been wrong. [24]

In his analysis of a detailed study of the results of a Community-wide poll conducted in September 1973, Inglehart wrote, of the lack of support in Britain for the Common Market, that,

> It is not wholly surprising that the British are hesitant to endorse an arrangement under which their country – one of the poorest in the Community – pays a substantial net subsidy to help solve the agricultural problems of richer countries such as France and Germany. [25]

It is not clear from the opinion poll evidence which we have reviewed that the British people saw it in quite these terms, but certainly their greatest resentment was one of rapidly rising prices on entry.

The evidence of British public opinion towards the Common Market fully reveals the major flaws in any simplistic *fait accompli* thesis. The nub of Kriesberg's argument was that the very existence of the ECSC, legitimated by the process of its creation in the member-states of the Six, sufficed to generate public support for economic integration in the coal and steel industries. Furthermore, the legitimacy accruing to the ECSC was such that, despite the difficulties experienced by the German coal consumer, support for the ECSC was still forthcoming from a majority of West Germans. Yet, in the case of Britain and the EEC, we have noted the growing acceptance of closer ties with Europe in the late 1960s and the perception that entry would mean economic growth and an improved standard of living in the long run. Despite these favourable views, and despite the three 'honeymoon' periods of the early 1970s, when the public appeared to rally to – or acquiesce in – the actions of a pro-European leadership, the majority of the British people expressing an opinion since entry have felt, for all but the first month of British membership, that entry was a mistake.

It does seem that, for short periods, the Government's advocacy of the

170

benefits of entry into the Common Market has led to temporary increases in support for British membership. It is in this rather limited sense that action by the government can generate some degree of increased support, albeit temporary, that the *fait accompli* thesis possesses an element of truth. But it is quite another argument to claim that inter-state integration necessarily generates mass support for further integration. This latter view, although it is a crude summary of its proponents' claims, does illustrate the deterministic element which is present in much integration theory. It is this element which the enlargement of the Six has brought into question, since support from the publics of all the member-states of the Community is no longer certain, and, from the British experience in the first eighteen months of entry, it is not enough to claim that in time the British people too will come to favour unification.

Yet the picture for the advocates of European unity which involves British participation is not wholly gloomy. If one of the major elements of neofunctionalist theory has been revealed as a construct of deterministic social science, there are still grounds for the pro-Europeans to be optimistic. One reason is the existence of majorities amongst the British public who express favourable opinions of the long-term effects of entry on Britain. We have seen that it is the fears of the short-term impact, particularly on prices, that explains the lack of sustained support for entry in the 1970s. To many it may seem surprising that perceived short-term effects can exert such a strong influence, but Hedges and Jowell sum up the reasons succinctly: 'Price increases are a painfully familiar phenomenon; economic growth is not. In that sense, the dice are loaded towards a short-term view.'[26]

We can readily see the basis of pro-Marketeer optimism if we look to the possible consequences of a referendum on the Labour Government's renegotiated terms. Here we must also recall the points which we made concerning the difference between opinion poll findings and the outcome of a referendum. Of course, the latter would follow a fiercely fought campaign, during which the issues would be crystallised. Such a situation is clearly very different from the conditions under which opinion polls are conducted, when the public is preoccupied with many other issues, particularly prices, and the longer-term issues have not been fully set out before them. It does not seem wholly unreasonable to argue that in a referendum the dice would not be quite so heavily loaded towards the short-term view. Indeed, considering that Britain's prospects for participating in world affairs and her future economic performance — plainly not issues which appear relevant to the public in their everyday lives — would be major issues in the referendum campaign. On such a momentous decision, the chances are that the dominance of the short-term effects would be at least partly vitiated.

We must avoid the pitfalls of deterministic neofunctionalism, but clearly, in any British referendum, much would depend on the re-commendations of a Labour Government. Although we have seen that the Labour leadership's decision to oppose entry on the terms negotiated by the Conservative Government followed a major swing against entry amongst Labour voters, it does seem that Labour's anti-Market stance from mid-1971 consolidated a party political polarisation of the public's views on entry. It therefore seems plausible to suppose that, were a Labour Government to recommend acceptance of their renegotiated terms in a referendum, with emphasis being placed upon the longer-term benefits of membership, the British people may well decide to remain in the Community.

The distinction between the short term and the long term is again central in the second factor which gives pro-Europeans grounds for optimism. The second factor is concerned almost totally with the work of the Michigan school, led by Professor Ronald Inglehart.[27] Inglehart distinguishes short-term influences on public attitudes — for example, the price of butter or sugar — from the long-term influences. A long-term influence on public attitudes is clearly very different from the sorts of long-term expectations that we have discussed, particularly in our examination of British opinions. While a long-term expectation is couched in terms of expected economic performance, world peace, and so on, Inglehart is far more concerned with the effects of environmental influences and outputs of the political system during a person's most formative years, or childhood. Inglehart is quite justified to contend that important changes in political socilisation may have been taking place in recent years as a result of the impact of the post-war European movement, increases in trade, the greater exchange of persons, and the establishment of European institutions.

In order to test his hypothesis, Inglehart studied the attitudes towards West European unification held by young people in four West European countries, and compared the findings with adult mass attitudes (see Tables 7.5 and 7.6). From Table 7.5, we can agree with Inglehart's conclusion that the percentages of young people in favour of unification are of landslide proportions in three of the countries.

As regards support for the four specific proposals (Table 7.6), we can see that the young people in the three member-states of the Six were more 'European' than the adults, although in the Netherlands the age-difference is less noticeable because of the strength of the support from the adults.

172

Table 7.5

Overall percentage 'strongly for' or 'for' European integration

	Netherlands	France	West Germany	Britain
Adults 1962	87	72	81	(65)*
Youth 1963	95	93	95	72

* An average of polls in 1955, 1956 and 1957

Source: Inglehart, op. cit., 1967, p. 92

Table 7.6

Percentages 'for' four proposals, 1963

	Netherlands	France	West Germany	Britain
1 *Abolish tariffs?'*				
Adults	79	72	71	70
Youth	87	83	89	74
2 *'Free movement of labour and business?'*				
Adults	76	57	64	52
Youth	64	65	75	65
3 *'Common foreign policy?'*				
Adults	67	50	60	41
Youth	80	71	74	56
4 *'Use "our" taxes to aid power European countries?'*				
Adults	70	43	52	63
Youth	82	68	72	57

Source: Inglehart, op.cit., 1967, p. 92

French youth in particular shuns the anxieties of its elders. Even British youth appears more 'European' than British adults. These observations are confirmed in the more detailed analysis presented in Table 7.7

Table 7.7

Average percentage 'for' the four proposals, by age-group

Age groups	Netherlands	France	West Germany	Britain
55 and over	70	47	52	49
40–50	73	58	63	57
30–39	71	59	64	61
21–29	72	58	67	60
16–19 (youth sample)	77	72	78	63

Source: Inglehart, op.cit., 1967, p. 93

The particular relevance of Table 7.7 to our fourth proposition lies in Inglehart's explanation, noted above in the description of the less detailed Tables 7.5 and 7.6, of the significant differences in the various responses. It is clear from Table 7.7 that those in the '55 and over' age group – and that is the group which holds most political power – are least in favour of European unification. The Dutch are exceptional, and it is instructive that, of the four countries under review, the Netherlands alone did not participate in the First World War. As a result, those Dutch people now in the oldest age-group were spared, in the early years of their lives, from the exposure to intense nationalism which their contemporaries experienced in Britain, France and Germany. The next oldest age-group (40–50 years of age in 1963) were at the most formative stage of their lives at a period of relative peace, and we can note a marked difference between them and their older compatriots in support for steps toward unification, except, of course, in the Netherlands. Lower down the age scales, there is little increase in 'Europeanness' amongst adults, with the Second World War constituting a further major nationalistic impact on the younger adults (21–39 years of age in 1963).

However, the youngest age-group (16–19 years of age in 1963) were born between 1944 and 1947 and have therefore gained their first political perceptions in a world where European collaboration seemed natural and right, and where extreme nationalism seemed archaic and dangerous. From this observation, Inglehart concludes that at least two elements are necessary for the establishment of a strong sense of being 'European'. First, there must be an absence of divisive memories. Secondly, there needs to be an awareness of positive participation in substantial common activities. Thus, the younger age-groups are more pro-European than their elder compatriots, but Britain, because she had not participated in the Community in 1963, possessed a relative lack of 'Europeanness' amongst her young people, compared to the young in the Six.

Inglehart is correct to stress the role of long-term trends in public opinion — his work parallels that of Butler and Stokes, who utilise the notion of age-cohorts in their study of long-term voting trends in British politics. [28] Central to the analysis of voting or opinion trends by the study of age-groups, or cohorts, is the notion of 'structural inertia' in concept formation. In simple terms, this means that once a person has formed a relatively detailed picture of his environment and is able to fit almost everything that he perceives into this framework, he is unlikely to change it to any great extent for the rest of his life. Since the young age-group studied by Inglehart will probably not dominate the positions of political power till the 1990s, at the earliest, it seems fair to assume that their Europeanism, although prone to a time-lag in its impact on the political system, will be increasingly important in the process of integration.

Cynics have argued that in later life today's young people will be less 'European', merely coming to reflect their parents' attitudes. But such cynicism is ill-founded — certainly Butler and Stokes effectively counter any suggestion that British voters, for example, come to vote Conservative rather than Labour as they grow older, and Inglehart is also able to refute any prophecies of 'senescent nationalism'. Feelings about Europe are matters of self-identification, which are not easily changed, particularly since these attitudes have been established at an early age. Nor can any sense of being 'European' be seen as a sign of teenage rebellion — we shall see later that the most prestigious social groups are very 'European' in outlook too. And, in his analysis of the Community-wide survey of September 1973, Inglehart is able to demonstrate that a sense of being European is not a product of age *per se*, but does in fact stem from a higher level of education and the relatively cosmopolitan sense of identity of the young people. [29]

The whole question of attitudes amongst the various age-groups in a population will be considered more fully in Chapter Nine. There we shall review the contradictory evidence from Denmark and Norway, and consider the implications for the future of the Community.

Conclusions

At least in its more simplistic form, the *fait accompli* thesis, a feature of deterministic integration theory, is incapable of providing a predictive insight into mass attitudes. But it does seem that Inglehart's study of the attitudes of the various age-cohorts in four European countries, in which he utilises the concept of 'cognitive mobilisation', shows that the operation of supranational institutions over a period of time can have some effect on the values of the younger age-groups. Also, with the growth of a strong affective component in the general support for unification – a growth seemingly generated by historical factors in Europe – a widespread popular support for European unity was created amongst the founder-members of the Community. This support was overwhelming amongst the young.

The neofunctionalists' attempts to formulate general, deterministic laws of integration have failed beacuse they failed to take into account the significance of special historical factors. Their omission reflects one of their domain assumptions, a commitment to European integration. Much neofunctionalist theory assumes that European integration is necessary and is good, *per se*. It follows that the public must inevitably come to support a goal which is unquestionably desirable. The evidence of public opinion from the new member-states of the Community appears to contradict *fait accompli* assumptions, although we are dependent on data which reflects less than two years' experience of membership. Nonetheless, it is clear that the levels of support accorded to integration by the publics of the Six were due to factors other than some automatic generation of mass support as a result of 'legitimacy' produced by the very existence of supranational institutions.

Throughout the Six, the creation of the Communities was linked in the public mind with the increases in economic growth and standards of living during the 1950s and 1960s; these were directly attributable to economic integration. In West Germany, the debate over entry to the ECSC had ceased to be a party political debate by the time of Kriesberg's survey, and with the two major parties expressing their support for integration, the public became less likely to express strong opposition. Moreover, in the 1950s, Adenauer was following a distinctly personal and largely popular foreign policy of allying West Germany quite clearly with the West, and West German commitment to European integration comprised a central plank in this ambition.

But, above all else, each of the Six had experienced the downfall of its national government in the course of the Second World War. This experience proved salutary, alerting the publics of Europe to the frailty of their national governments and political institutions. The lesson that was learned was that national political institutions were incapable of dealing

176

with certain crises, and therefore the publics of the Six were prepared to accept the legitimacy of newly created supranational institutions. The Danes and Norwegians also suffered the collapse of their national institutions, but both publics considered themselves Scandinavian rather than European and were thus more willing to accept some element of supranationalism independent from Europe. Furthermore, the Scandinavians considered joining the Communities only as a result of British initiatives — they felt there to be no choice but to follow Britain. We have already seen that the relative unwillingness of the British to join the Six stemmed from a lack of identity with Europe. But it is probable that the British have not become aware of the frailty of their national political institutions — not only did the British political system survive the war without experiencing collapse, but the British have enjoyed a unique continuity and stability of their political institutions for several centuries. The anti-Marketeers' emphasis on the loss of parliamentary supremacy is symptomatic of this unwillingness on the part of the British to transfer real legitimacy to supranational institutions. It is one of the supreme ironies of modern British politics that the self-styled defenders of parliamentary supremacy should press for a referendum on the issue of British membership of the Community.

Notes

[1] E.B. Haas, *The Uniting of Europe*, Stanford, 1958.

[2] For example, see K.W. Deutsch, 'Attaining and maintaining integration' in M. Hodges (ed.), *European Integration*, Penguin, 1972, pp. 108–23.

[3] L. Lindberg and S. Scheingold, *Europe's Would-be Polity*, Prentice-Hall, 1970; and E.B. Haas, 'The uniting of Europe and the uniting of Latin America' in *Journal of Common Market Studies* vol.5, no.4, 1967, pp. 315 and 327–8.

[4] K.W. Deutsch, 'Integration and arms control in the European political environment: a summary report' in *American Political Science Review* vol.60, no.2, 1966, pp. 354–65.

[5] R. Inglehart, 'An end to European integration', ibid., vol.61, no.1, 1967, pp. 91–105, and 'Public opinion and regional integration' in *International Organization,* 1970.

[6] D.J. Puchala, 'The Common Market and political federation in Western European public opinion' in *International Studies Quarterly* vol.14, 1970.

[7] Ibid., p. 34.

[8] Ibid.

[9] Ibid.

[10] J. Pinder, 'Positive integration and negative integration: some problems of economic union in the EEC' in M. Hodges, op.cit., 1973, pp. 124–50.

[11] Louis Kriesberg, 'German public opinion and the European Coal and Steel Community' in *Public Opinion Quarterly* vol.23, 1959.

[12] K.W. Deutsch, op.cit., 1966.

[13] D.J. Puchala, op.cit., 1970.

[14] Uwe Kitzinger, *Diplomacy and Persuasion: How Britain Joined the Common Market,* Thames and Hudson, 1973, pp. 352–70 and 411–21.

[15] Ibid., p. 362.

[16] Cited ibid.

[17] Ibid., p. 363.

[18] Ibid., p. 367.

[19] Ibid., p. 368.

[20] Ibid., p. 421.

[21] *Gallup Political Index*, no. 150, January 1973, and no. 153, April 1973.

[22] Ibid., no. 150, October 1973.

[23] Ibid., no. 163, February 1974.

[24] Ibid., no. 167, June 1974.

[25] R. Inglehart, *The 1973 European Community Public Opinion Surveys: Preliminary Findings,* University of Geneva and University of Michigan, May 1974, pp. 8–9.

[26] B. Hedges and R. Jowell, *Britain and the EEC: Report on a Survey of Attitudes towards the European Economic Community,* Social and Community Planning Research, 1971.

[27] In particular see R. Inglehart, op.cit., 1967.

[28] D.E. Butler and D. Stokes, *Political Change in Britain,* Pelican, 1971.

[29] R. Inglehart, op. cit., 1974.

8 Stability and Volatility

Proposition 5: Public opinion is 'moody' or unstable with respect to both desire for further integration and feelings of mutual sympathy and loyalty or identity.

Introductory discussion

A key notion in the development of public support for European integration is the extent to which mass attitudes and opinions are stable and reflective of some underlying sentiment, or are subject to great changes in short time intervals. Inglehart's evidence of the internalisation of attitudes favourable to integration by the young in Western Europe is significant because it appears to demonstrate the development of a long-term stability, attributable to changing political socialisation.[1] But it is arguable that large-scale setbacks in the process of integration, or even a lack, over a lengthy period, of progress toward further integration, could rob a particularly 'pro-European' age-cohort of its committed 'edge'.

We saw in Chapter One that the public's perception of the salience of issues and the strength of attitudes are important considerations in any analysis of public opinion. For historical reasons, and also because of their basic assumptions, the earlier neofunctionalists saw public opinion toward integration as characterised by apathy, and by the late 1960s Lindberg and Scheingold referred to the development of a 'permissive consensus'.[2] The argument that the public fails to perceive integration as salient, and lacks strong feelings on the issues involved, also seemed to gain credence from the British people's apparent lack of interest in the so-called 'Debate on Europe' in 1972.

Following Pentland's analysis, which we quoted in Chapter One, European integration seems to be an 'issue area' *sui generis,* possessing crucial features which distinguish it from the issue areas of domestic policy or foreign policy.[3] However, integration shares with foreign policy the likelihood that the public is relatively unaware of the complexity of all the issues, lacks information, and is influenced in its views, to a notable extent, by personality traits. These similarities are sufficient to give some attention to various studies of public opinion toward foreign policy. For instance, Gabriel Almond studied American opinion toward foreign policy between 1945 and 1950, and found large-scale shifts in mass attitudes over short periods (for example, 20 per cent to 30 per cent shifts occurred in three months on questions such as those relating to 'amount of satisfaction with the United Nations').[4] From his findings, Almond feared that because of the 'moody' nature of opinions on foreign policy issues, with people 'over-reacting' to changes in the contemporary political scene, policy-makers could be forced into untenable positions. Kelman, too, concluded that mass opinion on policy issues and perceptions of others is marked by a lack of structure and stability.[5] Yet V.O. Key Jr, in his study of American mass attitudes, admitted that the public did not possess a sophisticated understanding of complex foreign policy issues, but that on questions concerning the perception of the friendliness of other countries and policies supporting collaboration, stability rather than moodiness was the norm.[6]

Clearly, there are similarities between community policy and foreign policy as issue areas, and this must be kept in mind; but, in some important ways, integration also approximates domestic policy in the public eye. For example, the policies pursued by Community institutions are judged as domestic-type policies.[7] If the integrative process continues, this perception seems likely to become still stronger, since more policies formerly pursued at national level would be transferred to the Community – if the end-product of integration is to be a 'state-model' political system, then a larger domestic political system will have been created.

The most illuminating research on public perception of domestic policy issues is that presented by Butler and Stokes.[8] Amongst several other case-studies, they examined public opinion toward nationalisation, or public ownership, an issue which has been at the forefront of debate in domestic British politics since 1945, and an issue on which the two major parties have maintained comparatively clear and opposed views. Their findings were summarised in Chapter One: 'only 50 per cent were consistent in either supporting or opposing further nationalization over the three interviews', between 1963 and 1966.[9] Although the public may be better informed about domestic issues than foreign affairs, and although domestic issues are seen to be of more immediate salience than foreign policy issues, public opinion on domestic issues seems to be typified by a lack of detailed knowledge and constant shifts of individual opinions 'beneath the surface'.

Unfortunately, 'panel surveys' have scarcely been utilised in surveys of public opinion toward integration, but the opinion poll data which is available does enable us to test our fifth proposition effectively. First, some research has been undertaken on the consistency of opinions on European integration. Secondly, the use made of opinion poll data in this study is significantly different from attempts to predict election results from poll data. The British General Elections of 1970 and 1974, where most of the pollsters were unable to predict the result with precise accuracy, have shown that the polls' margins of error are too wide for effective predictions in a closely fought campaign. However, the concern here is not to forecast a 'winner' in an election, but merely to note the percentages of the public holding certain opinions on issues relating to integration and to observe any shifts in those opinions over time. If we note large majorities in favour of further integration, observing only a few minor shifts in those opinions over a lengthy time-span, then it would seem fair to conclude that there is clear and consistent public support for further integration. As Christopher Hewitt has argued, movements under the surface are far less significant if there have always been large majorities on one side or the other.[10] However, a large number of 'don't knows' in the polls, with large net shifts in public opinion over time, and contradictory responses, would seem to indicate that an issue is marked by an unstable and confused public opinion.

The evidence and its interpretation

Much of the evidence presented in the discussion of our first proposition appears to support the findings of V.O. Key, and therefore to reject our fifth proposition. An examination of the trends revealed in Figures 4.1 – 4.6 inclusive shows the relative stability both of mass support for unification and of mass feelings of mutual sympathy and loyalty in France and West Germany. If we compare Figures 4.7 and 7.1 with Figures 4.1 – 4.6, we can see that, until 1962, British public support for European unity ranked second to the level of support in West Germany and exceeded that in France. De Gaulle's veto was a blow to the British, but his second veto was seemingly 'the last straw'. Entry in 1973 has done little to dispel British opposition, pointing to British fears of the short-term effects and indicating that British support in earlier years, notably the 1950s, reflected a belief that European unity was good but that Britain would not be involved.

In Figures 4.1–4.6 we can see the dominant, favourable trends, distrubed only by certain major events. In the early 1950s, the establishment of the ECSC and the sense of a threat from without, which was strengthened by events in Korea, meant that support for unification increased. But in 1954 the French National Assembly rejected the EDC. Support for unification received a new boost from the Monnet-inspired *rélance,* which was consolidated by the Treaty of Rome and the rapid progress towards the Common Market by 1962. De Gaulle's veto of British entry in January 1963 caused the next fall in the levels of support.

Inglehart has analysed the impact of the French veto on the levels of support for unification amongst different age-groups of the Dutch, French and German publics.[11] Throughout the Six, he observed a decline, from 1962 to 1963, of slightly more than 6 per cent in the average level of support for the nine aims of European integration. Yet the percentages giving 'no answer' also increased by 8 per cent. Thus, the percentage expressing opposition to the nine aims actually decreased, despite the setback of De Gaulle's veto. Inglehart sees the increase in the percentage of 'no answer' responses as an emotional response to a discouraging event. He argues that during the talks on British entry more people became informed of the Communities, and, as the talks seemed to be going well, came to support integration. But with the veto these same people, who were the least stable adherents because of their short-lived conversion, reacted to the suddenly bleak outlook and became discouraged. Yet they did not express opposition to unification, and thereby were 'avoiding the psychic pain of acknowledging that they were "for" what appeared to be a losing cause'.[12]

Table 8.1

Levels of support for integration proposals (figures in percentages)

	February 1962	February 1963
Holland	78·5	73·0
West Germany	68·2	61·8
France	58·8	54·4

Source: Inglehart, op.cit., 1967, p. 98

Inglehart's hypothesis is strengthened by the fact that the countries with the publics most in favour of European unification lost the most supporters (see Figure 4.1 and Table 8.1). By reference to the evidence presented by Puchala, of public opinion in the Six between 1957 and 1962 (see Table 7.2), it would seem that the 'Europeanness' of these countries was increased by a significant proportion of relatively recent converts, and it was these countries which therefore suffered the largest falls in support for unification in 1963.[13] The French, however, were less 'European' to start with, and probably lacked such bandwagon support. This factor, combined with the fact that De Gaulle argued that British entry was incompatible with French and European interests, explains the relative stability of French support between 1962 and 1963.

Table 8.2

'Fall-out' from 1962 to 1963 by age-group,
four key measures (figures in percentages)

	Netherlands		France		West Germany	
	20–39	40+	20–39	40+	20–39	40+
Abolish tariff	−10	−14	−5	−15	−5	−11
Free movement, labour and business	+8	–	+9	−1	−2	−8
Common foreign policy	−13	−5	−8	−11	−13	−11
Aid poorer European regions	−10	−7	+8	−1	+2	−1
	−6·3	−6·5	+1	−7	−4·5	−7·8

Source: Inglehart, op.cit., 1967, p. 102

Table 8.1 confirms the trends evident in Figures 4.1 and 4.4. Table 8.2 serves to give further credibility to Inglehart's thesis by providing information on the ages of some of those who felt disillusioned in 1963. The West German public, who were strongly pro-European, portray a classic case of the bandwagon effect of successful economic integration generating widespread support. When a setback occurred, it was the older Germans, who were socialised in the days of intense nationalism, that were more likely to withdraw their support for unification. Table 8.2 also leads us to modify the conclusions we drew from Figures 4.1 and 4.4. It is clear from Inglehart's evidence that the older French, like the older Germans, were more susceptible to disillusionment with integration. But it is equally clear that the overall 'fall-out' rate amongst the French was reduced by a strong swing in favour of integration on the part of the younger age-groups. It is hard to explain this phenomenon — could it be that French youth suffered some form of 'lag' in their conversion to unification, or did the younger French feel reassured by de Gaulle's demonstration that France would not lose her voice by participating in Europe? The evidence from the Netherlands in Table 8.2 supports Inglehart's general thesis — the 'fall-out' of over 6 per cent of supporters of integration from a strongly pro-European public illustrates the extent of the bandwagon effect, while the lack of any marked difference between young and old vindicates Inglehart's emphasis on the significance of Dutch neutrality in the First World War.

Although the evidence from polls in the Six support our fifth proposition, the evidence from polls undertaken in three of the applicant-states of the early 1970s — Denmark, Norway and the United Kingdom — appears to refute any notion of stability. But it is at this point that the correct interpretation of the evidence demands that we note a crucial distinction between attitudes and opinions. We made this distinction in Chapter One, and for our present purposes it is sufficient to stress that, because of their very nature, attitudes are relatively stable and change only over long time-spans. On the other hand, opinions are more susceptible to short-term fluctuations. Furthermore, it is largely correct to conclude from the evidence presented in earlier chapters, that the affective and identitive components of support are more attitudinal in their origins, whereas the utilitarian and systemic components are more opinion-oriented. The distinctions between attitudes and opinions and between the various components of support are by no means exclusive or readily observable in practice, but they are useful aids for analysis.

Amongst the publics of the original Six, we have observed consistently positive affective, identitive and utilitarian support, and also signs that some systemic support is being generated. Such evidence is mainly supportive of our fifth proposition. But in Denmark, Norway and the United Kingdom, the evidence is not so clear-cut. In order to draw some useful conclusions from this somewhat confusing evidence, let us isolate several plausible ideal-typical situations which help to shed light on the nature of the publics' sentiments:

(1)   stable and positive affective and identitive components of support which reflect underlying favourable attitudes, together with stable and positive utilitarian and systemic components of support which reflect favourable opinions;
(2)   stable but negative affective and identitive components of support which reflect underlying unfavourable attitudes, together with stable and

negative utilitarian and systemic components of support which reflect unfavourable opinions;

(3) stable and positive affective and identitive components of support which reflect underlying favourable attitudes, but with unstable utilitarian and systemic components of support which may reflect favourable or unfavourable opinions at various points in time;

(4) stable but negative affective and identitive components of support which reflect underlying unfavourable attitudes, but with unstable utilitarian and systemic components of support which may reflect favourable or unfavourable opinions at various points in time;

(5) affective and identitive components of support which reflect conflicting attitudes, and unstable utilitarian and systemic components of support which may reflect favourable or unfavourable opinions at various points in time;

(6) affective and identitive components of support which reflect conflicting or contradictory attitudes, and stable utilitarian and systemic components of support, which may be (a) favourable or (b) unfavourable,

In view of the findings in Chapter Four, this last ideal-typical situation seems unlikely to be approximated in practice, although in the case of Franco-German relations the affective component of support has undergone gradual change while the identitive and utilitarian components have remained consistently positive.

In the case of the United Kingdom it seems that the public's instability and volatility on the issues of entry and membership were rooted in relatively stable, albeit contradictory, underlying attitudes. Looking at the attitudes, we observed in earlier chapters that the British have continued to possess relatively strong feelings of friendship and trust for other West European countries, together with a belief that Europe does possess a distinct identity. These attitudes helped to generate the support for European unification which was widespread in Britain in the 1950s, but which evaporated as the prospect of British entry became increasingly likely at various times in the 1960s. By the late 1960s, the British sense of not being part of the European identity, the existence of which was not questioned, was compounded by signs of a generally isolationist tendency is mass attitudes.

In Chapter One we referred to Nias's study of the correlation between personality types, underlying attitudes, and views on British entry to the Common Market; his findings certainly confirm the role of underlying attitudes in views on such an issue as integration. It is reasonable to conclude that the correlation between conservatism and opposition to integration is not confined to Britain, but it does seem that there are other factors in Britain which react with or reinforce any opposition to entry which stems from conservative attitudes. For example, in Chapter Seven we noted that the British public commonly expressed fears that entry would lead to domination. The inability to perceive that Britain may be a part of the European identity, and the unwillingness to transfer legitimacy to new institutions above those of the nation-state are also pertinent attitudinal features. In his commentary on the SPCR survey of the British public and the Common Market in 1971, Kitzinger writes,

> At an abstract level, while joining would 'force us to pull up our socks', it would also involve a threat to national identity — a serious matter in view of what the author called, 'complacent attitudes developed by being the head of a large empire': 'Thank God I'm British', 'We *do* feel unique, don't we' (acquiescent giggles from all), 'Our technicians and craftsmen are the best in the world', 'We've got more sense of humour'. Considerable sentimental ties with the Commonwealth also emerged: 'They're our family', 'We're of one blood'. (It should be noted that the Commonwealth was generally seen in the shape of the old White Dominions — very few mentions were made, even in the 2,030 interviews, of the sugar-exporting countries or of the developing countries in Asia and Africa.)[14]

Despite feelings of friendship and trust for other West European countries, the relatively stable underlying attitudes of the British have been incompatible with a commitment to participate in European unification. But it would be a misunderstanding of the significance of the evidence to conclude that such negative sentiments determined British opposition to entry. Had the experts given their wholehearted support to the European cause and had the public not feared the short-term effects of entry on prices in particular, then it is likely that a more stable and favourable public opinion on the subject of entry would have existed continuously from 1961, when Macmillan announced that Britain was applying for membership.

But the experts have been divided. Economists, politicians, and the media in general have presented conflicting arguments and facts to a public bewildered by the complexity of the issues involved. At the beginning of this chapter we quoted Christopher Hewitt's views on the indicators of volatility in public opinion. Two of these — large net shifts in opinions and contradictory responses — are certainly characteristic of the British on the European issue. The large net shifts are illustrated in Figure

4.7. The SPCR survey and the frequent opinion polls have revealed several basic contradictory responses. For example, Gallup found that a majority of the public in October 1972 expressed their opposition to British entry, but that a majority believed that in the long-term the British economy and standard of living would benefit from entry. [15] As we observed in the previous chapter, the major reason for opposition seems to have been the expected short-term effects on price-levels.

But the most striking feature of British opinions on entry remains that of deep bewilderment. Kitzinger writes of

> . . . . a feeling that this issue, while it would profoundly affect people's future, was out of their hands and could not really be put back there — any more than so much else of this modern trans-national technetronic world could be brought back into manageable packages under visible democratic control. It was this feeling to which Enoch Powell and Anthony Wedgwood Benn each in his way responded. [16]

Kitzinger would have been justified in pointing out that Powell and Benn have contributed to the confusion which they have proceeded to exploit. Powell was a member of Macmillan's Government which was committed to entry, and yet he did not speak out against entry until his departure from Heath's Shadow Cabinet in the late 1960s. Similarly, Benn was a member of Wilson's Government which applied for entry in 1967, and he accepted then that the decision on entry should not be put directly to the people in a referendum. He came to advocate a plebiscite only after Labour's electoral defeat of June 1970.

The experience of Britain provides evidence which partly questions our fifth proposition because the volatility of the public's opinions have been shown to conceal underlying stable (albeit negative) attitudes, which, in turn, have made it much harder for the British pro-Europeans to achieve the 'full-hearted consent' of the British public. The publics of the original Six, of course, appeared to refute any notion of inherent moodiness or volatility on issues related to integration by the long-term stability of their attitudes and opinions. But what can we learn from the evidence that has been presented on a public who rejected membership of the Community — the Norwegians?

At first glance the evidence from the Norwegian polls appears to refute our fifth proposition, but deeper analysis reveals that in several important ways the notion of stability of opinions and attitudes on the issue of integration is fallacious. [17] Unfortunately the Norwegian polls are infrequent over the years between the first major debate on the Common

Market issue in 1962 and the resumption of that debate towards the end of 1970. However, with regard to the question of entry, the polls conducted by two independent polling agencies from August 1971 to September 1973 provide a useful guide to the state of Norwegian public opinion before the referendum of September 1972 and also after the people's decision to stay out (see Figure 8.1).

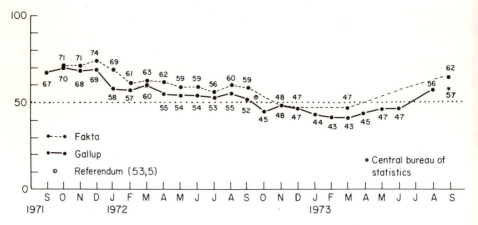

Fig. 8.1 Those intending to vote 'no' in a referendum on Norwegian entry into the Common Market, 1971–73

Source: O. Hellevik, N.P. Gleditsch and K. Ringdal, op. cit., University of Oslo, 1974, p. 3

The question asked has not been identical for the whole period, but has always referred to a dichotomous choice between yes and no to full membership in the EC. From May 1973 Gallup asked the respondents to choose between the trade agreement and full membership (the August poll was published by Scan Fact, an agency which cooperates with Gallup and for national surveys uses the interviewing organisation of Gallup). Fakta's September '73 survey had 'no relation' as a third response alternative in addition to membership and trade agreement: the 62 per cent 'no' divides into 56 choosing trade agreement and 6 no relation. The survey of the Central Bureau of Statistics asked whether the respondents would vote yes or no in a new referendum. For additional details on wording and results, see *Norsk opinion om EF: en tabellsamling* (International Peace Research Institute, Oslo, 1974), a relatively complete survey of all opinion polls on the EC issue from the 1950s.

From Figure 8.1 we can see that there was a shift of opinion shortly after the referendum, with a small majority coming to favour entry. But this small pro-Market majority was reversed to create, once more, a stance of opposition to entry by September 1973. The comparatively small size of the majorities seems to point to a general lack of volatility in contrast to the sudden and sizeable shifts of opinion experienced by the British. But, of course, this analysis is limited in its validity by its dependence on observations of trends on the 'surface' — we are in danger of drawing quite weighty conclusions from aggregate data.

Our caution is well-founded, since deeper analysis of Norwegian public opinion has revealed that our fifth proposition is supported by data from two sources. First, there is evidence of a sharp shift, which is observable in the aggregate data, but occurred before the regular polls on the Common Market issue began in 1971. Hellevik and Gleditsch quote earlier research, arguing that general interest in the Common Market issue

> .... seriously picked up only towards the end of 1970. At this point the 'Popular Movement against Norwegian membership in the EEC' (*Folkeberegelsen*) was formed. At the end of 1970 support for the membership alternative declined to about half its previous level. A majority could no longer be found even for continuing the negotiations. [18]

From this date, however, the public's responses in the polls indicate greater stability. But a panel survey conducted between November 1971 and July 1972 demonstrates 'that the total amount of individual changes was twice as large as the net change in aggregate opinion during this period'. [19] This panel study, with interviews in November 1971 and a mail questionnaire seven months later indicates that,

> While stable at the aggregate level, the 'against' group lost nearly a third of its members during this relatively short time span. But this was offset by gains from the two other groups. Contrary to the common impression, the 'no' group had recruited as many members from the undecided as had the 'yes' group' [see Table 8.3]. [20]

We noted in Chapter Five that the main reasons for Norwegian opposition to entry were the immediate and utilitarian fear of the effects on the primary sectors of the economy, and also the more deep-seated fear of domination, or loss of self-determination and independence. This latter fear is expressive of an underlying attitude amongst the Norwegian public which parallels a major cleavage in Norwegian politics between the centre and periphery. We shall say more about this cleavage in the

189

Table 8.3

Panel data on public opinion on the EEC in
November 1971 and July 1972 (figures in percentages)

Opinion in July 1972	Opinion in November 1971			Total
	For	Against	Undecided	
For	15	6	14	35
Against	1	30	14	45
Undecided	1	7	12	20
Total	17	43	40	100

One third of the November sample did not answer the mail questionnaire in July, with response rates 76 per cent for the 'yes' group, 65 per cent for the 'no's and 57 per cent for the 'undecided'. In the table the answers for the different groups are weighted so as to give the panel a distribution of November opinion equalling that of the entire sample. The data were collected by FAKTA for *Folkeberegelsen*

Source: Ottar Hellevik and Nils Petter Gleditsch, *The Common Market Decision in Norway: a Clash between Direct and Indirect Democracy*, International Peace Research Institute, Oslo, p. 3

following chapter. Although we lack any clear evidence, it is also plausible to argue that the Norwegians' affective and identitive ties are with Scandinavia first and Europe second.

The trend data in Denmark reflect attitudes and opinions amongst the public which appear to be similar to those present amongst the British and the Norwegians. [21] From April 1971 until the referendum in September 1972, Gallup found that between 52 per cent and 65 per cent of the people favoured entry. For economic and geographic reasons, the Danish case for entry appeared more convincing that the Norwegian or even the British case. But by May 1974, more Danes said that they would be 'relieved' (31 per cent) if the Common Market were scrapped than said they would be 'very sorry' (27 per cent) or even 'indifferent' (27 per cent). By this time, only 35 per cent felt the Common Market to be a 'good thing', whereas 31 per cent felt it to be 'bad' and 24 per cent 'neither good nor bad'. This shift in opinions since entry indicates precisely the situation observed in Britain and Norway — volatility and instability of opinions, with more stable but largely negative underlying attitudes towards integration.

By emphasising the distinction between attitudes and opinions we have been able to refute our fifth proposition even amongst those publics where 'moodiness' and instability seemed to be the most striking feature. In keeping with the general conclusions to Chapter Four, where we confirm our first proposition, it does seem that strong and positive affective and identitive sentiments are correlated with a desire for 'action' towards integration. But the evidence of this chapter illustrates that stable but negative affective and identitive sentiments amongst the public may well be correlated with unstable opinions on the Common Market issue, particularly when the political leadership of a country is itself divided.

These preliminary conclusions support the arguments advanced by Butler and Stokes, and, in order to probe a little deeper into our findings, we need to return to the concept of an issue's 'salience', which we discussed in Chapter One. Butler and Stokes develop this concept, which is central to the remainder of this chapter. [22] Basically, salience refers to the importance which people attach to an issue, and the relevance which they feel it has to their lives. In their description of the impact of issues on the people's voting behaviour at elections, Butler and Stokes argue,

> For an issue to have much impact in the whole electorate, the bond of issue to self must be formed in the minds of a substantial body of electors. Many issues have meaning only for tiny fractions of the electorate, but some are salient to much wider portions. The greater the proportion of people to whom an issue is salient and the subject of strong attitudes, the more powerful the impact it can have on the fortunes of the parties. [23]

We can draw two conclusions from this statement. First, what is the nature of the bond of the issue of European integration to self amongst the various publics? And, secondly, what proportion of people feel that European integration is salient, and for how many people is it the subject of strong attitudes?

At the outset of our reply, it is worthwhile to quote Kitzinger's review of the state of British public opinion during 1971 and 1972:

> Any study that focuses on a particular problem is liable to mislead as to the state of public opinion simply by the very fact of its focus. The first thing, therefore, to make clear is that outside certain circles of passionate or professional 'pros' and 'antis' and of politicians at

Westminster (and Labour politicians in particular, for whom the issue became politically and personally so much more critical than for most Conservatives) the country at large throughout this period had a great many other preoccupations. Prices were rising by 10 per cent during 1971, unemployment rose from 700,000 in January to 900,000 in October; there were industrial disputes, unrest in Northern Ireland, and a host of other problems on the public agenda. [24]

Community-wide polls confirm that Kitzinger's commentary is not confined only to the British. In 1963, Gallup International's survey of the Six revealed that amongst these seemingly committed publics there was little strong feeling or curiosity concerning the stages in the construction of Europe and that, although information about the Community was quite widely spread, it was of a superficial nature. [25] Subsequent polls in the Six have confirmed these conclusions, demonstrating that despite the seemingly strong public sympathy for the idea of Europe, a large section of the public does not question the judgement it has made and is only moderately interested in how matters develop from day to day.

A number of reasons have been advanced for the lack of interest in Europe, and the lack of a real understanding of the Community. In the last analysis, the most crucial factor is that the number of voters who state that they are interested in current political events is distinctly lower than that of those who express a preference for a party or for a political movement of some sort. It is a generally observed feature of political behaviour that for many people the basic political choice is choosing a party, and beyond this they are little interested in the course of current affairs (see Table 8.4). Certainly, for the vast majority of people on most issues, Butler and Stokes found that party preference was a much stronger influence on a person's views than was any notion of upholding with ideological consistency a position on some form of left—right political continuum. [26]

The most common measure of the degree of the public's information about the Community is the ability to name the member-states of the Six, or, since 1973, the Nine. In 1970, 36 per cent of the public of the Six named the member-states correctly, although 63 per cent of the Luxembourg public and 49 per cent of the Dutch were successful. Rabier makes a vital point for the interpretation of these figures:

These percentages may seem rather low; they are explained by the fact that many people add certain countries (for example, Switzerland) or forget one (for example, Luxembourg). In fact, the

Table 8.4

Political commitment and interest in Europe,
February–March 1962

	(1)	(2)	(3)
The Netherlands	95	54	45
West Germany	67	47	43
France	58	43	33
Belgium	58	30	30
Italy	63	33	29
Luxembourg	58	39	27

(1) Percentage who 'support a political party'
(2) Percentage who are 'strongly or moderately interested in politics'
(3) Percentage who 'think very often or often about European unity'

Source: Gallup International Survey in *Journal of Common Market Studies,* 1963, p.104

six countries are named on the average by more than half the people questioned: France and Germany by eight out of ten; Belgium, Italy, and the Netherlands by about seven out of ten; and Luxembourg by five out of ten. [27]

Taking the ability to name the member-states of the Community as a yardstick of the public's knowledge about the Community is very limited in its scope – it can only act as a rough and ready guide to superficial information. Equally, it would be meaningless to expect the publics to be as well informed on Community issues as the governmental and business elite whose major area for concern is integration. For our purposes, probably the best measure of public knowledge is subjective – in short, how well informed do the publics *themselves* feel on Community issues?

Community-wide polls which have probed the publics' feelings about the level of their information have revealed a widespread awareness of a lack of knowledge (see Table 8.5). In all Community countries only a little less than a third of those interviewed felt that they were sufficiently well informed on the problems dealt with by the Community, ranging from 40 per cent in West Germany to 22 per cent in Britain. In general,

Table 8.5

Assessment of degree of information on the main issues of the Community

	Belgium			France			Italy			Luxembourg			Netherlands			Germany			Denmark		Great Britain		Ireland	
	'71	'73	'74	'71	'73	'74	'71	'73	'74	'71	'73	'74	'71	'73	'74	'71	'73	'74	'73	'74	'73	'74	'73	'74
Sufficiently well informed	26	32	31	27	33	32	17	33	31	33	45	54	26	29	38	39	31	40	37	32	17	22	24	35
Not sufficiently well informed	56	43	48	63	52	53	77	53	51	51	37	37	61	53	35	55	54	42	55	44	76	70	71	56
No reply	18	25	21	10	15	15	6	14	18	16	18	9	13	18	27	6	15	18	8	24	7	8	5	9

The polls were conducted in July 1971, September 1973, and May 1974

In 1971 the heading read, 'Estiment qu'ils sont ou non suffisamment informés sur les problèmes concernant le Marché Commun.' The response wordings were 'Suffisamment informés' and 'Pas suffisamment informés'

In 1973 the heading read, 'Jugement porte sur le degré d'information en ce qui concerne les problèmes de la Communanté Européenne.' The response wordings were 'S'estiment: suffisamment bien informés/ pas suffisamment bien informés'

In 1974 the heading included the word 'importants', describing the sorts of issues which the interviewers had in mind

Source: Commission of the Communities, op.cit., Brussels 1971 and 1974

194

there does seem to have been an upward trend since 1971, but the essence of the conclusions reached from the poll of July that year still seems to apply. Even in the case of the Netherlands, where there seems to have been a marked improvement in the public's confidence in its own knowledge of Community issues, the Commission's conclusions remain plausible.

In 1971, the lack of sufficient information was felt particularly strongly in Belgium, France and the Netherlands. This appeared to present a contradictory situation in the Netherlands – the Dutch public was able to give positive replies to the more difficult questions, like the publics of Luxembourg and West Germany. Yet the publics of Belgium, France and Italy were less competent than the Dutch in answering the more difficult questions on specific Community issues – in the case of the Belgian, French and Italian publics, it seems that they were less informed than in the rest of the Six, and realised their relative ignorance. But in the Netherlands it seems that the public's level of information had reached a point which was leading them to demand even more knowledge. The fact that between 1971 and 1974 the Dutch became rapidly more satisfied with their awareness of Community issues seems to show that their demand for more information was met, at least to their general satisfaction.

It is also instructive that in May 1974 the publics were asked to identify the major problems which they had encountered in becoming informed on the important problems dealt with by the Community. In the interpretation of this data we face a great problem – we can take the percentage of 'no reply' responses as an indication of wide coverage of Community events in the media and also as a sign of interest on the part of the public in becoming informed, or these same figures may well indicate a lack of any effort whatsoever to become informed. The former interpretation seems largely correct, since the Dutch achieved the highest level of 'no reply' responses (68 per cent), closely followed by the Danes (66 per cent). Indeed, Britain and Ireland also exhibited fairly high 'no reply' percentages – 51 per cent and 52 per cent, respectively. Presumably, the new experience of membership is having some impact on the public's level of awareness. But the West Germans (54 per cent) exceeded the British and Irish levels of 'no reply' responses. The levels for the four remaining member-states confirm the observations of Table 8.5: Luxembourg, 46 per cent; Belgium 36 per cent; Italy, 34 per cent; and France 26 per cent. Indeed, these last four publics admit to being the most apathetic on issues dealt with by the Community, since the percentages stating that lack of time or interest prevents them from acquiring greater information are as follows: France and Italy, 28 per cent each; and Belgium and Luxembourg, 24 per cent each. In both Britain (13 per cent) and West Germany (14 per cent), there is some feeling that the media do not give European issues enough coverage, while in Britain (8 per cent) and Ireland (12 per cent), there is said to be a lack of 'objective' information.

With the Labour Party's commitment to a binding and final decision on British entry by the British people, the evidence of the level of information on Common Market issues and the interest of the public in these issues has become a live political issue in itself. As a basic measure of the perceived salience of the Common Market issue, Gallup's monthly question 'What would you say is the most urgent problem facing the country at the present time?' is a rough guide. The Common Market usually comes well down the public's list of national priorities, reaching second place only once, in June 1971, when the Conservative Government published the White Paper on entry (on this occasion it was mentioned by 19 per cent, with 'Prices, cost of living' mentioned by 41 per cent). But for most of the period since early 1971, prices, unemployment, Ireland, industrial unrest, and housing have taken a higher place in the public's reckoning of Britain's most urgent problem. [28]

Kitzinger discusses the evidence on public opinion on the question of an election or a referendum on British entry, and vividly illustrates some of the glaring inconsistencies. [29] First, a Gallup poll of February 1972 supports our conclusion earlier in this chapter that most people look to their parties for a lead on most issues. 48 per cent said that they would still vote for their party in an election on entry, whatever their views (41 per cent Conservative pro-Marketeers and 54 per cent Labour anti-Marketeers) with only 14 per cent (19 per cent Conservative anti-Marketeers and 13 per cent Labour pro-Marketeers) saying they would abandon their usual party allegiance. 22 per cent said they would not vote and 16 per cent did not know what they would do.

In February 1971, Harris found that 70 per cent said 'Yes' to a referendum when asked, 'Do you think we should have a national referendum to decide whether to join the Common Market or should the Government make the decision?' Only 17 per cent opposed a referendum. But in September 1971 NOP asked, 'Do you think the public as a whole has enough information on which to vote in a referendum on whether or not Britain should join the Common Market?', and only 17 per cent felt the public had enough information, as opposed to a massive 80 per cent who felt that they had not. Moreover, according to a Harris poll, the Labour Party's decision of early 1972 to campaign for a referendum led to a fall of 11 per cent between February and April in the percentage favouring a referendum. [30] This decline in support was almost totally due to the desertion from the referendum cause of 23 per cent of Tory voters who had previously advocated a direct say for the people. Curiously, the percentage of Labour voters advocating a referendum also fell, by a mere 1 per cent, but significantly the party's decision produced no immediate favourable reaction amongst its voters.

Conclusions

For the most part the evidence which we have examined in this chapter appears to refutes our fifth proposition, since it indicates the publics' general stability on the question of Europe. But a fuller inspection of the evidence reveals a number of exceptions to our general conclusion. These exceptions are explicable in terms of the distinction between attitudes and opinions and also by the varying nature of the debate over the idea of 'Europe' from nation to nation. Yet there are signs that even the publics of the Six, the original member-states, may come to experience more internal dissension on the subject of the Community and its problems than they have experienced to date.

We saw that in the Six the publics shared stable affective-identitive support for the European idea, whereas in the applicant-states the underlying attitudes were also stable but remained largely unfavourable to any participation in unification. Not surprisingly, the experiences of economic integration throughout the 1950s and 1960s have led to a favourable and stable climate of opinion within the Six. But opinions in Britain, Denmark and Norway reflect much greater uncertainty, rooted in unfavourable attitudes and encouraged by divisions over Europe amongst politicians and experts alike. The problems besetting the Community since its enlargement have nullified the predictions of the pro-European optimists and have appeared to vindicate all the warnings of the pessimists.

But our fifth proposition cannot be dismissed so easily. Any study of the levels of information of the publics throughout the Nine, and any analysis of the perceived salience of European issues, reveals that for most people Community affairs are still very remote from their day-to-day-lives. In the Six at least, acceptance of the Community is made possible by support for the European idea, and also by the lack of party political debate over the basic issue of belonging to the Common Market. But if the Community is to progress from negative integration to a more positive form of integration, to the closer economic and political union advocated in the Treaty of Rome, then clearly the Community issue-area must become more akin to a domestic issue-area. This would involve a necessarily greater public perception of the salience of Community issues. It is also quite likely that at some point the fundamental issue of political sovereignty would have to be faced.

In the applicant-states the question of joining the already-functioning Community brought into the political limelight some of the sorts of issues which the member-states may soon find themselves debating. If Pinder's prediction is correct, a failure to transform the Community along the lines of positive integration could create a situation where the negative integration achieved to date creates more problems than it has solved. Yet moves towards more positive integration will unleash new pressures and create new conflicts which could well lead to a growing dissensus on Europe amongst the publics of the Six. In its most acute form, conflict arising from positive integration could culminate in a crisis over political sovereignty. Despite strong affective-identitive and utilitarian-systemic support, the lack of clear affective-systemic or utilitarian-identitive support, and the apparent unwillingness to make personal sacrifices in the cause of European unification, could all be signs that if the question of sovereignty is raised too early, then a crisis could ensue, which could precipitate a collapse of the Community.

If we are to achieve a fuller understanding of the likely sources of support for or resistance to more positive integration, we must review the attitudes and opinions of the various groups within the national publics. We concentrate on this task in Chapter Nine.

Notes

[1] R. Inglehart, 'Trends and non-trends in the Western Alliance: a review', in *Journal of Conflict Resolution* vol. 12, no. 1, 1968.

[2] L. Lindberg and S. Scheingold, *Europe's Would-be Polity,* Prentice-Hall, 1970, pp. 38–45.

[3] C. Pentland, *International Theory and European Integration,* Faber and Faber, 1973, pp. 220–5.

[4] G. Almond, *The American People and Foreign Policy,* Praeger, 1960.

[5] H. Kelman, 'Societal, Attitudinal and Structural Factors in International Relations' in *Journal of Social Issues* vol. 2, 1953, pp. 42–56.

[6] V.O. Key Jr, *Public Opinion and American Democracy,* Knopf, 1961.

[7] C. Pentland, op.cit., 1973.

[8] D. Butler and D. Stokes, *Political Change in Britain,* Pelican, 1971, pp. 218–64.

[9] Ibid., p. 224.

[10] C. Hewitt, 'Policy-making in postwar Britain: a nation-level test of elitist and pluralist hypotheses' in *British Journal of Politics* vol. 4, part 2, 1974, pp. 187–216.

[11] R. Inglehart, op.cit., 1968, p. 102.

[12] Ibid., p. 98.

[13] Ibid.

[14] U. Kitzinger, *Diplomacy and Persuasion: How Britain Joined the Common Market,* Thames and Hudson, 1973, p. 359.

[15] *Gallup Political Index* no. 147.

[16] U. Kitzinger, op.cit., 1973, p. 353.

[17] O. Hellevik, N.P. Gleditsch and K. Ringdal, *The Common Market Issue in Norway: a Conflict between Center and Periphery,* University of Oslo, 1974.

[18] O. Hellevik and N.P. Gleditsch, *A Clash Between Direct and Indirect Democracy,* University of Oslo, 1973, p. 1.

[19] Ibid., p. 3

[20] Ibid., pp. 3–4.

[21] *Gallup Political Index* no. 147.

[22] D. Butler and D. Stokes, op.cit., 1971, pp. 230–9.

[23] Ibid., pp. 233–4.

[24] U. Kitzinger, op.cit., 1973, pp. 356–7.

[25] Gallup International, 'Public opinion and the European Community', edited and translated by M. Forsyth, in *Journal of Common Market Studies* vol. 2, no. 2, 1963, pp. 104–5.

[26] D. Butler and D. Stokes, op.cit., 1971, pp. 235–9.

[27] J.-R. Rabier, 'Europeans and the unification of Europe' in *Government and Opposition,* vol. 6, no. 4, 1970, p. 480.

[28] *Gallup Political Index* nos. 126–69.

[29] U. Kitzinger, op.cit., 1973, pp. 352–3 and 418–21.

[30] Cited ibid., pp. 419–21.

9 Support for Europe and Social Variables

Proposition 6: 'Class and party loyalty correlate closely with opinions toward European integration.

Introductory discussion

From our discussion in Chapter Eight, we can see that it is vital not only that the stability of public opinion be considered, but also that opinions amongst the various sections of the public be examined. Historically, certain groups of the population have expressed their opposition to integration and Community policy has been a subject of party political debate on several occasions in the member-states of the Community. Discussion and lobbying are, of course, natural processes in any political system, but the crucial question concerns the degree of any disagreements — are they conflicts over the means, while consensus exists on the ends, or is there a lack of consensus on the ends?

The neofunctionalists accept that conflict is central to any political system, but stress that while conflict is the essence of politics, consensus on ends, or values, is a requisite of any ongoing political system. Thus, Lindberg and Scheingold modify the earlier neofunctionalist thesis of the cumulative logic of integration, but their revision rests upon the existence of a 'permissive consensus' in favour of integration on the part of the public.[1]

Again, the distinction drawn by Pinder between negative and positive integration is particularly relevant to any discussion of consensus or dissensus for integration.[2] Pinder has shown that most of the major successes of the Community up to the late 1960s are examples of negative integration, although they all include at least some degree of positive integration. The customs union, the CAP, and cartel policy and the introduction of Value Added Tax all contribute to the removal of obstacles to free exchange between the states, although they also possess 'positive' potential. Only the successful negotiations in the Kennedy Round talks and successes through the Social Fund 'in enhancing the mobility of workers and the transferability of their security benefits throughout the Community' can clearly be seen as examples of positive integration, since common policy-making took place. But if common policy-making is to be achieved in the future, as the Community undertakes positive integration, clearly it is desirable that there should be a consensus that this more interventionist form of integration should take place.

Pinder's argument is that the Community must seek to pursue common policies, since the results of negative integration, unless they are followed quickly by positive integration, could be very damaging. The removal of obstacles to free exchange between the states had largely been achieved, but according to Pinder,

> Positive integration, particularly to solve the balance-of-payments problems of member countries now that their national economic defences have been removed, may be necessary to the success and even the survival of the Community. This may require (i) major common policies at Community level over a wide range of key subjects, including regional, social, monetary and fiscal policies with corresponding fiscal and loan-raising powers, and (ii) the co-ordination of the monetary, budgetary and incomes policies of the member states.[3]

Pinder concludes by posing two questions: 'Will the Community regain the political momentum and find the economic means to establish these essential elements of economic union?'; and 'Would Britain, if she became a member, contribute to or impede this process?'[4]

From these two questions and from the possible implications of positive integration listed by Pinder, we can see that any moves towards fuller economic union must raise ideological and philosophical questions concerning the purpose of economic policies, the extent of economic planning, the distribution of wealth, and so on. Of particular interest in view of Pinder's second question must be the opinions of various sections of the European publics. Despite the widely-spread benefits of economic growth, it is hard to see in what ways the results of negative integration could prove more attractive to the working classes and those who live in poorer regions than to the better-off groups.

Also, criticism of European integration has come most frequently from the more extreme Left, who have attacked the Community for its support of modern capitalism, and also from the traditional Right, who have been quick to recognise the threats which it poses for the nation-state. More recently, we have seen that there is evidence that opposition to integration is correlated with a high score on the 'conservatism scale' of attitudes. Bearing in mind that the working class are found to be more 'conservative' in their attitudes than the middle class, it seems that working-class support for integration is likely to be relatively weak and, therefore, that any 'push' by a working-class movement towards more positive integration seems unlikely, at least in the immediate future. The irony is that the sort of policies which would directly benefit the working class of the European Community can only be realised through positive integration, as the lone example of the Social Fund well demonstrates.

Our sixth proposition also leads to a consideration of the levels of information about the European Community. Again, it seems that, if our proposition is verified, there may be a 'vicious circle' (virtuous for any anti-Marketeer) which bars the growth of greater working-class support for integration. The point is that the Community may not seem salient to many people (and therefore their knowledge of it remains low) until it can provide them with the sort of benefits now provided by the nation-state, and, indeed, until it can mitigate the effects of problems which the nation-state is finding it increasingly hard to cope with. But without positive integration the Community is unable to intervene effectively, while its pluralistic format may well institutionalise negative integration, with possibly damaging effects. Thus, the image of the Community could become that of an unsuccessful effort to foster integration, unable to take the very actions which could generate support and facilitate further integration. It is no doubt for these reasons that the strategy of the European Movement and other 'pro-European' organisations has been primarily to increase the level of the public's information about the Community.

The evidence and its interpretation

Probably the most compelling demonstration of the correlation between class and opinions on European integration is to be found in the data presented by Puchala, on reactions to the Common Market amongst economic interest groups (see Table 9.1). Table 9.1 illustrates clearly the vital point that support for the Common Market has varied among different social groups. It must be noted that 'business' in Table 9.1 refers to small-scale businesses, such as shopkeepers, and that Table 9.2 is therefore far more helpful for a view of 'big business'. Both tables show clearly the consistently greater support integration receives from the business groups and upper-status groups.

Table 9.1

Reactions to the Common Market among economic
interest groups in France, Italy and West Germany, 1957–62
(figures in percentages)

Population	Year	Group	Approve	Disapprove	Don't know
France:	1957	Business	72	11	17
		Agriculture	52	14	34
		Labour	47	14	39
	1962	Business	83	6	11
		Agriculture	71	13	16
		Labour	68	12	20
West Germany	1957	Business	75	5	20
		Agriculture	77	7	16
		Labour	46	21	33
	1962	Business	86	8	6
		Agriculture	85	6	9
		Labour	63	19	18
Italy	1957	Business	73	3	24
		Agriculture	61	10	29
		Labour	54	6	40
	1962	Business	82	4	14
		Agriculture	74	3	23
		Labour	76	2	22

Source: Puchala, op.cit., 1970, pp. 54–5

Community-wide polls conducted since Puchala's findings confirm the
pattern that the most consistent support for the Common Market is to be
found amongst the relatively most privileged groups of society in the Six,
or the Nine. In 1962, Gallup International found that, in the Six, the
higher income groups, the industrialists and the professional classes, were
always amongst the groups in which there was the highest proportion of
people strongly in favour of European unity.[5] Conversely, groups in

Table 9.2

Reactions to the Common Market among 'upper status'
French, West German and Italian respondents, 1957–62
(figures in percentages)

Population	Year	Approve	Disapprove	Don't know
France	1957	73	15	12
	1962	90	6	4
West Germany	1957	84	19	7
	1962	91	5	4
Italy	1957	86	4	10
	1962	97	—	3

Source: Puchala, op.cit., 1970, p.39

which there was found to be the highest proportion of people strongly against European unity ranged from low income groups (8 per cent mentioned this in Belgium), to the farmers (11 per cent in West Germany), the supporters of the Left (20 per cent in France), and the 'non-political' (14 per cent in the Netherlands).

The pattern of the distribution of support for Europe amongst the social groups that the Gallup International Survey revealed in 1962 had been a marked feature of opinions on integration ever since the Schuman Plan was put into effect. In Chapter Five we saw that Kriesberg was able to establish some correlation between concern about household coal and evaluations of the ECSC in West Germany.[6] He subjected this finding to further analysis, and found that for those people who felt Germany had fared badly in the ECSC level of income was a determinant factor. In Table 9.3 we can see that at the lower income levels, those who bothered with household coal were more likely to say that it was a mistake to have joined the ECSC than those who did not bother with coal. At the higher income levels, even those who bothered with coal tended to say that joining the ECSC was not a mistake. Presumably, for those on lower incomes, the expense and inconvenience of the coal supplies led them to be more likely to reject the ECSC, because of a relatively greater sense of deprivation than that suffered by those on higher incomes.

Research on French opinion in the 1950s fully confirms Kriesberg's

Table 9.3

Evaluation of the ECSC in West Germany
by concern about household coal by income level
(figures in percentages)

DM per month	Who gets coal	Evaluation of ECSC				
		(1) Good	(2) Mildly favourable	(3) Bad, not anti	(4) Bad, anti	(5) Undecided
249 or less	Others	24	29	10	14	24
	Respondent	24	21	11	29	16
250–399	Others	25	32	13	9	20
	Respondent	17	26	18	18	20
400–599	Others	21	20	11	27	21
	Respondent	16	35	17	15	16
600 or over	Others	32	37	5	13	13
	Respondent	18	36	20	17	9

Source: Kriesberg, op.cit., 1959, p. 39

thesis. Not only were the industrialists and the members of the liberal professions far more likely to express support for Franco-German *rapprochement* shortly before the defeat of the EDC, but the upper income bracket have also given consistently greater support to the ECSC and all plans for further integration.[7]

In view of the differing levels of support for integration among different social groups within the Six, it is hardly surprising that differing levels of support also appear to be correlated with party identification, Again, Puchala has undertaken a comparison of the reactions to the Common Market among ideological predisposition groups in France, West Germany and Italy between 1957 and 1962 (see Table 9.4). Integration had ceased to be an issue in the party political debate in West Germany by the mid-1950s, but we can see that Communist opposition to the EEC in France and Italy still exerted the strongest influence on opinions in those countries. Also, in France and Italy, the 'Right' seem rather less favourable to the EEC than the Centre, but this is a relatively marginal difference and seems adequately explicable by reference to the typical values of the Right — nationalism and conservatism. On both counts, the EEC is unlikely to prove as attractive to the Right as it can to the more outward-looking and innovatory Centre. It is also worth stressing that in France and Italy the Socialist parties are unambiguously 'European' — indeed, the only occasion in France when working-class support and the support of the Left for unification has exceeded that of the upper-middle-class and 'Right' voters was when Guy Mollet's Socialist Government of 1956 gave integration legitimacy for the less privileged and more radical sections of the French population. In West Germany today, the Social Democrats have claimed the role of the most 'European' party.

The value of data for the Six, which demonstrates some differences among their publics on the Common Market issue along class and party lines, is that it refutes any notion of an overwhelming and inevitable consensus for integration in the most overtly pro-European countries. That some opposition, or at least mild scepticism, exists in the Six on the issue of unification is itself a crucial point, but that this opposition or scepticism is concentrated within particular social groups and also varies in strength by party preference could become of vital significance in the future development of Europe.

In view of the analyses presented by neofunctionalists, the extent of the variation of opinions within the Six may surprise some readers. But far less surprising is the existence of widely differing opinions on class and party lines within the applicant-states, particularly Britain, Denmark and Norway, where opinions on the Common Market have been divided since the issue of entry was first thrust into the political arena. Kitzinger's survey of the evidence from the British polls confirms the major findings of Gallup over the past decade or so.[8] The groups most in favour of British entry are the men, the young, the upper-middle and better-off class, the inhabitants of the South and the Midlands, and the conservative voters.

Kitzinger found the difference in opinions on Europe by sex to be significant in Britain. Only in May 1972 did there appear to be a majority of women in favour of entry. There seem to be plausible reasons for such consistent opposition amongst British women. Firstly, the effect of entry on prices has been a central feature of the debate in Britain, and it is likely to be the women who would experience the most immediate impact from rising prices. Secondly, many students of political behaviour have noted the predominance of 'conservative' values amongst women. Several theories have been advanced to explain the phenomenon of female conservatism, but with women's role in society undergoing rapid change

Table 9.4

Reactions to the EEC among ideologically predisposed groups in France, West Germany and Italy, 1957–62
(figures in percentages)

	Year	'Ideology'	Approve	Disapprove	Don't know
France	1956	Right	67	10	23
		Centre	67	10	23
		Christian Democrat	75	7	18
		Left	76	10	14
		Communist	32	47	21
	1962	Right	89	2	9
		Centre	94	–	6
		Christian Democrat	82	7	11
		Left	79	14	7
		Communist	51	42	7
West Germany	1957	Centre	78	10	12
		Christian Democrat	75	7	18
		Left	77	8	15
	1962	Centre	84	9	7
		Christian Democrat	88	4	8
		Left	92	4	4
Italy	1957	Right	70	10	20
		Centre	88	–	12
		Christian Democrat	68	1	32
		Left	61	9	30
		Communist	32	27	41
	1962	Right	87	–	13
		Centre	94	3	3
		Christian Democrat	80	1	19
		Left	83	5	12
		Communist	51	13	36

Table 9.4 continued

Basis of figures:

1957, France

Right	—	Independents
Centre	—	Radical Party
Christian		
Democrat	—	MRP
Left	—	Socialist Party

1962, France
As above, except Gaullists were added to 'Right' and PSU added to 'Left'

1957 and 1962, West Germany

Centre	—	Free Democratic Party
Christian		
Democrat	—	CDU/CSU
Left	—	Social Democratic Party

1957 and 1962, Italy

Right	—	Monarchists and Neo-Fascists
Centre	—	Centre Party, Republicans, Independents
Left	—	Social Democrats and Socialist Party

Source: Puchala, op.cit., 1970, pp. 52–3

there are grounds for expecting many women's attitudes to become less conservative. We shall return to the question of value-systems later in this chapter, but it is worth stressing that Butler and Stokes and also Nias have found a correlation between an anti-Market stance and high scores on an index of conservatism.[9]

Age also appears to be a significant variable in British views on Europe, but Kitzinger does not fully accept the theories of Inglehart which were reviewed in Chapter Seven.[10] Indeed, a poll of Britain commissioned by the Community in 1972 confirms the findings of the British polls in 1971 — it is the 25–45 year olds who are the most pro-European in Britain, with the 15–25 age-group usually being the 'runners-up'. If Inglehart's theory of 'cognitive mobilisation' was sound, we could reasonably expect the youngest age-group to be the most pro-European. Also Kitzinger does not ascribe the large proportion of anti-Marketeers among the over-64s to their experience of nationalistic socialisation alone. Other perfectly rational explanations undoubtedly do lie in their fears of radical change and fears of higher prices (many old-age pensioners are, after all, very poor). Nor can the elderly take much solace from the expected long-term benefits of British entry, because of their shorter biological reach. Again, we shall return to the whole question of 'cognitive mobilisation' later in this chapter.

In Britain it is the analysis of opinions by class, region and party which is particularly fascinating since it is within certain groups which are observable by these variables that some significant shifts in opinion have occurred. In May 1971, a small majority of the upper and middle professional class (ABs) opposed entry, but by late July there was a 22 per cent majority in favour of entry within this group. The lower-middle-class grouping (C1) of clerical, administrative, civil-service and supervisory grades began to move in favour a fortnight after the more highly ranked ABs. The upper working class (C2) 'seem to have started shifting in the same direction as the C1s some ten days later'.[11] Finally, the DE grouping of manual workers shifted dramatically towards a pro-European stance just two months after the ABs, taking only two weeks to move from a 53 per cent majority against entry to an 'anti-' majority of only 10 per cent. But Kitzinger concludes, 'Nevertheless, in every single reading throughout the chart as one went down the social scale, one always found less support for entry and almost always a greater percentage in opposition to it.'[12]

Indeed, this conclusion tallies with probably the most sobering evidence ever to be collected by the pollsters as regards the Common Market (see Table 9.5). Kitzinger writes:

> In a way the most disturbing table of all is the one showing the very definite profile in the popular view of the sort of people who would benefit, and the sort who would suffer if Britain were to join the Common Market. If the campaign for entry had set out to persuade the country of the benefits, it certainly did not seem to have brought home personal benefits to the bulk of individual voters. Even if the very harsh class differentiation of the summer seemed to be softening a little in the autumn, the issue remained one on which Britain seemed (as on so much else) divided into two nations.[13]

Regional differences were also apparent in the levels of support for entry. In early summer 1971, the Scots appeared to be the most strongly anti-Market group, but two large-scale shifts occurred in July and late August–early September, with the result that the 'antis' fell from 81 per cent to 50 per cent, while the percentage in favour increased from 14 to 43 per cent. The North remained the most 'anti-' region of England, and

Table 9.5

British views on beneficiaries and victims of entry,
Gallup 1971 (figures in percentages)

	Benefit			Suffer		
	August	September	October	August	September	October
Manufacturers, exporters	36	29	29	2	1	1
Financiers, bankers, commerce	26	27	24	1	–	–
Well-to-do people, upper class	13	19	19	1	1	–
Professional people	13	10	9	1	–	1
Working people	8	8	8	39	35	31
Housewives	2	2	2	31	27	28
Old-age pensioners			2			33
Farmers	8	6	7	22	19	15
Fishermen	1	1	1	22	14	13
Others	9	10	8	17	21	14
Nobody	6	4	7	8	8	8
Don't know	18	14	18	12	9	12

Source: Kitzinger, op.cit., 1973, p. 370

opposition was also stronger in the West and Wales than along the more prosperous London–Birmingham axis. But our data for the regions is limited in its value, since the pollsters only achieve a representative sample nationally, with the result that their regional samples may well be unrepresentative.[14]

But it is party identification which is the most interesting and by far the most complex variable for any student of British public opinion on the Common Market issue. Fortunately, Gallup have for many years charted the fluctuating opinions of the voters on the European issue at fairly frequent intervals (see Tables 9.6(a) and 9.6(b)). In Table 9.6(a), we can see that, as British entry into the EEC became more closely identified with a Labour government's policy, so Conservative and Liberal supporters, who were once the keenest advocates of British membership, became increasingly hostile to the idea of entry. It seems significant that the highpoint of British support for entry was in March 1965, when the Common Market was not an item of party political debate and the problems which Britain would face on entry were not being brought to the public's notice by an active opposition.

We quoted Kitzinger's analysis extensively in Chapter Seven, and certainly Table 9.6(b) appears to show that the Labour Party's increasingly anti-Market stance followed a shift which had already taken place amongst their voters. Certainly, at the 1970 election, Labour had not adopted an anti-Market posture, and therefore it does seem that Labour's shift to a more anti-European policy reflected a groundswell of

Table 9.6

Attitudes towards entry of the EEC by political party
(figures in percentages)

(a)   'If an opportunity occurs for Britain to join the Common Market, would you like to see us try or drop the idea altogether?'

	January 1964	March 1965	September 1969
Conservatives			
Try to join	36	59	21
Drop idea	45	23	65
Don't know	19	18	14
Labour			
Try to join	34	58	34
Drop idea	38	22	47
Don't know	28	20	19
Liberals			
Try to join	45	57	31
Drop idea	38	22	62
Don't know	17	21	7

Source: *Gallup Political Index* nos 61 and 114

Table 9.6

(b) *'On the facts as you know them, are you for or against Britain joining the Common Market?'*

	Early July 1971	October 1972
Conservatives		
For	41	64
Against	40	22
Don't know	19	14
Labour		
For	15	22
Against	68	55
Don't know	17	23
Liberals		
For	25	
Against	56	
Don't know	19	

Source: *Gallup Political Index* nos 132 and 147

opposition amongst its supporters. Moreover, the shift of Labour voters to a position where the anti-Market majority was cut seems to reflect independence of mind on the part of many British electors. But the foregoing analysis overlooks the increase in opposition to entry that occurred among the supporters of the major Opposition party in the mid-1960s. The Tories had spoken of their pro-Market intentions during the 1970 election campaign and during the year preceding the publication of the July 1971 White Paper on entry. Similarly, a growing and an increasingly vociferous element within the Labour Movement had been outlining its case against British entry from the 1960s, and began planning for the adoption of an anti-Market policy by the major Opposition party on Labour's electoral defeat in 1970. Is it not likely, therefore, that the people were indeed following political cues before July 1971? The Tories' White Paper did serve to rally their forces dramatically, even making some impact on Labour voters, but Labour voters had previously moved to an anti-Market position apparently as a result of a natural opposition to any decisions made by a Conservative government and also as a consequence of the newly acquired respectability of being anti-Market within the Labour Party, a view that was being legitimised by many Labour politicians, including, most notably, Douglas Jay, Michael Foot, Peter Shore and Tony Benn.

Further support for our modification of Kitzinger's analysis comes from a recognition of the changes that have occurred in the content of the political debate in Britain since the mid-1960s. For the period 1963–66, the panel survey conducted by Butler and Stokes showed that entering Europe was more usually associated with views typically held by the Left – the toleration of immigration, the renunciation of nuclear weapons, and the view that the unions were not too powerful being good examples of other 'Leftist' views.[15] Equally, one could argue that opposition to entry would appear to be more natural to those who held views associated with the Right.

In 1963, Gaitskell had been opposed to entry and Macmillan in favour, thus reversing the seemingly more natural situation of the Left favouring entry with the Right opposing. It may be that this juxtaposition of the party's policies helps to explain some of the ambivalence evident in the opinions of the parties' supporters in the 1960s. But, in the 1970s, the significance of party preferences seemed to become much more marked. It seems plausible to argue that Labour has found it far easier than in the 1960s to link opposition to entry with its Leftist philosophy of the 1970s, which put great emphasis on the right of the individual to have a say in his destiny. By this philosophy, the ballot-box at General Elections is no longer sufficient in a modern democracy – people must have a say in the affairs of their workplace, and also the people must be allowed to decide directly on British membership of the Community. When it is also remembered that Labour voters are predominantly working-class, and that the working class tend to achieve high ratings on any index of 'conservatism', then the logical consistency of British-Leftist opposition to the Community becomes even more evident. Thus, we can see that a party which is heavily dependent on support from a section of the population which tends toward 'conservatism' has been able to adopt an anti-Market stance free from serious internal inconsistencies. It has done so largely by emphasising the threat which integration is often seen to pose for self-determination and for the living standards of the working population.

The traditional twentieth-century cleavage of class and party in British politics thus seems crucially relevant to opinions on the Common Market, and this imposition of a traditional, national political cleavage upon the Common Market debate is also vividly manifested in Norway. In their study *The Common Market Issue in Norway: a Conflict between Center and Periphery*, Hellevik, Gleditsch and Ringdal make the following observation:[16]

> Cross-tabulating against the standard social background variables used in opinion polls we find a pattern of stable and in some cases quite sizeable differences in the level of support for Norwegian membership of the EC. Starting with the variables showing the greatest differences in opinion, we find that:
>
> — those living in *central* parts of the country more often support membership than those living in the geographical *periphery,*
> — those living in *towns* more often than those living in the *countryside,*
> — those with a *high family income* more often than those with *low income,*
> — those with *high education* more often than those with *low education,*
> — those working in *the tertiary or secondary sector* of the economy more often than those in the *primary sector,*
> — those with a *high occupational position* more often than those with a *low occupational position,*
> — *men* more often than *women,*
> — the *middle-aged* more often than the *young* and *old.*[17]

In common with the findings for the rest of Europe and Britain, it is in the categories which are least rewarded socially and have least prestige that the percentage levels against unification are highest.

Some people are high status on almost all counts — income, occupation, education, residence, age and sex — while other may be low status on all counts; and, indeed, others may be high status on some counts and low status on others. Galtung developed a simple cumulative index of the total social rank of an individual, with the score on the 'social position index' (SP index) indicating the number of high status on the rank variables listed above.[18] Hellevik *et alia* elucidate:

> The index spans great differences in social position. At the low extreme (the social periphery) we would find for instance a female old-age pensioner in the rural parts of Northern Norway with just primary education. A lawyer in his forties living in Oslo with an income above the median would be situated at the other extreme

(the centre of society).[19]

In Figure 9.1 we can see that these differences in social situation coincide with clear variations in opinions towards the EEC. Hellevik *et alia* conclude, 'An overwhelming majority in the periphery was against joining the EC, while the majority in the centre was almost as large in favour of joining.'[20]

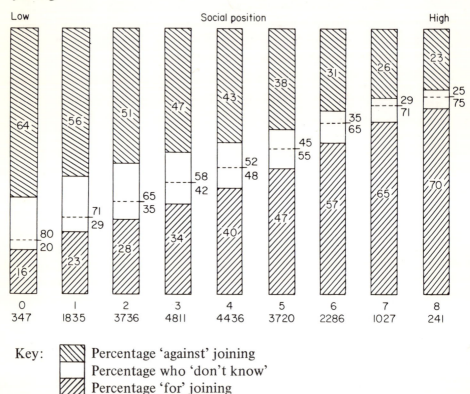

Key:

◢◣ Percentage 'against' joining
☐ Percentage who 'don't know'
▨ Percentage 'for' joining
---- Percentage $\frac{against}{for}$ joining, of those who took a position

Fig. 9.1 Social position and opinion on the European Community in Norway, 1972. The figures under the bars represent the number of cases in each SP category

Sources: O. Hellevik, N.P. Gleditsch and K. Ringdal: University of Oslo, 1974, p. 7; polls of Fakta and Gallup, May–December 1972. Total number of respondents: 22,466, divided into 44 per cent against, 17 uncertain and 39 in favour of joining, 53/47 against/for with DKs excluded

216

Using the Social Position Index, Hellevik *et alia* are able to present a refined analysis which illustrates the effect of each variable on EC opinion. This shows that the variables of education, income, occupational position and occupational sector all possess a large contributory element from the other variables in creating any effect on EC opinion. Age and sex turn out to have an unchanged, although low, impact. But by far the most significant variables, which are highlighted clearly by means of this refined analysis, are those of geographical residence (e.g. Oslo or the North) and ecological residence (e.g. urban municipality or rural municipality). Furthermore, education appears to have the same moderate effect, whatever the social position. But residence and sex appear to have most impact in the 'periphery', while income, occupational position, occupational sector and age appear to become more significant variables in the 'centre'.

Having shown quite conclusively that 'In Norway the EC issue was a centre-periphery conflict', Hellevik *et alia* then examine the impact of the varying opinions held by social position on the political system. They argue that,

> One of the best documented findings in political behaviour research is the tendency of low-status groups to participate less in political affairs. This tendency has been documented for Norway as for many other countries. Several studies have made use of the index of social position and found centrality to be associated with electoral participation, organization membership, media consumption, knowledge and opinion formation, etc.[21]

In Table 9.7 we can see the findings of Ringdal's analysis of the relationship between social position and knowledge of, interest in, and opinion of the EEC issue. It is immediately clear that the periphery is less interested in the EEC issue, knows less about the EEC and has less access to some important channels of information. Also, the periphery has less confidence in its knowledge on issues. The political consequences of these findings are that members of the social periphery are less frequently elected as representatives in any system of indirect democracy, and also the periphery is at a relative disadvantage with regard to possible access to and influence on their representatives. Indeed, the higher the level in a representative hierarchy, the scarcer the periphery element. Studies on recruitment to the Norwegian Storting and the British Parliament and Cabinet confirm this general hypothesis.

Hellevik *et alia* summarise the bias towards the centre in a representative democracy: 'There is a slight overrepresentation of the social centre

Table 9.7

Social position and interest, knowledge and opinion-holding with regard to the EEC issue in Norway (figures in percentages)

	Social Position								
	Low 0	1	2	3	4	5	6	7	High 8
(a)	7	14	16	19	21	24	48	49	70
(b)	40	42	46	49	52	68	76	89	96
(c)	37	49	51	58	67	76	84	93	92
(d)	79	76	82	87	91	95	97	100	
(e)	21	28	29	34	39	43	56	71	
(f)	21	30	35	34	35	39	40	60	59
(g)	66	63	65	67	67	70	73	85	76
(h)	55	67	68	67	68	74	76	72	86
(j)	77	76	77	77	79	82	86	89	92
(k)	89	83	83	87	89	90	93	95	94

(a) 'Is very interested in the EEC issue' (Fakta, October 1971)

(b) 'Can name four or more countries of the six member countries' (Gallup, August 1972)

(c) 'Has heard of the government information pamphlets' (Fakta, August 1971)

(d) Has heard of the People's Movement (anti-EEC)' (Fakta, August 1971)

(e) 'Has heard of the European Movement (pro-EEC)' (Fakta, August 1971)

(f) 'Feels competent to take a stand on the EEC issue' (Gallup, September–December 1971)

(g) 'Takes a stand on the EEC issue' (Gallup and Fakta surveys, September–December 1971)

(h), (j), (k) As (g), but referring to January–April 1972, May–September 1972, and September–December 1972, respectively.

among those who vote compared to those entitled to vote, a strong overrepresentation among those nominated and an even stronger one among those elected.'[22] And once elected, the representative's contact with the periphery become even less frequent – he mixes with other representatives, civil servants and journalists daily, but has to make a very great effort to maintain contacts with the periphery. Hellevik *et alia* calculate the effects of this gap between voters and representatives – of the 23 per cent more representatives in favour of entry than voters in the referendum, approximately 15 per cent of the gap appears to be the result of the different composition by the centre-periphery factor.[23]

The conclusions reached by Hellevik *et alia* lead them to question Inglehart's concept of 'cognitive mobilisation'. Hellevik *et alia* do emphasise their lack of data, which prevents them from undertaking a detailed analysis, but they present enough evidence to question the usual explanation offered on the social variations in opinion at the voter level, which maintains that, 'A favourable attitude to supranational integration is seen as dependent on information about and familiarity with the new political system, on the "ability to cope with remote roles and situations".' However, Hellevik *et alia* found that when they examined the impact of the social position variable and the information variable on opinions on the EEC issue, the former had the greater impact. Moreover, Hellevik *et alia* found that, 'If instead of actual knowledge about the EC we look at the subjective feeling among the respondents of being sufficiently informed on the EC issue to take a position, we find no difference in EC opinion between those who feel competent and those who do not.'[24]

Indeed, these conclusions could equally well be applied to Denmark and Britain. Again, a flaw has been revealed in neofunctionalist theory, since the proposition that technical information can in some way transcend social and political cleavages is disproved. 'Cognitive mobilisation' had credibility when it applied to countries where the issue of European integration did not coincide with basic conflicts, but in Britain, Denmark and Norway no such harmony of interests can be perceived and the various antagonists in the respective internal conflicts of these countries suspected the motives of those parties seeking membership.

It is here that the image of the European Community becomes directly relevant, for the social periphery of Britain, Denmark and Norway have all expressed one common fear – a loss of autonomy. Such a fear is quite realistic – how could the section of any nation-state's population which senses a lack of real influence in the national political system possibly hope to prevent a still further decrease of its influence in a supranational organisation? The present structure of the Community, reflecting the neofunctionalist logic of a technocracy guiding the people to their new destiny in a fully integrated system, scarcely helps to nullify the fears of groups who already have the most restricted access to their respective political systems.

Much research on public opinion and European integration has shown education to be a key factor in determining a person's support for further integration. By the use of multivariate analysis of the Community-wide poll of September 1973, Inglehart shows the level of education to be an even more significant determinant of 'Europeanness' than occupation or income. [25] Although education is a reflection of social class differences, it seems that education has an even stronger impact than this would lead us to expect. Inglehart again refers to the cognitive impact of education when he argues that '. . . those who are more educated are more likely to discuss politics, read political news, and are substantially better informed about European events than the less educated. In the current European context, this process seems conducive to the development of support for European integration.' [26] In so far as this statement reflects the assumptions underlying the concept of 'cognitive mobilisation', we have seen that it is based on the experience of the Six and that it may not be applicable as an explanatory theory in countries where the Community debate has reflected internal rifts within society.

Inglehart also suggests that,

> The development of support for European integration also seems linked with a process of intergenerational value change. . . . Briefly, this process seems to lead to the development of a less parochial, more cosmopolitan sense of identity. The younger generation throughout Western Europe (and the United States) is markedly more likely to feel they belong to such geographical units as 'Europe' or 'the Western World' than are older age groups. [27]

But Inglehart continues by pointing out that whether or not such a general cosmopolitan sense of identity is transformed into support for supranational European integration largely seems to depend 'on the institutions present in a given country, and the political parties in particular'. Indeed, with the use of multivariate analysis, Inglehart is able to support our conclusions on the very significant role of parties in opinion formation in Britain and also in Denmark, stating that,

> Membership in the European Community has been a matter of heated partisan debate in both countries, and sharp cleavages exist among the respective electorates. In relative support for European political union, there is more difference between a Conservative and Labourite in Britain than between a Communist and a Christian Democrat in Italy. Political party differences are greater still in

Denmark, where 40 to 50 per cent of the Liberals, Radicals and Conservatives support European union — as compared with 23 per cent of the Social Democrats and a bare 12 per cent of the Socialist People's Party. [28]

The spread of a more cosmopolitan orientation among the young age-groups is part of a much broader process of intergenerational value change. Among the older age groups, a 'materialist' set of values tends to be predominant, placing top priority on economic growth, combating inflation and crime, and maintaining order. But the younger age-groups are more likely to reflect a 'post-materialist' set of values, which emphasises the need for belonging, self-expression and intellectual and aesthetic goals. Inglehart states that, according to his research, 'The materialist type predominates among the oldest cohorts by a ratio of about ten to one; among those born since 1945, post-materialists are almost as numerous as materialists.'[29] It is the post-materialist types who are more likely to have a cosmopolitan orientation, identifying with political units larger than the nation-state. Again, Inglehart is wary of presenting any hasty conclusions, for he states that 'the relationship is a complex one, conditioned by the political context of the respective countries'. [30]

Indeed, there are two further grounds for advocating caution in developing any predictive theory on the course of integration which is based on the spread of post-materialist values. First, the rationale of European integration since its inception with the Schuman Plan has rested on aspirations of an openly materialist type — economic growth, higher standards of living, the elimination of barriers to trade, and so on. Indeed, in Chapters Five and Six, we established that much of the support for integration in the Six was utilitarian in its origins. Although we also observed the existence of strong and widespread affective and identitive support, it is not inconceivable to foresee a situation at some point in the future where the utilitarian (or materialist) image of the Community could come to act as a handicap in the generation of further public support.

The September 1973 poll also included questions on the respondents' feelings of dissatisfaction or satisfaction with their lives — standards of living, the quality of life, and nature of society, and so on. Inglehart feels that, 'The 1973 survey results indicate that West European publics are predominantly satisfied with the economic aspects of their lives — but slightly more dissatisfaction than satisfaction is expressed in regard to the sociopolitical domains.'[31]

One of the most fascinating findings, and one which lacks any satisfactory explanation, is that the five most satisfied publics are the publics of the five smallest countries – Belgium, Denmark, Eire, Luxembourg and the Netherlands. [32] There are certainly no grounds for regarding this apparent correlation between size of country and level of satisfaction as an 'iron law of politics', but it should prompt us to question any assumptions that we may hold that the unification of states and the subsequent creation of larger units necessarily results in 'the greatest happiness for the greatest number'. No doubt the federalist proponents of a United States of Europe would claim that their proposals for smaller units than the present large member-states within the unified whole would secure the best of both the worlds of unification and decentralisation. In view of the materialistic bias of the present Community, with the assumption that satisfaction and support for integration can be created on a utilitarian basis, it is worth noting that the wealthier regions do not necessarily express higher levels of satisfaction.

Conclusions

Class and party loyalty do indeed correlate closely with opinions towards European integration. The findings of the research conducted in the Six by Puchala and Kriesberg in the 1950s and early 1960s support our sixth proposition. More recent research in the applicant-states of the early 1970s reflects similar conclusions, particularly in the United Kingdom, where opinions on Europe illustrate the continuing dominance of class and party antagonisms in society. In Norway too, the traditional societal cleavage, running along 'centre-periphery' lines, has been superimposed on the European debate.

Although our sixth proposition appears to have been verified, it is far from providing us with a satisfactory conclusion in itself. Indeed, the evidence which we have analysed in this chapter points to the existence of even stronger correlations between certain social variables and opinions on European integration than exist between class and party identification and views on Europe. For instance, it is clear that in any survey the respondent's nationality is probably the most powerful determinant factor of all. The extent to which the variables of class and party relate to views on Europe clearly varies greatly from nation to nation. Moreover, the exact role of varying levels of education or the impact of contrasting value-systems are also seen to depend on nationality. And the reason why nationality appears to be such a determinant factor is that it symbolises the different political contexts within which the publics receive and interpret any information about 'Europe', 'the Common Market', and so on.

In Norway and the United Kingdom, the debate over entry of the Common Market came to mirror traditional socio-political cleavages for historical and sociological reasons. Certainly, a lack of identity with Europe, and, in Britain's case, confidence in the strength of national institutions, have contributed to the underlying opposition – or at least, scepticism – felt for involvement in the 'new Europe'. In the Six, such fundamental 'anti-system' feelings for a supranational experiment were not present, except from the Communists in the early years. Consequently, we can observe differing levels of support for integration amongst the publics of the Six, but these variations according to social group or party identification reflect some degree of disagreement of a procedural nature, over 'means' and not 'ends', since the substantive issue of whether or not to participate in the Community has been resolved. But in Denmark, Norway and the United Kingdom – and, to a lesser extent, Eire – disagreement remains on the fundamental question of 'ends', since the problem of whether or not to participate had not been finally resolved in the early 1970s.

In the applicant-states, the debate has remained of a substantive nature, reflecting traditional socio-political cleavages. For this reason, any notion that greater technical knowledge of the Community can promote support in such an antagonistic political context is clearly fallacious. Clearly, the 'image' of the Community must count for far more. Also, the ability of party leaders to enlist the support of their party loyalists was questioned by the experience of the Norwegians. However, we found evidence of a particularly strong link between party and opinion on Europe amongst the British, and we did suggest that a Labour government's recommendation to vote for continued membership of the Community in any referendum or election could persuade a politically volatile public to support membership. But prediction is made difficult by the very volatility of the electorate, the underlying, negative attitudes of the British toward integration and the experience of a referendum campaign in which many leading politicians would continue to advocate withdrawal. Should the Labour Government remain reticent, or even recommend withdrawal, then the outcome would be far more predictable.

Notes

1 L. Lindberg and S. Scheingold, *Europe's Would-be Polity,* 1970, pp. 41–9.

2 J. Pinder, 'Positive integration and negative integration: some problems of economic union in the EEC' in M. Hodges (ed.), *European Integration,* Penguin, 1972, pp. 124–50.

3 Ibid., pp. 148–9.

4 Ibid., p. 149.

5 Gallup International, 'Public opinion and the European Community, edited and translated by M. Forsyth, in *Journal of Common Market Studies* vol. 2, no. 2, 1963, pp. 116–23.

6 Louis Kriesberg, 'German public opinion and the European Coal and Steel Community' in *Public Opinion Quarterly* vol.23, 1959.

7 Jean Stoetzel, 'The evolution of French opinion' in D. Lerner and R. Aron (eds), *France Defeats EDC,* Praeger, 1957, pp. 72–101. See also *Sondages,* quarterly reports for the 1950s.

8 U. Kitzinger, *Diplomacy and Persuasion: How Britain Joined the Common Market,* Thames and Hudson, 1973, pp. 366–7.

9 D. Butler and D. Stokes, *Political Change in Britain,* Pelican, 1971, pp. 240–64; D. Nias, 'Psychology and the EEC' in *New Society,* March 1973, pp. 529–31.

10 U. Kitzinger, op.cit., 1973, p. 364.

11 Ibid., p. 365.

12 Ibid.

13 Ibid., p. 370.

14 Ibid., pp. 365–6.

15 D. Butler and D. Stokes op.cit., 1971, pp. 240–64.

16 O. Hellevik, N.P. Gleditsch and K. Ringdal, *The Common Market Issue in Norway: a Conflict Between Center and Periphery,* University of Oslo, 1974, p. 4.

17 Ibid., p. 6.

18 Ibid.

19 Ibid.

20 Ibid., p. 10.

21 Ibid., pp. 11–12.

22 Ibid., p. 14.

23 Ibid., p. 17.

24 Ibid., p. 19.

25 R. Inglehart, *The 1973 European Community Public Opinion Surveys: Preliminary Findings,* University of Geneva, May 1974, p. 5.

224

[26] Ibid., pp. 5—6.
[27] Ibid., p. 8.
[28] Ibid., p. 9.
[29] Ibid., p. 11.
[30] Ibid.
[31] Ibid., p. 13.
[32] Ibid., p. 14.

10 Conclusion: the Need for Democratic Legitimacy

There are three major areas which warrant further discussion. First, what are the theoretical implications of our findings? Secondly, what have we discovered about the more detailed aspects of the nature of public opinion on European integration? Thirdly, and this is probably the most crucial area for discussion, do our conclusions suggest any guidelines for future policies or reforms for those who wish to see the Community of the Nine solve its present and future crises?

Turning to the theoretical implications of our findings, we have found that the role which is assigned to public opinion in the integration process, by neofunctionalist theorists in particular, is quite inadequate. Neofunctionalism has its origins in the first phase of European integration and became, in effect, the Communities' legitimising ideology. Reflecting Jean Monnet's faith in the ability of economic integration to lead inevitably to political integration, there was little emphasis in the earlier neofunctionalist writings on the potentially vital role of national political elites or public opinion. Indeed, the neofunctionalists' deterministic concept of the 'cumulative logic of integration' even seemed able to accommodate the defeat of the EDC by the French National Assembly in 1954. It was contended that the French rejection merely demonstrated that the more extreme federalist proponents of political unification had been trying to push events along far too quickly. This example illustrates the neofunctionalists' limited view of the real role of public opinion – integration is seen to be essentially an elite-pull phenomenon rather than mass-push, but some form of 'permissive consensus' for integration should exist amongst the public of a liberal-democracy before integration of a political nature can be introduced by the elites.

Neofunctionalist reasoning appeared to be confirmed in the 1950s and early 1960s by the acquiescence of the publics of the Six in their governments' European policies. But the increasing intransigence of President de Gaulle in 1962–63 presented the problem of accommodating a 'dramatic political actor' into a theoretical framework centred upon the notion of a cumulative logic of integration. The French boycott of 1965 shattered any hopes of effective accommodation and

227

gave greater credibility to those critics who had stressed the ongoing reality of the nation-state. The Luxembourg Settlement of 1966, which comprises the conditions on which the French representatives returned to the Communities' institutions, had the effect of institutionalising a pluralistic concept of *L'Europe des Patries*.

Paradoxically, since the setback of 1965–66, the neofunctionalists have increasingly turned for solace to the study of mass attitudes and opinions. There appear to be two basic reasons for this. First, there has been a growing realisation that, as integration progresses, so it must come to have less in common with the foreign policy issue area and must become more akin to the domestic policy issue-area. In an effort to uphold the twin concepts of 'elite-pull' and the 'cumulative logic of integration', the neofunctionalists claim that the result of the increasing similarity between the community policy and domestic policy issue-areas is that the public will come to see Community policies as more salient, while turning to the Community more and more for the solution of problems and the fulfilment of needs and demands. Although the Community may never approximate a full federal union, clearly it must assume an ever increasing number of responsibilities from the national level.

Secondly, many studies of long-term opinion formation do appear to reach conclusions which support the neofunctionalist case. For instance, it is argued by Lindberg and Scheingold that in the Six in the 1960s a 'permissive consensus' favouring integration existed amongst the publics, and Inglehart's concept of 'cognitive mobilisation' refers to the strengthening of this support over the years to come.[1] However, our detailed examination of the evidence from the polls and surveys suggests that 'permissive consensus' and 'cognitive mobilisation' are not very sure bases on which to construct a revised version of neofunctionalism.

With regard to the notion of the existence of a 'permissive consensus' for further integration in the Six, we wrote in our conclusions to Chapter Five that,

> Much of the data relating to opinions on the ECSC or the EEC does indicate strong utilitarian support, but to a certain extent the replies merely mirror the nature of those particular institutions and the subsequent wording of the questions put to the publics.

While we recognise that the Common Market certainly did receive much support because of its image of promoting a rise in prosperity, and that there was strong affective-identitive support for unification, we also observed that,

228

... the most optimistic and pro-European publics of the Six could not see political unification as being anything but a long-term achievement. This fact, together with a perception of more national gains than benefits for the individual, and a residual nationalistic strand amongst the publics, all help to explain the reluctance of many people to be willing to accept some personal sacrifice in the cause of European unification.

Furthermore, in the conclusions of Chapter Six, we indicated that,

> ... a careful analysis of the common policies which receive the greatest support reveals that the publics, even in the pro-European Six, are wary of common policies which may require some form of sacrifice in the common, 'European' good. Also, those common policies which are most indicative of support for unification appear to be less popular than the more technical policies or defence policy, where common interests are usually more easily perceived.

In view of the positive affective-identitive and utilitarian-systemic support for integration which we did observe within the Six, it would be presumptuous of us to deny that Lindberg's and Scheingold's concept of a 'permissive consensus' does contain a good deal of truth. But we must avoid making a deduction that a neofunctionalist perspective would encourage. Neofunctionalism, with its emphasis on the socio-economic determinants of integration and its view of the integrative process as an 'elite-pull' phenomenon, leads to an interpretation of the opinion poll data in which any 'permissive consensus' for integration is seen to exist as yet another phase in the irreversible process whereby economic integration results in political integration. Indeed, in its ability to visualise a clear progression through a series of historical phases to some ultimate political situation, or goal, neofunctionalism shares the deterministic essence of Marxism. When Lindberg and Scheingold refer to the probability that the integrative process in Europe will not culminate in a fully federal state, it is on a par with the early Marxists concluding that the dialectical process would in some way be checked before full Communism could be achieved and that the 'dictatorship of the proletariat' would be the end-product.

We must be far more prudent. Although some form of strong public support for economic integration does exist in the Six, we should not ignore the evidence which demonstrates a lack of strong utilitarian-identitive or affective-systemic support. And if the publics of the Six are unable to conceive of truly common European needs or interests, or find it difficult to express loyalty and support for the Community in its present form, then the implications for the prospects of further integration are profound. Is it not possible that the publics would resist, through their national political leaders, any further integration? However, by Pinder's analysis such an outcome would be disastrous for the Community, since negative integration unleashes forces which can be controlled only by further, more political integration. Thus, unless the whole Community is to collapse and revert to the nationalistic 'self-contained uncertainty' envisaged by Hoffmann, further positive integration must be introduced. This is the crux of the issue — can the Community enter a new phase of integration, or will the publics' ambiguity or, at best, acquiescence, develop into opposition as the Community moves from 'negative' to 'positive' integration?

As we saw in the previous three chapters, it is by reference to the concept of 'cognitive mobilisation' that Inglehart seeks to reassure us.[2] Basically, he argues that the younger age-groups in Western Europe have experienced a change in values compared with their parents' generation. This shift in values over the generations is the product of historical factors, such as the collapse of European nationalism after 1945, and also results from differing levels of mass education and information in the post-war era, compared to the years before the war. But in later work it becomes clear that Inglehart is referring not only to a greater 'Europeanness' amongst the younger age-groups, but that he is describing a general value-change which encompasses opinions on materialism, the quality of life, geographical identity, and so on.[3]

In so far as the geographical identity of youth is more likely to reflect a cosmopolitan orientation, rather than reflecting the ideals of nationalism, it would seem that the publics of the Community will become increasingly willing to see the transformation from 'negative' to 'positive' integration take place. The problem is that this scenario is dependent upon too many unfounded assumptions. In the first place, the physical replacement of the older, more nationalistic age-groups by the younger, more cosmopolitan age-groups can only occur in the long term — it would take 20 or 30 years for the young to succeed to the positions of power and influence, by which time they would also comprise the overwhelming majority of the population. Yet the transition to positive integration has to occur within the short or medium term. Moreover, the failure of the Community to cope with the crises which have actually been caused by the essentially negative integration of the 1960s could create a widespread sense of disillusionment with integration amongst the young brothers and sisters of the 'young' age-groups who have been interviewed over the past decade or so.

Yet there is an even more fundamental criticism. Can we be sure that post-materialist values, incorporating a cosmopolitan orientation, will necessarily generate support for the European Community? The answer must surely depend on the image projected by the Community, and the interpretation of that image by the young people who do possess post-materialist values. Chapter Nine shows that the individual's national political context is a crucial determinant in the interpretation of the Community's image, and that certainly in Denmark and Norway the young are the least favourably predisposed to the Community. A survey of the British in 1972 found that generally the youngest adults (18–34 years old) were slightly more pro-European than their immediate elders (35–44 years old), although Kitzinger cites contradictory evidence.[4] In the Six, the widespread support for the 'European idea' (affective-identitive support), combined with the successful economic image of the Community, could well contribute to large-scale support amongst the young for further integration. However, the ambiguities which exist in the publics' support for unification may make even the support of the young in the Six more problematic than some theorists now appear to realise.

However, it is the image of the Community's institutions which gives cause for the greatest concern. They have been unable to generate any affective support to speak of amongst the publics of the Six, while they appear to have generated real suspicion amongst the publics of the applicant-states. Undoubtedly, there are national factors which help to explain variations in the popularity – or lack of popularity – of the Community's institutions, but we do not have to look far for the main cause of the lack of mass support accorded to the institutional framework.

The fault lies in the original image of integration as it was expressed in the Communities of the Six. In particular, this flaw in the theory is given institutional expression in the role of the European Commission. Andrew Shonfield has analysed the situation accurately:

> ... the ideological bias of the first phase [of integration], which purported to give the European Commission the status of an overlord in the process of European integration – an incipient European governmental power speaking with growing authority to obsolescent national governments – gets in the way of the efficient management of European affairs.[5]

Shonfield's analysis highlights the federalist and neofunctionalist assumptions upon which the ECSC and the EEC were based. The federalist contribution is to be found in the image of the Commission as the executive branch of a future European Government, which would

231

eventually come to be responsible to the European Parliament, which itself would become a directly-elected legislative body. The neo-functionalist contribution is to be found in the role ascribed to the Commission — it would comprise the technocrats who would create the new Europe as the nation-state inevitably became 'obsolescent'.

Clearly, democratic legitimacy is the missing ingredient in the institutional superstructure. Nor can this be readily conferred by the concentration of legislative power, including the power of veto, in the hands of the representatives of the member-governments who constitute the Council of Ministers. At best, the vesting of the Council of Ministers with the law-making power ensures that no member-state's vital national interests can be overridden. And Shonfield is certainly correct to emphasise the great dangers of a hasty transformation of the Community to a fully federal system in the vain hope of securing democratic legitimacy.[6] A far more likely result would be a damaging, potentially ruinous, secession from the federal Community by a member-state whose public felt that their vital national interests had been sacrificed to the common European 'good'.

But the Community need not allow the risk of secession to prevent the implementation of any reform which is designed to bestow democratic legitimacy upon its institutions. At the heart of any reform must be a basic change in the relationship between the Commission and the European Parliament. This is because at present the popular image of the Commission remains one of a body of remote technocrats who are vested with the power to create a fully unified Europe, but who are not responsible to any other body and who are quite incapable of actually coping with the crises facing the Community.[7]

The irony in all this is that, in popular opinion, the real power of the Commission may well have increased since the Luxembourg Settlement of 1966, which actually decreased its power. But this popular misconception is quite plausible, particularly in the new member-states, which have had to assimilate a mass of detailed Community laws since entry. The source of the misconception lies in the Commission's loss of its function as the guide to the 'ever closer union' referred to in the preamble to the Treaty of Rome. As a result, the Commission is seen to be concerned primarily with the exercise of detailed regulatory functions. Indeed, Shonfield argues persuasively that,

> The fascination of exercising direct governmental power may prove so great that the European Commission will confine itself to a role which finds it closest analogy in the federal regulatory agencies of

the United States — the Federal Trade Commission, the Inter-State Commerce Commission, and so on. This would be because it preferred certain power here and now, however limited its extent, to the exercise of an uncertain but much more profound influence over the shape of political events in the future.[8]

Developments since the Luxembourg Settlement and the Davignon Report seem to confirm Shonfield's fears. In fact, the very apolitical, neofunctionalist assumptions on which the Communities' institutions were established have resulted in the emergence of politics within a pluralistic or nationalistic framework — any clashes in the Community are seen only to involve national political leaders, who risk 'losing face'. Professor Coombes provides us with a lucid exposition on the current situation and its origins, when he writes:

> Alas, however, the Communities were founded on an assumption of consensus and over the years the Commission has come to see its role increasingly (under the pressure of circumstances and not always by its own will) as that of a mediator or arbitrator, whose task is primarily the technical one of finding the right split among the different demands of the Member States' governments. One cannot help feeling that it is mainly this institutional failure which lay at the heart of the crisis of the Communities in 1973, for that crisis arose essentially from the failure to respond to a number of severe external challenges and from the failure to cope with the political issues inherent in the idea of economic and monetary union.[9]

In short, Coombes concludes that '. . . the factors normally used to force a compromise — external threat and internally conflicting demands cutting across different sectors — proved too much for the institutional machinery of the Communities'.[10]

It is now quite clear that the question which faces us is plain and simple — what is to be done? The answer lies in drawing together the various strands which have been developed throughout this book and, in particular, in this final chapter. Above all, we must face the fact that with the gradual creation of negative integration — for instance, a free customs union — problems arise which can only be solved by further, positive integration. Coombes identifies the urgency of this task:

> The longer it takes to get on with that task of agreeing to common positive measures, the worse will be the inequalities and anomalies of the Common Market as it is; in other words, the more critical will be some of the features to which Labour opponents of membership object.[11]

Secondly, we must remember that this transition to a qualitatively different stage of integration demands political guidance and skilled leadership. The institution best suited for this task is, of course, the Commission, but it is just this vital political function which the Commission has lost. Indeed, unless action is taken to change the popular image of the Commission, its intervention as a guide to further integration could well be counterproductive.

Thus, it is the third and final strand in our answer — the need to establish democratic legitimacy for the Community — which is the most fundamental issue. Yet there is no easy solution here, for, as we have argued previously, any attempt to establish a fully federal political system in Europe would increase greatly the risks of secession by one or possibly more of the current member-states of the Nine. Furthermore, it is worth reiterating our findings in Chapter Six, that the majority of people in the Six, who are supposedly the most 'European' publics in the Community, favour a form of political unity where the nation-state maintains considerable power. Full-blooded federalism is clearly a very real threat to European unity.

The nub of the issue is the creation of democratic legitimacy for the Community without making secession its likely, and potentially disastrous, by-product. The key to any solution surely lies in the nature of the political systems of the member-states, and, as we observed in Chapter One, the Community can effectively include only liberal-democracies. The very essence of the Community method, with its emphasis on bargaining over conflicting interests and striking mutually beneficial agreements, demands that the member-states be liberal-democratic. All of the member-states of the Nine do contain minorities, some being larger than others, who reject liberal — or parliamentary — democracy, but the majority of peoples in the Community confer legitimacy on their respective national political systems because they are liberal- or parliamentary-democracies.

Thus, the Community must be reformed if it is to secure the democratic legitimacy which would enable it to survive the vital transition to more positive integration. And the most effective reform in terms of securing fairly immediate results, without provoking a secession, would be to institutionalise in the Community a key component of liberal-democratic political systems, namely political opposition. Like elections, which involve the mass of adults directly in their political system, the existence of political opposition serves to confer legitimacy on that system. But unlike direct elections to the European Parliament, political opposition could develop very quickly and would not involve such detailed or lengthy

234

discussions on the exact procedures to be followed.

The attractiveness for the publics of a political opposition within the Community would lie in demonstrating that the executive — the Commission — *is* responsible and that the 'technocrats' *do* have to defend their actions, fight for their ideals and generally *have* to 'face the music'. Moreover, no really radical reform is needed for the Community to develop an effective political opposition. Already, the European Parliament has the power to 'force the Commission to resign as a body by passing a motion of censure on its activities by a two-thirds majority vote and a majority of its members'.[12] The members of the European Parliament can also put oral and written questions to the Commission, who are obliged to reply. Coombes indicates that,

> Against this background the Commission's general report on the activities of the Communities (published annually, again according to the treaties, 'not later than one month before the opening of the session of the Assembly') must be seen as a document of constitutional importance, being one of the chief expressions of the political responsibility of the Commission and of its public accountability for its functions.[13]

Amongst other things, the Commission's annual report to the European Parliament contains an outline programme for the current year. If the Parliament became quicker to use its very real powers, the Commission could be invested with some form of party political backing for a particular programme, a development which seems more likely as a result of the Parliament's newly acquired budgetary powers. Following the argument put forward by Coombes, the result would be that the Commission would have to come to 'represent one (or some) political strains in the Parliament'.[14] Indeed, had the Parliament deployed its powers previously, Coombes argues that,

> ... it would have forced the Member States' representatives in the Council to be far more realistic about the implications of what they decide, or rather most often fail to decide, and would have helped to make the Community far more flexible than it has seemed. Thus 'renegotiation' might have become a perfectly normal process, but one carried on within the stabilising and adjusting process of parliamentary government.[15]

Coombes also argues that this change in Commission–Parliament relations, which would restore to the Commission its more political 'guiding' functions and which would lead to the emergence of an Opposition within the Parliament, would also lead 'to irresistible pressures for directly electing the Parliament'. [16] This may well be an effect, although the demands for direct election, which are now supported by European Conservatives, are already becoming more insistent. Shonfield clearly has a valid point when he argues that the European Parliament should not seek to compete for power with the national parliaments, although he does appear to overstate the implications of direct elections to the European Parliament. Quite simply, Shonfield asserts that the Community 'is not a federation of states with a central government but a Community of nations feeling its way forward to a number of collective decisions'. [17]

We must bear in mind Shonfield's view that the objective of the European enterprise is integration but not a merger. The problem now becomes that of institutionalising political opposition and thereby conferring democratic legitimacy on the Community, without seeming to adopt a blatantly federalist schema. If this latter impression were to be conveyed to the public, the whole exercise of institutional reform could be jeopardised, with all the resultant dangers that would follow as the Community proved unable to adopt a more positive form of integration. Yet the acceptance of direct elections by the European Conservatives does signify that the existence of directly-elected MPs may not be seen as a 'blatantly federalist schema'.

The most effective solution therefore seems to be to involve the national parliaments more and more in the process of European legislation. Shonfield elaborates on this idea by proposing that a network of parallel parliamentary committees should be established in the member-states, and he suggests that the European Parliament could become a 'committee-of-committees'. Shonfield argues,

> The fact that the European Parliament is composed of national MPs with a double mandate puts it in an excellent position to orchestrate the whole process. Orchestration means in this context arranging joint meetings of parliamentary groups and committees drawn from different countries, working out a timetable which does not conflict with the main programmes of legislative business in the national parliaments, and, most important, arranging for parallel moves to be taken in the different national parliaments to put simultaneous pressure on several members of the Council of Ministers. [18]

The European Parliament, as presently constituted, may be well suited to this task, but there is no reason why a directly-elected Parliament, at some

236

date after 1980, should not be able to perform a similar role. Shonfield continues to advocate his case by arguing that

> ... its closest analogy is with the United States Congress, whose Committees are certainly the most powerful parliamentary force in the contemporary democratic world. In the end, European members of parliament, like other interest-groups in the Community, would develop their own powerful network of transnational relations.[19]

We can certainly agree with Shonfield that his proposals would 'provide the visible evidence that effective opposition politics had been injected into the Community process'.[20] But Shonfield's proposed reforms do not concentrate solely on the functions of the European and national parliaments. Clearly, a real change in the Commission—Parliament relationship, involving the introduction of opposition, cannot be effective without a reform in the role of the Commission. Again, Shonfield's major proposal accords with our demands — he urges that the individual nation-states should be allowed to harmonise their own economic, industrial or welfare regulations, for example, and that the Commission should not seek to impose uniformity on the Nine.[21] Indeed, with the institutionalisation of political opposition within the Community, the Commission will be able to act as the guide which can help to bring about more positive integration, using its political skills to solve the major problems which the Community must face. Its regulating function would have to be jettisoned.

Throughout this book, we have seen that the idea of European unification conjures up confused and often distorted images. Misconceptions of the true nature of the European Community today stem from the original theoretical bases on which the Community's institutions were established, and also from the early developments in the history of European integration. For instance, the Commission and the European Parliament embodied the notion that a single European will would come to exist, and that this 'inevitable', logical result of economic integration must be actively encouraged. Also, the Commission came to exercise its political functions of leadership less and less, and became constrained in the role of a classic, technocratic and irresponsible organisation which seeks integration through the undemocratic imposition of petty regulations.

But, in truth, the European objective has not been to eliminate its constituent national identities. Instead, European integration has reflected the desire to establish a unique form of transnational collaboration which reflects the realities of the modern world and which therefore is far better equipped than the isolated nation-state to overcome the crises which face the people of Western Europe today and which will face them in the future. Yet it was the crises which the Community faced in 1973 that served to demonstrate that, unless institutional reforms which enable the Community to pursue a more positive form of integration are effected, then the outlook for the Nine is indeed bleak. We must conclude that the Community can be sure of successfully negotiating this transitional phase in its development only if the reforms that are introduced also secure for the Community's institutions a large degree of democratic legitimacy.

Notes

[1] L. Lindberg and S. Scheingold, *Europe's Would-be Polity,* Prentice-Hall, 1970, p. 41; R. Inglehart, 'Cognitive mobilization and European integration' in *Comparative Politics,* 1970.

[2] R. Inglehart, op.cit.

[3] R. Inglehart, *The 1973 European Community Public Opinion Surveys: Preliminary Findings,* University of Geneva, May 1974.

[4] Commission of the Communities, *Les Britanniques et l'unification de l'Europe,* December 1972, pp. A5, A7, A9, A10.

[5] A. Shonfield, *Europe: Journey to an Unknown Destination,* Pelican, 1973, p. 85.

[6] Ibid., pp. 70–1.

[7] Ibid., pp. 34–5. Shonfield also cites the views of Professor Ralf Dahrendorf, whose criticism of the Commission appeared in two articles entitled 'Wieland Europa' in *Die Zeit,* 9 and 16 July 1971.

[8] Ibid., p. 86.

[9] David Coombes, 'The Annual Report of the EEC' in *Political Quarterly* vol. 45, no. 4, October–December 1974, p. 486.

[10] Ibid., p. 487.

[11] Ibid., p. 488.

[12] Ibid., p. 485.

[13] Ibid., p. 486.

[14] Ibid.

[15] Ibid.

[16] Ibid.

[17] A. Shonfield, op.cit., pp. 70–1.

[18] Ibid., p. 82.

[19] Ibid.

[20] Ibid.

[21] Ibid., pp. 77–80.

Bibliography

Abramson, C., and Inglehart, R., 'The development of systemic support in four Western democracies' in *Comparative Political Studies*, January 1970.

Almond, G., *American People and Foreign Policy*, Praeger, 1960.

Aron, R., *Peace and War*, New York 1966.

Barber, J., and Reed, B. (eds), *European Community: Vision and Reality*, Croom Helm, 1973.

Beloff, J., 'Britain, Europe and the Atlantic Community' in Wilcox and Haviland, *The Atlantic Community*, Praeger, 1963.

Best, J., *Public Opinion: Macro and Micro*, The Dorsey Press, 1973.

Bogart, L., 'No opinion, don't know and maybe no answer' in *Public Opinion Quarterly*, 1967, pp. 331–45.

Bottomore, T.B., *Sociology: a Guide to Problems and Literature*, revised edition, George Allen and Unwin, 1972.

Bracher, K., 'Democracy' in Mayne, R. (ed.), *Europe Tomorrow: 16 Europeans look ahead*, Fontana, 1972.

Buchan, A. (ed.), *Europe's future, Europe's choices: models of Western Europe in the 1970's*, Chatto and Windus, 1969.

Butler, D., and Stokes, D., *Political Change in Britain: Forces shaping Electoral Choice*, Pelican, 1971.

Camps, M., *European Unification in the Sixties*, Oxford University Press, 1967.

Camps, M., 'Is Europe obsolete? in *International Affairs*, July 1968.

Camps, M., 'European unification in the seventies' in *International Affairs*, 1971, reprinted in Hodges, M. (ed.), *European Integration*, Penguin, 1972.

Central Information Office, *Britain: an Official Handbook*, London 1961, 1964, 1968–72.

Cobb and Elder, *International Community: a Regional and Global Study*, Holt, 1970.

Commission of the European Communities, *Les Européens: Oui à l'Europe*, Brussels, May 1970.

Commission of the European Communities, *L'Opinion des Européens sur les aspects régionaux et agricoles du Marché Commun, l'unification politique de l'Europe et l'information du public*, Brussels, December 1971.

Commission of the European Communities, *Les Britanniques et l'unification de l'Europe,* Brussels, December, 1972.

Commission of the European Communities, *Europe as the Europeans see it,* Brussels, November 1973.

Commission of the European Communities, *L'Europe vue par les Européens,* Brussels, January 1974.

Commission of the European Communities, *L'Europe vue par les Européens,* Brussels, March 1974.

Commission of the European Communities, *Satisfaction et insatisfaction quant aux conditions de vie dans les pays membres de la Communauté Européenne,* Brussels, April 1974.

Commission of the European Communities, *Euro-Barometer* no. 1, Brussels, July 1974.

Commission of the European Communities, *L'Europe vue par les Européens,* Brussels, August 1974.

Coombes, D., *Politics and Bureaucracy in the European Community,* George Allen and Unwin, 1970.

Coombes, D., 'The Annual Report of the EEC' in *Political Quarterly* vol. 45, no. 4, 1974, pp. 489–9.

Dahrendorf, R., 'A new goal for Europe' in Hodges, M., (ed.), *European Integration,* Penguin, 1972.

Davison, W.P., (ed.), *International Political Communities,* Praeger, 1966.

Deutsch, K.W., *Nationalism and Social Communication: an Inquiry into the Foundations of Nationality,* Wiley, 1953.

Deutsch, K.W., *Political Community at the International Level: Problems of Definition and Measurement,* Doubleday, 1954.

Deutsch, K.W., *Political Community and the North Atlantic Area: International Organization in the light of Historical Experience,* Princeton University Press, 1957.

Deutsch, K.W., *The Nerves of Government,* Free Press of Glencoe, 1963.

Deutsch, K.W., 'Integration and arms control in the European political environment: a summary report' in *American Political Science Review* vol. 60, no. 2, 1966, pp. 354–65.

Deutsch, K.W., *France, Germany and the Western Alliance: a Study of Elite Attitudes on European Integration and World Politics,* Scribner and Sons, 1967.

Deutsch, K.W., *The Analysis of International Relations,* Prentice-Hall, 1968.

Deutsch, K.W., and Merritt, R.L., 'Effects of events on international images' in Kelman, H. (ed.), *International Behaviour,* Holt, 1965.

Duchêne, F., 'Europe's role in world peace' in Mayne, R. (ed.), *Europe*

Tomorrow: 16 Europeans Look Ahead, Fontana, 1972.

Durant, H., 'Public opinion, polls and foreign policy' in *British Journal of Sociology,* 1955, pp. 149–58.

Duren, A., 'Multinational companies as a political problem' in Barber, J., and Reed, B. (ed.), *European Community: Vision and Reality,* Croom Helm, 1973.

Easton, D., *A Systems Analysis of Political Life,* Wiley, 1967.

Etzioni, A., *Political Unification,* New York 1965.

Farrell, R.B. (ed.), *Approaches to Comparative and International Politics,* Northwestern University Press, 1966.

Fawcett, J.E.S., 'The issue of parliamentary sovereignty' in *The World Today* vol. 27, no. 4, April 1971.

Finer, S.E., *Anonymous Empire,* Pall Mall Press, 1966.

Gallup International, 'Public opinion and the European Community', edited and translated by Forsyth, M., in *Journal of Common Market Studies* vol. 2, no. 2, 1963.

Gallup Polls: see Social Surveys, Gallup Poll Ltd.

Galtung, J., *The European Community: A Super-power in the Making,* George Allen and Unwin, 1973.

Gilmour, I., *The Body Politic,* Hutchinson, 1971.

Giner, S., *Sociology,* Martin Robertson, 1972.

Gouldner, A., *The Coming Crisis of Western Sociology,* Heinemann, 1971.

Haas, E.B., *The Uniting of Europe,* Stevens, 1958.

Haas, E.B., *Beyond the Nation State,* Stanford University Press, 1964.

Haas, E.B., 'The uniting of Europe and the uniting of Latin America' in *International Organization,* 1970.

Haas, E.B., and Schmitter, P., 'Economics and differential patterns of political integration: projects about unity in Latin America' in Davison, W.P. (ed.), *International Political Communities,* Praeger, 1966.

Hansen, R., 'Regional integration: reflections on a decade of theoretical efforts' in Hodges, M. (ed.), *European Integration,* Penguin, 1972.

Hartley, A., 'Transnational political forces' in Barber, J., and Reed, B., *European Community: Vision and Reality,* Croom Helm, 1973.

Hedges, B., and Jowell, R., *Britain and the EEC: Report on a Survey of Attitudes towards the European Economic Community,* Social and Community Planning Research, 1971.

Hellevik, O., and Gleditsch, N.P., *A Clash between Direct and Indirect Democracy,* International Peace Research Institute, University of Oslo, 1973.

Hellevik, O., Gleditsch, N.P., and Ringdal, K., *The Common Market Issue in Norway: a Conflict between Center and Periphery,* International

Peace Research Institute, University of Oslo, 1974.

Hewitt, C., 'Policy-making in postwar Britain: a national-level test of elitist and pluralist hypotheses' in *British Journal of Politics* vol. 4, part 2, 1974.

Hodder-Williams, R., *Public Opinion Polls and British Politics,* Routledge and Kegan Paul, 1970.

Hodges, M. (ed.), *European Integration,* Penguin, 1972.

Hoffmann, S., 'The fate of the nation-state' in *Daedalus,* Summer 1966.

Holt, S., *The Common Market: The Conflict of Theory and Practice,* Hamish Hamilton, 1971.

Inglehart, R., 'An end to European integration?' in *American Political Science Review* vol. 61, no. 1, 1967.

Inglehart, R., 'Trends and non-trends in the Western Alliance: a review' in *Journal of Conflict Resolution* vol. 12, no. 1, 1968.

Inglehart, R., 'Cognitive mobilization and European integration' in *Comparative Politics* V, 1970.

Inglehart, R., 'Public opinion and regional integration' in *International Organization* vol. 24, no. 4, 1970.

Inglehart, R., *The 1973 European Community Public Opinion Surveys: Preliminary Findings,* University of Geneva, 1974.

L'Institut français de l'Opinion publique, *Sondages,* 1951—74, Quarterly.

Jacob, P.E., and Teune, H., 'The integrative process' in Jacob, P.E., and Toscano, J.V. (eds.), *The Integration of Political Communities,* Lippincott, 1964.

Jahoda, M., and Warren, N. (eds), *Attitudes: Selected Readings,* Penguin, 1966.

Jay, D., *After the Common Market: a Better Alternative for Britain,* Penguin, 1968.

Kelman, H., 'Societal, attitudinal and structural factors in international relations' in *Journal of Social Issues* vol. 2, pp. 42—56, 1953.

Kelman, H., (ed.), *International Behaviour,* New York 1965.

Kelman, H., 'Three processes of social influence' in Jahoda, M., and Warren, N. (eds), *Attitudes: Selected Readings,* Penguin, 1966.

Key, V.O., Jr, *Politics, Parties and Pressure Groups,* Crowell, 1958.

Key, V.O., Jr, *Public Opinion and American Democracy,* Knopf, 1961.

Kitzinger, U., *The European Common Market and Community,* Routledge and Kegan Paul, 1967.

Kitzinger, U., *Diplomacy and Persuasion: How Britain Joined the Common Market,* Thames and Hudson, 1973.

Kriesberg, L., 'German public opinion and the European Coal and Steel Community' in *Public Opinion Quarterly* vol. 23, pp. 28—42, 1959.

242

Lerner, D., and Aron, R. (eds), *France Defeats EDC,* Praeger, 1957.

Lindberg, L., and Scheingold, S., *Europe's Would-be Polity,* Prentice-Hall, 1970.

Lowell, A.L., *Public Opinion and Popular Government,* Longmans, 1919.

McCloskey, H., 'Personality and attitude correlates of foreign policy orientation' in Rosenau, James N. (ed.), *Domestic Sources of Foreign Policy,* The Free Press, 1967.

McCloskey, H., *Political Inquiry,* Collier Macmillan, 1969.

Mackintosh, J.P., 'The House of Commons and the European Parliament' in Barber, J., and Reed, B. (eds), *European Community: Vision and Reality,* Croom Helm, 1973.

Macmillan, H., *Pointing the Way,* Macmillan, 1972.

Macmillan, H., *At the End of the Day,* Macmillan, 1973.

Mahotiére, S., de la, *Towards One Europe,* Pelican, 1970.

Mayne, R., *The Recovery of Europe,* Weidenfeld and Nicolson, 1970.

Mayne, R. (ed.), *Europe Tomorrow: 16 Europeans Look Ahead,* Fontana, 1972.

Merritt, R.L., and Puchala, D.J. (eds), *Western European Perspectives on International Affairs: Public Opinion Studies and Evaluations,* Praeger, 1968.

Mitchell, J.D.B., 'The governance of Europe – a new dimension in international relations' in Barber, J., and Reed, B., *European Community: Vision and Reality,* Croom Helm, 1973.

Mitrany, D., *A Working Peace System,* Quadrangle Books, 1966.

Moodie, G.C., and Studdert-Kennedy, G., *Opinions, Publics and Pressure Groups: an Essay on Vox Populi and Representative Government,* George Allen and Unwin, 1970.

Nias, D., 'Psychology and the EEC', in *New Society,* 8 March 1973, pp. 529–31.

Parkin, F., *Class Inequality and Political Order,* Paladin, 1971.

Pentland, C., *International Theory and European Integration,* Faber and Faber, 1973.

Pinder, J., 'Economic growth, social justice, and political reform' in Mayne, R. (ed.), *Europe Tomorrow: 16 Europeans Look Ahead,* Fontana, 1972.

Pinder, J., 'Positive integration and negative integration: some problems of economic union in the EEC' in Hodges, M. (ed.), *European Integration,* Penguin, 1972.

Puchala, D.J., 'The Common Market and political federation in Western European public opinion' in *International Studies Quarterly* vol. 14, 1970.

Puchala, D.J., 'Transactions analysis' in *International Organization* vol. 24, no. 4, 1970.

Queener, L., 'The development of internationalist attitudes: hypotheses and verifications' in *The Journal of Social Psychology* vol. 29, 1949.

Rabier, J.-R., *L'Opinion publique et l'Europe des Six,* University of Brussels, 1966.

Rabier, J.-R., 'Europeans and the unification of Europe' in *Government and Opposition* vol. 6, no. 4, 1971.

Reader's Digest Association, *Products and People,* London 1973.

Rock, P., *Deviant Behaviour,* Hutchinson University Library, 1973.

Rosenau. J.N., 'Pre-theories and theories of foreign policy' in Farrel, R.B. (ed.), *Approaches to Comparative and International Politics,* Northwestern University Press, 1966.

Rosenau, J.N. (ed.), *Domestic Sources of Foreign Policy,* The Free Press, 1967.

Runciman, G., *Relative Deprivation and Social Justice,* University of California, 1962.

Russett, B., *Trends in World Politics,* Macmillan, 1965.

Schattschneider, E.E., *The Semisovereign People,* Holt, 1960.

Scott, A., 'Psychological and social correlates of international images' in Kelman, H. (ed.), *International Behaviour,* New York 1965.

Shonfield, A., *Europe: Journey to an Unknown Destination,* Pelican, 1973.

Sidjanski, D., 'Pressure groups and the European Economic Community' in Barber, J., and Reed, B., *European Community: Vision and Reality,* Croom Helm, 1973.

Social Surveys (Gallup Poll Ltd), *Gallup Political Index,* 1960–74, nos. 1–169.

Spinelli, A., 'The growth of the European Movement since the Second World War', in Hodges, M. (Ed.), *European Integration,* Penguin, 1972.

Stoetzel, J., 'The evolution of French opinion' in Lerner, D., and Aron, R. (eds), *France Defeats EDC,* Praeger, 1957, pp. 72–101.

Taylor, P., 'The concept of Community and the European integration process' in *Journal of Common Market Studies* vol. 7, no. 2., 1968.

Teer, F., and Spence, J.D., *Political Opinion Polls,* Hutchinson University Library, 1973.

Ullmann, M., 'Public information' in Mayne, R. (ed.), *Europe Tomorrow: 16 Europeans Look Ahead,* Fontana, 1972.

Uri, P. (ed.), *From Commonwealth to Common Market,* Penguin, 1968.

Vredeling, H., 'The Common Market of political parties' in Barber, J., and Reed, B., *European Community: Vision and Reality,* Croom Helm, 1973.

Wallace, H., 'The impact of the European Communities on national policy-making' in Hodges, M. (ed.), *European Integration,* Penguin, 1972.

Windlesham, Lord, *Communication and Political Power,* Jonathan Cape, 1966.

Index

Indexer's note: Certain page references may only be to the indice numbers relating to footnotes. If a reference cannot be found in the text on the page number quoted, the reader should turn to the notes at the end of the chapter for the necessary lead.

249